SECOND LANGUAGE WRITING
Series Editor, Paul Kei Matsuda

Second language writing emerged in the late twentieth century as an interdisciplinary field of inquiry, and an increasing number of researchers from various related fields—including applied linguistics, communication, composition studies, and education—have come to identify themselves as second language writing specialists. The Second Language Writing series aims to facilitate the advancement of knowledge in the field of second language writing by publishing scholarly and research-based monographs and edited collections that provide significant new insights into central topics and issues in the field.

Books in the Series

The Politics of Second Language Writing: In Search of the Promised Land, edited by Paul Kei Matsuda, Christina Ortmeier-Hooper, and Xiaoye You (2006)
Building Genre Knowledge, Christine M. Tardy (2009)
Practicing Theory in Second Language Writing, edited by Tony Silva and Paul Kei Matsuda (2009)

For my parents, Vicki and Dwight Tardy

Building Genre Knowledge

Christine M. Tardy

Parlor Press
West Lafayette, Indiana
www.parlorpress.com

Parlor Press LLC, West Lafayette, Indiana 47906

S A N: 2 5 4 - 8 8 7 9

Library of Congress Cataloging-in-Publication Data

Tardy, Christine M.

Building genre knowledge / Christine M. Tardy.

p. cm. -- (Second language writing.)

Includes bibliographical references and index.

ISBN 978-1-60235-112-7 (pbk. : alk. paper) -- ISBN 978-1-60235-113-4
(alk. paper) -- ISBN 978-1-60235-114-1 (adobe ebook)

1. English language--Study and teaching--Foreign speakers. 2. Interdisciplinary approach in education. 3. Academic writing--Handbooks,
manuals, etc. I. Title.

PE1128.A2T279 2009

808'.0420711--dc22

2009022501

Cover design by Paul Kei Matsuda
Printed on acid-free paper.

Parlor Press, LLC is an independent publisher of scholarly and trade
titles in print and multimedia formats. This book is available in paper,
hardcover, and Adobe eBook formats from Parlor Press on the World
Wide Web at http://www.parlorpress.com or through online and brick-and
mortar bookstores. For submission information or to find out about Parlor
Press publications, write to Parlor Press, 816 Robinson St., West Lafayette,
Indiana, 47906, or e-mail editor@parlorpress.com.

Contents

Acknowledgments

As with any work of this length, I owe a great debt of gratitude to many. First and foremost, I thank the four writers who allowed me to intrude into their graduate studies and put their words under a microscope. I also thank the writing instructor for allowing me to sit in her class and talk with her students about that class. Their willingness to allow me to observe them, audio-record them, and analyze their writing and their words is a remarkable display of trust. Without these individuals, this project simply could not have come to fruition. I sincerely hope that I have not represented any of them or their experiences in a way that they would find misleading.

I owe thanks as well to the many people who have influenced my understanding of genre and writing through their work. Their voices run throughout this book and continue to challenge and motivate me. On a more personal level, I am grateful to Margie Berns, Graham Smart, and Irwin Weiser for their comments and help on the research that led to this monograph. Many thanks also to John Swales, whose work first sparked my interest in genre many years ago and who has been remarkably supportive of me from my days as an undergraduate to the present. And I owe special thanks to Tony Silva, who has taught me much more about research and second language writing than he knows. His careful and cutting-edge work has inspired me as a researcher, and his encouraging words and calm demeanor helped me keep my sanity while swimming in binders and files of data.

I am also very thankful for the support I've received at DePaul University, especially from my department chairs Bill Fahrenbach and Peter Vandenberg, and my past and present colleagues in rhetoric and composition (Pete, Darsie, David, Roger, Heather, Julie, Melinda, Matthew, Shaun, René, and Tony), who have indulged my attempts to bridge disciplinary divides. DePaul's College of Liberal Arts and Sciences also provided helpful support through a summer research grant.

At Parlor Press, I am grateful to David Blakesley, who provided very helpful guidance and support along the way, and to Paul Kei Matsuda for his belief in this work from its earlier stages and his always helpful conversations in moving forward to this stage. I am also indebted to Anis Bawarshi for his thorough read and insightful suggestions on an earlier version of the manuscript. Any remaining faults in this work are mine alone. Finally, I thank Matthew for putting up with the endless anti-social evenings that have gone into this project and for engaging my obsession with seeing the world through genre.

Building Genre Knowledge

1 Genre and Genre Knowledge

Linguistic diversity in higher education is on the rise. According to the Institute of International Education (2008), the number of international students in U.S. universities has jumped from about 34,000 in 1954 to just over 580,000 in 2007. Similarly, the international student population has continued to grow in the United Kingdom, with over 330,000 international students in the United Kingdom in 2005, making up 13% of the total student population in higher education (UK Council for International Student Affairs, 2008). In both countries, the international student enrollment is slightly higher at the graduate level than the undergraduate level, with the majority of international students studying in the fields of engineering, business and management, and physical and life sciences. Indeed, in the U.S. it is not uncommon for engineering graduate programs at research universities to enroll more international students than domestic students. In both the U.S. and the U.K., the majority of these students are multilingual English speakers, who have already completed many years of English language study.

Of course, international students are not the only multilingual students on campus. U.S. postsecondary institutions, for example, are serving a growing number of foreign-born U.S. residents as a result of an increase in immigration in recent decades. Some of these students may have moved to the U.S. as babies or young children, but many arrived in middle school or secondary school. These students, often referred to as "Generation 1.5" (not traditional first generation or traditional second generation), were usually given very limited ESL instruction in school and were instead quickly "mainstreamed" into monolingual classrooms. Although English may be these students' dominant language, they often continue to face linguistic challenges in academic literacy, due to the limited support they have received in English language learning *and* in literacy development in their first language. Unfortunately, gathering data regarding this student population is rare at most universities, so their numbers, languages spoken, and fields of study are largely unknown.

The challenges of English-language academic literacy are also not limited to multilingual students in the contexts of English-dominant countries. As academic research and the global economy have increasingly adopted English as a common language, learners around the world have been forced to develop advanced English language skills, including students at English-medium universities worldwide, international scholars and researchers who have never studied outside of their home countries, and countless professionals around the globe in business, science, and other fields. With the post-World War II explosion in science and technology, access to and management of information has become vital to international scholarship, and English has, in many cases, become a common language of scholarship. Journal databases like the *Science Citation Index* (*SCI*), for example, illustrate a growing dominance of English-language publications, with English making up 95% of *SCI* publications in 1995; the remaining percentage was made up of French, German, Russian, and—at about 0.5 to 0.7%—all other languages (van Leeuwen, Moed, Visser, & van Raan, 2001). Now, even beyond the hard sciences, journals wishing to establish or maintain an international reputation must publish in English, putting great pressure on scholars to write in English. This preference for English-language publication trickles down to undergraduate education, where students in many countries rely on English-language textbooks or even attend English-medium universities. Overall, it is estimated that multilingual users of English will greatly outnumber native English speakers within the next few decades (Graddol, 1997), if they have not already.

This linguistic landscape is characterized by inequity. While native English speakers may take language for granted in their scholarly endeavors, numerous students around the world spend years studying English and face the challenges of academic reading, writing, and networking in a second or additional language—part of this challenge includes learning the valued genres of academic communication. Undergraduate students, for example, may need to write essays, research papers, lab reports, response papers, and project reports; graduate students engage in genres that bridge academic and professional participation, such as journal articles, conference papers, and grant proposals. Learning such genres goes beyond the learning of form. Students must learn the discursive practices of their discipline, including the preferred ways of constructing and distributing knowledge, the shared content knowledge, and the intertextual links that build and reference such knowledge (Kamberelis, 1995); they must also develop a knowledge of the labels given to commonly used genres, the communicative purposes of different genres, the sociocultural context in which genres operate, the formal text features associated with genres, and the cultural values embedded in genres (Johns, 1997). Individual success in this process is influenced by many individual, social, political, cultural, and linguistic factors—all of which may make the learning of "disciplinarity" (and thus disciplinary genres) more time-consuming, difficult, and frustrating. Factors like language proficiency, prior (perhaps conflicting) genre experiences, and the sociopolitical networks that learners are (or are *not*) a part of are all relevant to genre learning—and may pose barriers for linguistically diverse students. The question of how to facilitate the learning of disciplinary genres for these students has, as a result, gathered much attention by both researchers and teachers, especially within the context of higher education.

This book explores the challenges of disciplinary writing development, offering a framework for understanding how knowledge of disciplinary genres is developed over time in various settings. Specifically, the book follows the paths of four multilingual graduate students through their participation in an ESL writing course, disciplinary content courses, and disciplinary research. It describes the contexts in which the students wrote during different stages of their graduate study and the knowledge of different genres that they built over time. I focus on the genre learning of multilingual writers because these writers are increasingly the "typical writer" in a mobile world that often uses English as an academic *lingua franca,* and also because I believe that these writers' experiences have much to tell us about the complexities of genre learning. Although my research is situated within the context of international graduate student learning at a U.S. university, I believe the issues examined here are relevant to a range of populations, monolingual and multilingual, in English-dominant countries and contexts in which English is a second or additional language.

In this chapter, I lay the groundwork for the subsequent chapters, outlining the debate over genre and writing pedagogy; defining the important constructs of practice, task, discourse, and genre; introducing the crucial importance of genre networks; and presenting relevant models of expertise. Building on these theoretical foundations, I present a theory of genre knowledge and a descriptive model for developing this knowledge as a multilingual writer. This model will be illustrated through the stories of four such writers in the remainder of the book and elaborated in the final chapter.

GENRE AND WRITING INSTRUCTION

The research in this book grows out of the questions that I've returned to repeatedly as a teacher of writing: What writing tasks should I include in my courses? To what extent can and should I teach discipline-specific writing? What will the writers actually take away from my course, if anything? Whether my classroom was in the workplace in Asia or at universities in the United States and the Middle East, I have found the notion of *genre* to be useful in understanding the written communication that learners hope to master. While my workplace students needed to write within the four memo formats carefully prescribed by their multinational company, the graduate students that I have taught have had far more diverse and less predictable needs: article reviews, collaborative term projects, lab reports, proposals, conference papers, master's theses, dissertations, and journal articles, to name only a few. In both cases, viewing these texts as genres—that is, typified responses to repeated situational exigencies—seemed to provide both me and my students with a useful heuristic for increasing their understanding of these writing demands.

Genre is of course not a new concept in writing instruction, where genre-based teaching has been both championed and critiqued for nearly two decades. Genre-centered approaches rely on the belief that an awareness of texts' forms, functions, and social contexts will facilitate learners' development of writing expertise (Hyland, 2003). In U.S. first-year composition instruction, genre has become a popular organizing principle for textbooks and course syllabi in which students examine and write texts like letters, reviews, profiles, and research papers. In many of these instances, genre has become merely a substitute for discourse modes and is presented as a fairly static and a-rhetorical text type. But approaches that could more aptly be called "genre-based" have been outlined by Bawarshi (2003) and Devitt (2004), who advocate the critical analysis of genres in the classroom. Textbooks that adopt this orientation (Devitt, Reiff, & Bawarshi, 2003b; Jolliffe, 1999) teach writers ways to explore genres rather than teaching students to use specific genre features.

Genre-based approaches have enjoyed considerably more favor in second language classrooms. In attempting to address the needs of students who are often culturally and/or linguistically marginalized from sociorhetorical practices in educational, academic, and workplace settings, many practitioners have turned to genre as "a way in" to the power structures of society. The genre-based pedagogy adopted in Australia in the 1980s, for example, arose out of concerns that process pedagogy failed to serve traditionally marginalized students with its less explicit approach to writing instruction. Australian educationists like James Martin, Frances Christie, and Joan Rothery drew upon Hallidayan systemic-functional linguistics to articulate a new pedagogy that aimed to make visible the underlying textual features of "genres of power." Teaching these genres in K-12 and workplace instructional settings, practitioners in this so-called "Sydney School" see genre as a key resource for academic or workplace literacy. (See Cope & Kalantzis, 1993; Martin, 1993a, 1993b; Martin & Rothery, 1993 for more detailed discussions of the history and curricular applications of this approach.)

While the Sydney School approach has evolved amidst the unique concerns of the Australian educational and workplace contexts, a separate approach to genre-based pedagogy has become popular among practitioners of English for Specific Purposes (ESP). The most extensive work in this area has been found in ESL academic writing contexts (outlined most thoroughly by Flowerdew, 1993; Johns, 1997, 2002b; Martin, 1993b; Swales, 1990; and Swales & Feak, 1994b; Swales & Feak, 2000). A hallmark of the ESP approach to genre-centered pedagogy is its emphasis on rhetorical consciousness-raising. Genre analysis (an explicit sociorhetorical analysis of genres) has become central to a pedagogy that asks students to explore the relationship between texts and their social domains (that is, between generic *form* and generic *content*). Theoretically, this pedagogical approach appears to facilitate the development of genre knowledge for writers like international graduate students, scholars, and professionals faced with high-level writing demands in a second language; nevertheless, several criticisms have been raised against genre-centered teaching.

Some critics of both the Australian and ESP models have pointed to the danger that teaching genres in the classroom can serve to reify the power structures in which they are embedded; these critics advocate a more critical approach through which academic norms are challenged rather than accepted (Benesch, 1995, 2001; Pennycook, 1997). Others problematize the emphasis that genre-centered approaches place on mastery of genres as access to power, overlooking the many other forms of capital (e.g., gender, race, and class) that "may significantly preclude or enable social access" (Luke, 1996, p. 329). Canagarajah's (1996, 2003) work has also highlighted the additional non-discursive elements that can work against writers from developing countries who are disadvantaged by virtue of a system of scholarly publication largely controlled by countries like the United States and Great Britain.

Freedman (1993a, 1993b, 1999) has further argued that discursive practices such as genres are impossible to teach, given the shifting nature of the disciplinary ideologies out of which genres evolve. Related criticisms come from a belief that generic staticity is implicit in any pedagogical application—"unless genres are static, why should they be, and how can they be, taught?" ask Freedman and Medway (1994b, p. 9). Yet, as Swales (2004) notes, such reasoning would discount the validity of much education, particularly in fields like computer science, where knowledge changes at a particularly rapid rate. While the dangers of staticity and prescriptivism are easily recognizable by teachers (Kay & Dudley-Evans, 1998), some have pointed out that there is nothing inherently prescriptive in genre-based approaches (Hyland, 2003; Swales, 1990). Less direct criticism of genre-centered ESP or English for Academic Purposes (EAP) is found in arguments against the teaching of discipline-specific writing in general, as such an approach may require an understanding of disciplinary content as well as disciplinary practices of knowledge construction and dissemination—an understanding that few ESP/EAP instructors could claim outside of their own discipline (Spack, 1988).

Related views argue that writers need to participate in a discipline in order to learn the discipline's writing (Spack, 1988) and that genres can therefore only be acquired within the specific milieu in which they exist (Freedman, 1993a; Freedman, Adam, & Smart, 1994). These claims quite accurately emphasize the situatedness of genre learning and the very real distinctions between classroom and non-classroom writing; what they fail to account for, however, is the often fuzzy nature of the boundary between these two contexts. In many cases of ESP or EAP instruction, for example, the classroom is embedded within the larger disciplinary or professional world. Learners come to classrooms with writing tasks that they are completing in their content courses, at work, or in their independent research. They leave the writing classroom and go directly to their lab, to a study group, or even to a research conference. In a sense, the classroom is a part of the disciplinary domain in which genres are best learned; in workplace ESP, these boundaries may be even less distinguishable. Yet in both cases, there remain important differences between the classroom and non-classroom contexts, as I shall show throughout this book.

The lively debate over the role of writing instruction in the development of genre knowledge remains important for those who teach in contexts where mastery of specialized genres is one key to success. Over a decade ago, Aviva Freedman (1993a), in a well-known impeachment of "explicit teaching"[1] of genre in the classroom, called for empirical investigations of genre teaching. In a follow-up article, she reiterated this call unequivocally, stating: "It should not be the task of the skeptics to argue against a pedagogic strategy but rather the work of the proponents to bring forward convincing research and theoretical evidence—preferably before its wholesale introduction" (Freedman, 1993b, p. 279). Despite the echoing of this need for more empirical research (Hyland, 2000; Hyon, 1996; Parks, 2001; Swales, 1990, 2000), studies of genre and instruction have so far remained primarily theoretical and anecdotal. A fairly sizable number of studies have investigated how writers develop knowledge of genres and discourses through disciplinary or workplace practice, but fewer studies have looked at this development systematically within writing classrooms. Particularly lacking is research that follows the same writers as they negotiate both of these intermingling and interacting contexts (see Tardy, 2006, for a comparison of studies in various contexts).

PRACTICE, TASK, DISCOURSE, AND GENRE

Before delving into the complicated task of defining genre knowledge and its development, I need to address what underlies the theory and practice of specialized writing. I see four constructs as fundamental: practice, task, discourse, and genre. In my view, these are somewhat parallel concepts, with *practice* and *discourse* describing broad levels of interaction and communication channels, while *task* and *genre* describe more specific, typified instances of the larger categories.

Taking a social view of written communication, *practice* may be defined as *doing*, where the meaning and the structure of that doing is constructed by its social and historical context (Wenger, 1998). Examples of practice include conducting research, reading, and writing. Through practice, writers interact with the artifacts and people within the given sociohistorical contexts, making meaning and building knowledge (Prior, 1998). A related concept is that of *activity*, such as participation in monthly laboratory meetings, collaboration on a journal article, or presentation of a conference paper. These events are defined by their sociohistorical context, their goals, and the "tools" and "objects" (e.g., genres or technology) used to carry out those goals. The term *activity* is associated with Vygotskyan sociocultural perspectives on learning, in which "object-directed, tool-mediated" interactions are referred to as activity systems (Russell, 1997). Activity has served as a powerful theoretical construct for many ethnographic studies of writers and writing contexts. However, I will limit its use throughout this book—at least in its more theoretical sense as part of activity theory—for several reasons. First, the research I share in this book is not fully ethnographic, in that I did not observe extensive social interactions in most of the writers' contexts (with the exception of the writing classroom); it is in this careful ethnographic account of social practice that I believe *activity* becomes such a useful concept. Additionally, while activity theory has had much to contribute to studies of genre practice, I found myself often becoming lost in its terminological web when bringing it to the overlapping domains and communities that I follow in this book. As a result, I have turned instead to the concept of *task*.

As an alternative to activity, task may offer a more robust construct for studying the actual practice of individuals. Swales (1990) defines *task* as:

> One of a set of differentiated, sequenceable goal-directed activities drawing upon a range of cognitive and communicative procedures relatable to the acquisition of pre-genre and genre skills appropriate to a foreseen or emerging sociorhetorical situation. (p. 74)

Though he describes task in the context of teaching methodology, I will use the term to refer to specific goal-oriented, *rhetorical* literacy events in both disciplinary and classroom domains—for example, writing a master's thesis, collaborating on a conference paper, or completing a classroom assignment. Bracewell and Witte (2003) similarly propose *task* as an important construct for studying workplace literacy, defining it as "the set of goals and actions that implement these goals, which are developed in order to achieve a solution to a complex problem within a specific work context" (p. 528). While this definition shares similarities with that of activity, it is more localized in time and space and may therefore foreground individualized actions; writers engage in activities through tasks. Because the writers in my study often worked independently and because my research tended to focus more on these writers' individual actions than on group participation, *task* in many cases provided a more useful metaphor for understanding their writing practice at given points in time. At the same time, I acknowledge that a focus on activity has much to offer the study of writing development; indeed, I see these theoretical approaches as complementary.

Key channels of participation in academic literacy practices and tasks include *discourse* and *genre.* In contrast to practice/task, which focus on social interaction, I use these terms to emphasize a focus on the language—oral, written, and even visual—used to mediate social interactions. On one level, discourse is the language, broadly speaking, used by particular groups and/or in particular situations. Corpus-based language analysis, for example, has illustrated that academic discourse can be characterized by certain linguistic features that distinguish it from other registers, such as conversation, news, or fiction (Biber, 1988). More recent work has studied discourse variation among academic disciplines, finding linguistic differences between disciplines like history and biology (Conrad, 2001) or, more broadly, the soft sciences and the hard sciences (Hyland, 2000). While this primarily linguistic use of the term is focused on structural patterns, discourse also encompasses the ideologies and worldviews that shape and are shaped by communication. The term *disciplinary discourse,* for instance, captures the meaning of "thinking and talking like an engineer" (or biologist, or philosopher, and so on). Discourse is, as Gee (1999) describes it, more than language; it is an "identity kit." Discourses shape our perceptions of the world, including how we communicate, act, interact, and understand.

When discourses become typified—that is, when the same events are carried out repeatedly through the same practices—they may be referred to as *genres*. Examples of written genres include dissertations, research articles, manuscript reviews, or submission letters, and each of these may be carried out uniquely by different social groups. Dissertations, for example, differ in a range of ways across institutions, disciplines, and geopolitical contexts. Becoming an accepted member of a disciplinary community (in both its local and global manifestations) is at least partially dependent on mastery of its discourse and unique use of genres, or the preferred means for arguing and evaluating within the field (McNabb, 2001; Said, 1982). Genre theory offers one means for understanding this type of conventionalized disciplinary communication.

Since the mid-1980s, many in applied linguistics, rhetoric, and education have turned to a view of genre as social action (Bazerman, 1988; Berkenkotter & Huckin, 1995; Kamberelis, 1995; Miller, 1984; Swales, 1990). Miller (1984) argues that a rhetorical view of genre must center on the action that a genre carries out, rather than on its formal features or "text type"; it is through this social action that people create the knowledge that is necessary in reproducing the generic structure (Miller, 1994). Genre is therefore a product or byproduct of repeated, specialized practice. At the same time, genres themselves may shape activities over time, providing a structure or scaffolding for practice (Bazerman, 1988; Kamberelis, 1995). More recently, Devitt (2004) has described genre as not so much a response to a recurring situation, but rather a "nexus between an individual's action and socially defined context" (p. 31). This metaphor accounts for the structurated nature of genres as they act and are acted upon by individuals and in social contexts. In this thoroughly rhetorical view, learning to use genres requires much more than learning text types and forms; it requires learning the social contexts, actions, and goals that give genres their meaning.

To this point, a sizable body of research has analyzed genres with the aim of uncovering the rhetorical functions that give rise to certain discoursal features. Ken Hyland's (2000) work, for example, has convincingly shown how features like generic move structure, citations, and hedges and boosters reflect the ideologies and epistemologies of their authoring communities. Genres that carry heavy weight in the academic world have been studied in the most depth, giving rise to rather detailed descriptions of research articles across disciplinary, cultural, and linguistic communities. In the early days, such work appeared to be motivated by an interest in uncovering "teachable" textual features to second language writers. More recently, this research seems to be more concerned with complicating our understanding of text types and their dynamic and social nature. In both cases, it is clear that genres act not only as channels of communication but also as barriers for novices or outsiders. Genres have a way of regulating communication among groups, and as their features become conventionalized, the values embedded in them too become assumed and often unquestioned. Given the hierarchical nature of many disciplinary communities, genres may therefore benefit the expert, who can use the genres in rhetorically effective ways, and further exclude or alienate the novice, for whom the values and conventions are more mysterious or perhaps even distasteful. This dynamic is clearly evident in academic discourse, as students struggle to play the game of academic writing, but it also exists in professional and public spheres.

NETWORKS OF GENRES

While a focus on individual genres is an important step toward understanding texts—what they look like in various contexts, what ideologies and goals they index, how and why they are (re)produced—this individual focus artificially strips away much of what gives a genre its meaning. As genres are used by a social group to carry out particular social actions, they rarely—if ever—function alone; instead, they interact with layers of other genres used to accomplish other, related goals. Kamberelis (1995) depicts this fluid and interconnected nature of genres as he writes:

> Any given field of practice is constituted by many related and partially overlapping genres . . . Additionally, fields of practice are themselves highly interconnected . . . Finally, individuals simultaneously belong to multiple, overlapping, and sometimes contradictory communities of practice, often moving in and out of them quite seamlessly. With all this overlap of fields, practices, texts, and people, the forms, functions, and practices of different genres leak into one

> another in a kind of metonymic or interdiscursive
> process of social semiosis. (p. 139)

In contemporary genre theory, the move toward a more integrated orientation to genre was first proposed by Amy Devitt (1991) in her exploration of the genre sets of tax accounting. Devitt (2004) has argued that viewing genres as intertextual and dialogic "allows us to see the inherent relatedness of genres within the same social group and its actions" (p. 55). In other words, studying genres as sets, systems, or clusters highlights how they respond to one another in order to accomplish a group's goals and activity.

The notion of genre network grows out of Bakhtin's (1986) insistence that genres are intertextual by their very nature. They are born out of prior texts and retain traces of those texts. This intertextuality not only gives a genre meaning, but also serves as a *modus operandi* for learning. That is, as new users of genres attempt to find the preferred ways of constructing genres and texts within a social setting, they often turn to previous texts that they have encountered (Kamberelis, 1995). They may borrow explicit textual fragments, they may draw on textual conventions or practices, or they may look to support genres like guidelines, feedback, or prior texts to learn how to communicate effectively. Learners may also draw on *oral* encounters surrounding texts, such as conversations with mentors, class discussions, or feedback from peers. Ivanič (1998) refers to these interactions as "intermental encounters" and illustrates through her research how such encounters may exert significant influence on writers.

It should be clear from this discussion that genres relate to one another in a variety of ways. At the most general level, genres are intertextually networked, containing traces of prior texts. Beyond this level, scholarly terminology becomes confusing and even somewhat haphazard. Genres exist in conversation, as responses and rejoinders (Bakhtin, 1986), or uptakes (Freadman, 1994). Devitt (2004) refers to these dialogical relationships as *genre sets,* while Swales (2004) uses the term *genre chains,* drawing on Räisänen's (1999) use of the term in describing crash safety; this latter metaphor seems to best capture the chronological and essentially interlinked nature of dialogue.

A third level of generic relationship is Devitt's (1991) originally-labeled *genre set,* which she has since re-named *genre repertoire* (Devitt, 2004), defining it as the set of genres owned by a given group. Devitt

(2004) distinguishes a repertoire as larger and less tightly knit than a genre chain:

> *Repertoire* is an especially helpful term . . . for it con-
> notes not only a set of interacting genres but also a set
> from which participants choose, a definer of the pos-
> sibilities available to the group . . . The genres within
> a repertoire do interact, though often in less obvious
> ways, with less clear-cut sequencing and more indirect
> connections than exist in a genre system." (p. 57)

At the risk of adding more confusion to an already murky pool of terms, it seems to me that both *repertoire* and *set* are terminological-ly useful. While a repertoire might refer to *all* of a group's available genres, a set might best refer to the genres available for a given rhetori-cal goal (e.g., genres for job promotion, genres for laboratory safety). Application of these terms immediately highlights their overlapping nature, yet I believe it is at times useful to distinguish sets from a full repertoire when considering the learning process. While the ultimate goal for novices may be access to a group's full genre repertoire, this process is likely to occur through accumulated engagement with dif-ferent genre sets.

While a genre repertoire includes all of the genres owned by a given group, a *genre system* would include genres owned and used by mul-tiple groups, all toward an ultimate rhetorical goal. Bazerman (1994) describes a genre system as

> . . . the full set of genres that instantiate the participa-
> tion of all the parties—that is the full file of letters
> from and to the client, from and to the government,
> from and to the accountant. This would be the full
> interaction, the full event, the set of social relations as
> it has been enacted. (p. 99)

For simplicity in referring to this myriad of intertextual relationships, I will use *genre networks* as an umbrella term. In cases where it is im-portant to distinguish the different relationships among genres, I will use the more specified terms described above.

A growing body of research has examined genre sets, repertoires, and systems, including those of tax accounting, patent law, psycho-therapy paperwork, faculty tenure files, grant funding, and electronic communities (Bazerman, 1994; Berkenkotter, 2001; Devitt, 1991; Hyon & Chen, 2004; Samraj, 2005; Tardy, 2003; Yates & Orlikowski, 2002). In this book, however, I will push the notion of genre networks a bit further to consider what it has to offer to an understanding of genre *learning*. A focus on genres as discrete entities, for example, masks many of the important influences on the process of genre learning and on how writers' involvement in larger social and textual systems may help or hinder that process. In the subsequent chapters, I will explore some of these influences as well as the ways in which participation in genre networks might help learners develop a more sophisticated understanding of the system's core genres, including an understanding of how to manipulate those genres for their own purposes. In academic settings, these core genres might include research articles or proposals; in workplace settings, they might include project reports or presentations. These are the high-stakes, prestige genres.

Before turning to a discussion of genre knowledge and how such knowledge is developed, I will briefly outline relevant models of expertise. Theories of expertise are useful at this juncture because they offer a framework for understanding what it means to be an expert writer in a specific domain and how novices might develop such expertise.

Expertise

Theories of expertise have been situated mainly, though not exclusively, within the field of cognitive psychology. Notable theorists Carl Bereiter and Marlene Scardamalia define expertise as "effortfully acquired abilities . . . that carry us beyond what nature has specifically prepared us to do" (1993, p. 3). They claim that experts are better problem solvers in their own local domains because they are able to draw on knowledge that allows them to think *less* than non-experts. Outside of their domains of expertise, however, experts work harder and appear to work toward extending their knowledge instead of utilizing the knowledge they already possess. Bereiter and Scardamalia (1993) describe how experts continually reinvest their mental resources, allowing them to address problems at increasingly higher levels. Useful to an understanding of writer expertise in particular are Bereiter and Scardamalia's (1987) models of *knowledge-telling* and *knowledge-transforming*. Knowledge-telling is a model of text composing generally adopted by inexperienced writers who utilize only the topic, genre constraints, and text as sources of knowledge. These sources provide novices with strategies for composing without additional support, using readily available knowledge and discourse production skills that they already possess. Expert writers, according to Bereiter and Scardamalia, go beyond knowledge-telling to rework or transform their knowledge. In this knowledge-transforming model, writers actively transform their ideas as they move between developing knowledge and developing text.

This two-way interaction between content and rhetoric is termed the "dual problem space" by Bereiter and Scardamalia (1987). It is this space that Geisler (1994) further explores in her model of expertise. In Geisler's model, abstractions play a key role; it is in the domain-content space where experts develop abstractions that lead them to go beyond lay knowledge, and it is in the rhetorical-process space where experts "develop the reasoning structures that enable them to bring those abstractions to bear upon the contexts in which they work" (Geisler, 1994, p. 84). Geisler suggests that it is the shifting between these two spaces that leads experts to go beyond knowledge-telling and into knowledge-transforming. Applied to disciplinary writing, this model would suggest that experts build disciplinary knowledge and develop discursive and rhetorical skills simultaneously, with each process interacting and building upon one another.

Geisler goes on to outline an acquisition process of expertise that encompasses three distinct periods. In the first period, writers engage in knowledge-telling, viewing texts as autonomous. In this stage, the rhetorical domain is generally collapsed within the content domain. In the intermediate stage, writers begin to work increasingly with abstractions through tacitly acquired knowledge, yet they continue to hold relatively naïve representations of the rhetorical space. In the final stage, writers are able to reorganize and abstract the rhetorical-problem space as distinct from the domain-content space; that is, they begin to view texts as having authors, claims, credibility, and temporality. At this stage, writers work with abstractions in both the rhetorical-problem space and domain-content space, engaging in the "dynamic interplay that produces expertise" (1994, p. 87). This importance of the rhetorical-problem space is echoed in ethnographic research by Smart (2000) in which workplace writers engaged in domain-specific writing simultaneously developed an "increased awareness of the rhetorical situation and textual conventions associated with the genre" (p. 240).

An alternative pluralistic theory of expertise is offered by Carter (1990), who views performance-guiding knowledge as a continuum from general knowledge to highly contextualized local knowledge. This theory describes a complementary relationship between these two types of knowledge, acknowledging that both are important in writing expertise. According to Carter, when writing in unfamiliar domains, novices apply global strategies to guide their performance, allowing them to acquire more local knowledge, which in turn allows them to rely less on global strategies. Thus, when expert writers encounter new tasks in their local domain, they can draw on highly-contextualized strategies.

Carter applies his global-local knowledge continuum to five stages of expertise described by Dreyfus and Dreyfus (1986). The first level is the novice stage, then "advanced beginners," followed by "competence." Local knowledge becomes crucial after the level of competence, and "it is only when writers work in one or more domains for a while that they begin to develop the local knowledge of that domain" (p. 282). Carter suggests that such knowledge is gained through experience in reading and writing within a local domain, as well as through guidance from teachers. He describes a cyclical process in which "as students continue to work in a domain, their knowledge becomes more local as their experience grows and their domain becomes more specific" (p. 282).

Applying expertise theory specifically to L2 writing, Cumming (1989) examines the relationship between writing expertise and second-language proficiency in an empirical study of adult ESL writers. Cumming's main finding is that both writing expertise and second-language proficiency contribute to writing processes and products, but to different aspects of writing. The characteristics of writing expertise that Cumming outlines for second language (L2) writers reflect characteristics of expert writers performing in their first language, such as the use of heuristics in problem-solving. An additional important finding in Cumming's research is that L2 writers seem to improve their writing performance as their language proficiency increases. However, increased proficiency may not affect *qualitative* changes in the writers' processes of thinking or decision-making as they compose. Cumming concludes that writing expertise may be an intelligence that is separate from L2 proficiency, employing cognitive skills that are applicable across languages rather than being specific to a first or second language.

These theories of expertise have illuminated an understanding of writing performance as encompassing a range of interacting domains. It appears that expert writers draw on strategies at various levels as well as domain-specific experience in their problem-solving process. While Cumming's work suggests that expertise may not be a language-specific skill, there remain questions as to how language proficiency and expertise may interact in domain-specific writing tasks.

GENRE KNOWLEDGE

In order to communicate actively, appropriately, and successfully within a specific domain or disciplinary discourse community—that is, to communicate as an expert—writers must develop[2] *genre knowledge.* At the outset, I need to emphasize that I see genre knowledge as related but not identical to general second language (or even first language) writing skills. In a thorough and thoughtful exploration of the construct of writing, Grabe (2000) lays the groundwork for moving toward a theory of second language writing. He argues that a useful starting point for theory building is to generate a taxonomy of research on aspects of writing, or "conditions on learning to write" (Grabe, 2000, p. 52). Along with categories like knowing the language, processing factors, and social context, Grabe lists "discourse, genre, and register knowledge" as one category that needs to be fully researched in order to gain a more complete picture of L2 writing. Exploring this category is the goal of this book; the first hurdle is to define the construct of genre knowledge.

On the most salient level, genre knowledge is an understanding of text form, including elements like text organization, disciplinary terminology, or citation practices (Beaufort, 1999). But genre knowledge extends beyond form to less visible knowledge such as an understanding of a discourse community's ideologies and discursive practices, or even domain-specific content knowledge (Berkenkotter & Huckin, 1995; Bhatia, 1999). Knowledge of genre also requires writers to understand a text's rhetorical timing, surprise value, or *kairos,* including a sense of how a text may be received at a given time within a given community. In addition, expert writers share an understanding of genre membership, knowing the in-group generic label (Johns, 1997) or recognizing prototypes or exemplars of the genre (Paltridge, 1997; Swales, 1990).

In her research of specialized writing in the workplace and disciplinary content classrooms, Beaufort (1999, 2004) has mapped the knowledge domains that constitute disciplinary writing expertise. Her model foregrounds "discourse community knowledge" as encompassing the overlapping domains of writing process knowledge, subject matter knowledge, rhetorical knowledge, and genre knowledge. Another model of disciplinary writing is proposed by Jolliffe and Brier (1988), who describe writer's knowledge in academic disciplines as composed of knowledge of discourse community; subject matter and methods of investigating subject matter; organization, arrangement, form, and genre; and ways of speaking. These components correspond roughly to four of the five canons of rhetoric: audience, invention, arrangement, and style, respectively. Both of these models are intended to describe disciplinary writing knowledge, of which genre is considered one element. In these models, genre knowledge itself is represented as essentially textual knowledge that intermingles with knowledge of discourse community, rhetoric, subject matter, and writing processes. Both models aptly situate genre knowledge as embedded within broader knowledge of disciplinary discourse, but if we adopt a fully rhetorical view of genre, genre knowledge (as a category) must represent more than form.

Because of my interest in the learning and teaching of specialized genres, I focus here specifically on defining and theorizing genre knowledge. In the model I offer, genre knowledge cannot exist separately from *formal, process, rhetorical,* or *subject-matter knowledge;* instead, it is a confluence of these four dimensions. Drawing on my earlier discussion of genre theory, I see genres as social actions that are used within specialized communities; that contain traces of prior texts in their shape, content, and ideology; and that are networked with other genres in various ways that influence their production and reception. Taking this definition, expert genre knowledge must contain knowledge in all of these areas. While the architecture of this model implies distinct knowledge domains, it is important to stress that the boundaries here merely serve a heuristic purpose. Rather than representing any kind of epistemic reality, they provide a framework for understanding the writers' knowledge at different points in time and the ways in which various practices influence knowledge development.

I use the term *formal knowledge* to refer to the more structural elements of genre—the genre's prototypical form(s), discourse or lexico-grammatical conventions of the genre, the contents or structural moves that are common to the genre, and the various modes and media through which the genre may be communicated. This knowledge focuses on the textual instantiation of the genre, in either oral or written form. Knowledge of a genre's contents or modality is used here to refer to a relatively "arhetorical" understanding based primarily on knowledge of conventionalized form rather than a focus on the rhetorical context. Formal knowledge also includes knowledge of linguistic code—an issue that is of special relevance to those writing in their second language or dialect.

Process knowledge refers to all of the procedural practices associated with the genre—that is, how a genre is carried out. Such knowledge would encompass the process(es) that users of the genre go through in order to complete their intended action, such as the oral interactions that might facilitate effective reception of a genre or the actual composing processes that aid the writer in text completion. Process knowledge also encompasses an understanding of the distribution of the genre to its audience and the reading practices of the receivers of the genre. Finally, process knowledge includes knowledge of the larger genre network and a grasp of how the networked genres work together in chains, sets, or systems.

Both formal knowledge and process knowledge have great potential to overlap with *rhetorical knowledge,* which captures an understanding of the genre's intended purposes and an awareness of the dynamics of persuasion within a sociorhetorical context. Writers need, for example, a sense of what the genre is intended to do within a local context and how power is distributed within that context. They also need to anticipate the readers of the genre, in terms of their purposes for reading the text, their expectations for the text, and their values that may influence their reception of the text. Rhetorical knowledge further includes the writer's understanding of his or her own positioning vis-à-vis the context and the specific readers. A writer's age, professional status, and perceived linguistic abilities are just some factors that are likely to influence the writing and reception of any genre.

Finally, *subject-matter knowledge* is an important, yet often overlooked (Jolliffe, 1995), domain of genre knowledge. When writing a research article in biomedical engineering, for example, a writer's knowledge of the relevant content within biomedical engineering is crucial for his or her success in writing the text. Other genres, such as résumés, require less subject-matter knowledge. However, when interacting with other knowledge domains, subject-matter knowledge is essential in pushing writers toward expertise for many genres.

While the construct of *knowledge* is certainly more abstract than much of my discussion here might imply, I nevertheless find categorization of knowledge domains to be useful in tracing writers' knowledge development in different contexts. Are certain knowledge dimensions developed more efficiently in some contexts than in others? Do strategies for developing different knowledge domains differ? Following writers and attempting to peer inside their minds and texts, I have come to see knowledge as an awareness (conscious or unconscious) that can deepen and extend as it is applied in new situations and as writers pull together various knowledge features to greater or lesser degrees. As I traced the formal, rhetorical, process, and subject-matter dimensions of genre knowledge, I saw them become increasingly integrated with growing expertise—inseparably so.

Figure 1 provides a visual metaphor for this increased integration, where writers' knowledge of unfamiliar genres may artificially separate the genre's form, subject matter, rhetorical goals and context, and procedures that surround its distribution and reception.

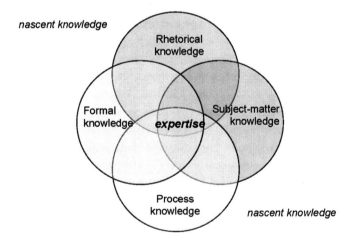

Figure 1. Integration of genre knowledge.

When first approaching the task of writing a job application letter, for example, the writers I followed tended to think of form and
content as distinct from issues of the rhetorical context or procedures.
They asked themselves questions like *what is the proper form?* or *what
do readers expect to find in this letter?* But they did not ask what I might
call more "integrated" questions like *how might I modify the organization of my letter for this particular employer?*—at least not in their first
encounters, which took place within a classroom environment.

In early genre encounters, writers are faced with the demands of
attending to multiple generic issues, and the cognitive load becomes
heavier as multiple layers of requisite knowledge are added to picture,
such as linguistic elements or the composing process. Furthermore,
general distinctions between first and second language writing would
suggest that these demands are even more complex for second language writers. But as writers re-encounter the same genre, certain dimensions of genre knowledge eventually become more or less "second
nature," so that the writer no longer needs to attend explicitly to those
features (Jolliffe & Brier, 1988; Kamberelis, 1995). This process reflects very closely that of cognitive theories of language learning relating to processing and automaticity (see, for example, Segalowitz,
2003). As McLaughlin (1990) describes it, when a complex task is first
approached, people attend to various features of the task; with a great
deal of practice, the component skills become automatic.

With practice, boundaries between the components, or dimensions
(as in Figure 1), become fuzzier. Writers integrate some dimensions
but still focus on other individual elements in isolation. The extent of
overlap or discreteness among dimensions depends on the situational
context and task to which the writers are responding. Additionally,
writers may find themselves foregrounding or backgrounding different knowledge dimensions when responding to different tasks (Prior,
1998; Tardy, 2003). In a writing classroom, for example, writers may
be more apt to focus predominantly on form; on the other hand, in
a disciplinary exam such as a doctoral preliminary paper, they may
focus on subject-matter content. This tendency may provide some insight into the issue of whether or not different dimensions are better
developed in different domains (Freedman, 1993a, 1993b; Freedman,
Adam, & Smart 1994). As I'll illustrate in later chapters, the writers
in my research were able to develop some rhetorical knowledge in the
writing classroom, but their primary focus in that setting tended to be

on form. In their disciplinary courses, on the other hand, the writers often attended more to subject-matter and rhetorical dimensions than to formal dimensions.

Genre knowledge development, like all writing development or language development, more broadly, does not occur in simple linear fashion. Rather, learners seem to go through a process of restructuring, so that new knowledge results in qualitative changes to the internal organization of knowledge, rather than simply in the addition of new structural knowledge. In McLaughlin's (1990) words:

> Restructuring can be seen as a process in which the components of a task are coordinated, integrated, or reorganized into new units, thereby allowing the pro-cedure involving old components to be replaced by a more efficient procedure involving new components. (p. 118)

In other words, writers do not accumulate new knowledge as some-thing like an expanding bulleted list; rather, every new "bit" of knowl-edge becomes integrated with existing knowledge, resulting in a fun-damental change to the learners' larger understanding.

As the writers described in this book became more expert genre users, they spoke of texts and textual practices in a way that considered form, rhetoric, procedure, and subject matter as inseparable. In doing so, their previous understanding of dimensions like form was revised. For instance, as one writer spoke of his attempts to organize a confer-ence paper, he drew simultaneously on his understanding of process, form, rhetoric, and subject matter. In analyzing data from this writing task, I found these categories of knowledge to be of little use as they no longer captured the delicate shades of genre knowledge that the writer held at that point. While other genre knowledge theories (e.g., Berkenkotter & Huckin, 1995; Bhatia, 1999; Jolliffe & Brier, 1988; Paltridge, 1997; Swales, 1990) do consider multidimensionality, they lack an explicit explanation of development. There is an implication in such theories that writers either hold knowledge of particular dimen-sions or they do not (cf. Beaufort, 1999); instead, it seems to me that writers can feasibly hold all of the requisite knowledge of a genre, yet fail to synthesize this knowledge in actual practice. In contrast then to a view of genre knowledge as simply made up various dimensions, a model that can account for increased *integration* of those dimensions offers a more flexible and dynamic picture of writers' knowledge over time.

How then do multilingual writers move from relatively fragmented nascent knowledge toward more integrated expertise? This is the main question that I hope to answer through the stories of the writers in this book, and in exploring this question, I move into the social nature of language and knowledge development. Much work on writing and genre development has foregrounded the extent to which writers learn through mentoring and social support, through what Jean Lave and Etienne Wenger term legitimate peripheral participation, or LPP. However, as the case studies in this book illustrate, LPP is not always available to writers—and even when it is, it does not always play a primary role in development. Rather, writers draw on a broad range of strategies and resources as they encounter genres in new contexts and tasks. The book is organized around the sociorhetorical contexts and tasks of writing that the four learners in my research engaged in as graduate students and researchers; this organization allows for a glimpse into the ways in which contexts and tasks both afford and constrain opportunities for genre learning for individuals as they move among overlapping domains of practice.

In chapter 2, I introduce the research context, the four writers, and the social and individual histories that they brought to their graduate studies. Chapters 3 and 4 move to the domain of the writing classroom, illustrating how the writers built genre knowledge in the classroom as they wrote job application cover letters and disciplinary texts as classroom assignments. These chapters trace links between classroom activities, teacher feedback, textual exposure, and the writers' evolving understanding of specific genres, even as they engaged in these genres outside of the classroom. Chapter 5 brings together a range of learning contexts, tracing the writers' practices with and knowledge of the multimodal genre of presentation slides. Exploring the writers' histories and current uses of this genre in classroom and research settings, the chapter illustrates how accumulated exposure and practice can build increasingly sophisticated genre knowledge over time. Chapter 6 moves from the writing classroom into the disciplinary content classroom, showing the strategies and resources that two of the writers drew upon as they attempt to make sense of the learning-based genres of lab reports and reviews. This chapter also considers the extent to which strategies learned in the writing classroom were later adopted by the writers in their disciplinary writing tasks. Moving up through the ranks of academic genres, chapters 7 and 8 explore two of the writers' challenging processes of learning the more prestigious genres of scholarly research—theses and research articles. It is in these chapters that we see the writers begin to integrate forms of knowledge, gradually building the kind of sophisticated and multidimensional genre knowledge characteristic of experts. As I examine these four writers' learning processes over time and in multiples spaces, I will explore the theoretical issues raised in this chapter; in chapter 9, I return to these issues with an eye toward the nature of genre knowledge development and the role of the language and writing classroom in facilitating such knowledge.

2 The Researcher and the Writers

As Casanave (2005) notes, research is primarily told through narrative—that is, through "a complex reconstruction of many tales designed to end with a message of significance" (p. 22). In order to make meaning, narrative weaves together various stories, tidying up the details along the way to help us make sense of a larger whole. In this chapter, I share the background to the research narrative that unfolds throughout the book. I begin by sharing my own paradigm of inquiry and the research methodology I have adopted, and I then describe the context in which my research took place and the writers whom I followed.

APPROACH TO INQUIRY

Ideology and inquiry paradigms are contentious aspects of knowledge construction, serving to distinguish sciences from social sciences from humanities, and even causing friction within many disciplinary fields of study. I use the term *ideology* here to refer to ontology (the nature of reality), epistemology (the nature of knowledge), axiology (the nature of value), and methodology (the procedures for knowledge construction). (See Silva, 2005, for a much more in-depth treatment of ideology and paradigms of inquiry.) In line with Harklau and Williams (in press), I believe strongly in the value of researchers examining and sharing their own ideologies and inquiry paradigms with readers, so I attempt to do so here.

The paradigm of knowledge construction that underlies the research in this book is best characterized by what Silva (2005) refers to as *humble pragmatic rationalism (HPR)*, also known as critical rationalism. Drawing on the work of Karl Popper, Silva defines HPR as follows:

... HPR's ontology is that of a modified realism; that
is, reality exists, but can never be fully known. It is
driven by natural laws that can only be incompletely
or partially understood. HPR's epistemology is inter-
actionist—a result of the interaction between subject
(researcher) and object (physical reality), wherein a
human being's perceptual, cognitive, and social filters preclude any totally objective or absolute knowledge. Regarding axiology, HPR values knowledge—
knowledge that is tentative, contingent, and probabi-
listic. HPR's methodology is multimodal—involving
the integration of empirical study (qualitative as well
as quantitative) and hermeneutic inquiry (the refine-
ment of ideas through interpretation and dialogue,
through conjecture and refutation). (p. 9)

Throughout the book, I try to stay true to this paradigm. In studying the knowledge development of individual writers, I believe that
there is some physical reality involved in this process that can be *partially* understood through inquiry. I also acknowledge that, without
doubt, my own experiences and identities (as a privileged White, native speaker of English, as an ESL/EFL teacher, as a graduate student
at the time of the research, as someone who has lived and functioned
in a second language) influence my understanding of this reality, and
that my "meddling around" as a researcher has influenced the shape of
the reality. I don't believe that inquiry into a social phenomenon like
writing can uncover an absolute truth, but I do believe it can contribute to tentative and contingent knowledge. Given these beliefs, I see
value in multiple modes of inquiry, or methodologies.

In hoping to understand more closely the processes of genre knowledge building, I have turned here to situated qualitative research as a
primary methodology. I wholeheartedly agree with Atkinson (2005)
that "efforts to study human behavior by limiting its influence, variability, or naturalness are in this sense illusory and misguided" (p.
63). Along those lines, the writers' stories that follow are highly variable and individualized. As a researcher, I remained more interested
in following than controlling the often random and unpredictable influences that seeped into the research context, affecting the writers'
behaviors and processes in a multitude of ways. I struggled often with

the question of to what extent I could or should tidy up their stories, and how doing so would affect not only my own understandings but also those of my readers. With these heavy reservations at the fore, I dove in to the study, in Atkinson's (2005) words, "*doing* the impossible" (p. 63).

RESEARCH CONTEXT

This research follows four international graduate students studying at a U.S. university. While the study began in the confines of an ESL writing course, it continued by following the independent trajectories of the students through their disciplinary programs and research. My goal in following the paths of four writers was to understand better the nature of genre knowledge and how it changes over time, in different contexts. Researchers commonly distinguish a writer's declarative knowledge (the conscious knowledge that the writer can describe) as well as more tacitly held understandings, also called procedural knowledge. In order to access both declarative and procedural knowledge to the extent possible, and to identify such knowledge from various perspectives, I integrated multiple sources, including the writers' texts, texts the writers drew upon or were guided by in their writing tasks, oral interviews with the writers and their writing course instructor, audiotapes of the writers' conference with their writing course instructor, observations and field notes of their writing class sessions, and, in some cases, written feedback from the writers' disciplinary instructors and mentors. I provide a more extensive description of the research design and methodology in Appendix A; information about collected texts, interviews, and instructor conferences are outlined in Appendices B, C, and D.

Midwest University

The Electrical Engineering Building at Midwest University is a three-story red-brick building with large, shiny glass windows and a towering atrium. Pictures of men in suits and gold-plated award plaques hang in the lobby. The white, tile-floor hallways are flanked by rows of closed doors bearing small nameplates, computer-generated images, and flyers for various engineering conferences. Voices at times echo through the halls, scheduling an appointment or discussing a problem encountered in the lab. The voices are usually male; you may hear the American-accented English typical to the evening news, but you are more likely to hear Chinese, Korean, or Indian accents and languages. Thousands of international students studying the sciences and engineering spend their days and evenings—for four or five years—in settings just like this.

For two years, from 2002 through 2004, I spent much of my time trying to learn more about the disciplinary writing development of four of these students at a large, state university in the Midwestern region of the United States (referred to here as "Midwest University"). As a research university with particular strength in engineering and technology fields, Midwest University enrolled the largest number of international students at a U.S. public university at the time of the study. In the fall of 2002, the total enrollment of international students was 4,695; the overall enrollment of international graduate students was 2,670. During the 2002–2003 academic year, almost 43% of the graduate students at the university were considered international students, with the greatest number of these coming from India, People's Republic of China, and South Korea. Many of these students were enrolled in the university's nationally-recognized programs of Computer Sciences (CS) and Electrical and Computer Engineering (ECE). In these departments, the diversity of the student population reflects that of the faculty, many of whom are originally from Asia or Europe.

International students in particular often come to these programs with extensive workplace experience and jobs to which they plan to return after completing their degrees. While some graduate students in these departments prepare for an academic career, many pursue work in industry; in their departmental websites, both CS and ECE stress their ties to the private sector. Because the departments do not necessarily prepare students for academic careers, as is more often the case in the humanities and social sciences, the *academic* environment of graduate school, and all of the norms and values of that environment, may at times conflict with some students' experiences before and/or after their graduate study.

The Writing Classroom: WCGS

Three times a week, a small number of engineering and science graduate students from across the Midwest University campus leave the cul-

turally and linguistically diverse hallways of the engineering and science buildings to come to the comparatively White and monolingual
"Marshall Hall"—the building that houses the university's English
department. Here, the students converge for 50 minutes to participate
in a course entitled Written Communication for Graduate Students
(or, "WCGS," as I'll refer to it). WCGS is a no-credit, pass/fail writing
course for graduate students for whom English is a second language.
While some departments on campus (such as electrical engineering)
require the course for second language students, other departments
and advisors encourage individual students to enroll. While students
largely appreciate the writing support that the course offers, the lack
of course credit or a grade lead many students to give the course low
priority in comparison with their other courses. Several sections of
WCGS are offered through the English department every semester,
with approximately 60 to 80 students completing the course each year.
The class size is limited to ten students, who come from various departments and programs at the university but are primarily engineers.
While a diverse population of students take WCGS, the majority are
males from East Asian countries.

The course is regularly taught by an English department faculty
member or one of a number of graduate Teaching Assistants (TAs)
with an interest in second language writing. Instructors have a great
degree of autonomy in course design, but they generally cover genres
that are likely to be encountered in academic and professional settings,
such as a curriculum vitae/résumé, conference abstract, grant proposal,
or manuscript review. WCGS students are encouraged to use their current research projects as the content for these assignments. Because of
the small class size, instructors can be fairly flexible in their choice of
assignments and content covered in the course. Some instructors focus
heavily on process and revision, while others may highlight generic
aspects of texts, and still others may require assignments that incorporate interview or ethnography-like tasks that explore social aspects of
writing. Although the class is scheduled to meet for three 50-minute
sessions per week, many instructors choose to hold individual writing
conferences with students (in lieu of class) as they work on composing
and revising their writing for each assignment.

In the course section that I observed, students wrote five major
assignments: a writer's autobiography, a CV/ résumé, a cover letter, a
conference poster or presentation, and a final project chosen by each

individual student. The students each participated in six individual conferences with the instructor during the semester, roughly one conference for each major assignment. The course instructor saw the conferences as serving several purposes, including learning more about the students and their work, tailoring the course to individual student needs, and—with newer students—talking with them and reassuring them about graduate school more generally.

Aside from the major paper drafts, students were not assigned additional homework; given the lack of credit received for the course, the instructor hoped to make it as low-stress as possible. She strove to find paper assignments that the writers could tailor to their individual needs, and believed that students could get out of the course what they wanted to. Class materials included a coursepack designed by the instructor that included numerous sample texts for each assignment, some published examples and some written by previous WCGS students. In addition, the teacher often created handouts for classroom activities, in many cases drawing on materials from Swales and Feak's books (1994a) *Academic Writing for Graduate Students* and (2000) *English in Today's Research World*.

The Instructor: Michele

Prior to the semester that I began my research, the course instructor (who was also a personal friend), "Michele," agreed early on to let me observe her section of WCGS for my research. In her 10 years of teaching writing, Michele (herself a native speaker of English) had taught students of diverse backgrounds and needs, including so-called basic writers, ESL writers, and mainstream students. During the semester that I observed her course, Michele was beginning the fourth and final year of her doctoral study in Rhetoric and Composition. This was her third time teaching WCGS, and she described the students as fairly typical in terms of their stage in their degree programs and level of writing ability.

At the start of the semester, Michele described herself to me as "a social constructivist at heart" and explained her general philosophical approach to teaching as making "invisible practices visible":

> So, it's like, there's all these practices that you need to
> be able to do to gain entry into certain groups, and
> if you don't *do* them, sometimes people aren't even

> aware that you're not doing them, but they'll think you're wrong or off somehow. So, my goal I guess is, I'll help students do what they want to do by making those practices that are hidden and no one's gonna tell them about *visible* . . . Where no one's gonna tell them until after the fact otherwise. (August 28, 2002)

Toward this goal, Michele explained that she planned on including many activities in the class in which students would look at sample texts, discussing the subtleties of texts that might be interpreted in different ways—for example, what she called the "formal informality" of American academic discourse. She hoped to discuss examples of writing in terms of the social interactions conveyed through text. In doing so, her goal was to help students develop strategies for dealing with the situations they may encounter as graduate students:

> I hope students leave the class with an approach to tackle similar situations. So, if they're in a situation where they don't know how they're supposed to write something, they can have some sort of a way they can try to figure it out. So, we look at- one of the things we do is- I hope they look at lots of examples of things. So, they're like, "OK, how do I write a research grant? I'll look at seven other research grants in this field, and- both for large structural things and specific wording kinds of things." And most of them do that already, but, I don't know, "heightened rhetorical awareness" is what I'm looking for. (August 28, 2002)

One of her initial goals was to make the class flexible in addressing individual student interests. Throughout the semester, she encouraged students to bring in papers they were working on outside of the class, to practice delivering upcoming presentations, and to share their professional experiences and questions with others in class.

Michele also explained that she did not tend to view herself as a professorial figure in the classroom, but more a "native speaker friend who happens to have rhetorical training" (August 28, 2002). She explained that many of the students felt somewhat isolated at Midwest

University and that this isolation was impeding their ability to succeed in many of their tasks.

> Sometimes I'm not sure if they really *need* me. I mean, I think they need the *course*. I'm not so sure if they- I think maybe the greatest value of the course is to give students a chance to sit and, you know, have a couple hours a week where they talk about their writing and what they're trying to do with their writing, and how they see their field and the written work they do in their field. It matters less, like, what specific activities you do or who's teaching the course, in a way. It's giving students a structured space to reflect every week about writing, and I think that's maybe the *most* useful part. Because these are smart students. They can figure out some of the specific things taught in the class by themselves. But it's more it gives students an opportunity set aside that they *have to* do that every week that I think is the most useful part. (August 28, 2002)

Michele saw herself, then, as a kind of native-speaker, graduate student informant, facilitating the discussion and practice of scheduled writing tasks.

The Class Members

I began attending WCGS on the first day of the semester, sitting with the students at the tables that circled the room. At the end of the first week, after the class enrollment had stabilized, I presented the details of the project to the 11 class members, explaining why I would be sitting in class with them throughout the semester. I asked for their permission to use their words in my research, and they all decided to sign the Informed Consent Form. The class demographics were representative of the overall demographic of international graduate students enrolled at Midwest University; the majority were males from the Far East studying in fields like computer science, mechanical or electrical engineering, or biological-mechanical-electrical-micro-systems (known as "bioMEMS").

During the semester, the class members appeared to gradually become more and more accustomed to my presence, my notebook, and my small tape recorder. For the most part, I sat in the back corner of the classroom between two students, quietly taking notes. At times, however, I interacted more closely with class members. During their poster sessions, for example, I engaged them in short conversations about their work. Later in the semester, Michele on occasion asked for my ideas on a given topic that was being discussed in the class. Although these "intrusions" were minimal, I mention them because they illustrate that I was a constant presence in WCGS.

THE WRITERS

The four writers whom I focus on in this book—Paul, John, Chatri, and Yoshi—were selected because of their willingness to participate in the research and to discuss and share their writing, and also because they together provided me with a range of backgrounds, interests, and experiences, without differing radically from one another. Paul and John were each beginning the second year of their master's programs, while Yoshi was in his first year of a master's program, and Chatri was beginning his fourth semester of a doctoral program. The four also differed in their professional experiences prior to my research; John and Paul had both begun their graduate work almost immediately after completing their undergraduate degrees, while Yoshi and Chatri both spent several years working before beginning their graduate studies in the United States. All four writers had completed all of their prior education in their home countries outside of the U.S. John, however, had lived in the U.S. from birth through elementary school. Their directions after completing their degrees were uncertain at the start of my study.

The length of time that the writers participated in my research varied because of their different dates of graduation (see Figure 2). As John and Paul both left Midwest University after completing their master's degrees, their participation ended earlier than Yoshi and Chatri. Below, I describe each writer in greater detail, providing further insight into their individual writing histories.

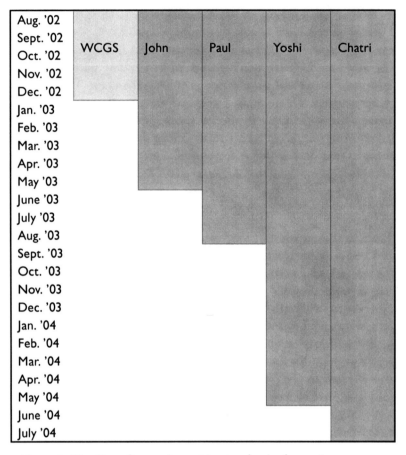

Figure 2. Timeline of research participation for the four writers.

Paul

At the start of the study, Paul was beginning his second year in a master's program in computer sciences. Paul's interest in computer science dated back to his childhood when he loved playing computer games:

> As I mentioned, I like playing games very much. I think since the first computer appeared in China, I was playing, almost. My dad is also in this area, and actually he's an expert on computer science. When I was a child, he brought a computer home and I played

> games on it. So I was getting interested in computer
> science. (September 3, 2002)

A native of China, Paul finished his bachelor's degree in engineering at
a top Chinese university and then worked for one year at a computer
company in China. He described this work as "very tiring" and decided that he wanted to continue his education instead of staying on at
the company. He applied to Midwest University because of its reputation in computer science and because he had a friend at the school who
had recommended it to him.

In our first meeting, Paul explained that his research interest was
"to investigate operating system and compare techniques to find the
solution for hand-held device. The goal is to reduce energy consumption" (September 3, 2002). In his first year in the master's program, he
began working as a Research Assistant (RA) on a research team with
five other graduate students and a professor—all Chinese. Though
the group all shared a native language and home country, they always
spoke in English when the advisor was in the lab. The collegial atmo-
sphere of his research group seemed to play a major role in Paul's interest in staying on for doctoral work in the CS program:

> . . . because both my colleagues and my advisor are
> very nice, and they also help me while I encounter
> some difficulty. I think I learned many things from
> them since I come here. And I think I will continue
> to make progress if I stay here. (September 3, 2002)

At the beginning of my study, Paul was already well on his way to continuing in the graduate program, having completed three of the four
required qualifying exams for PhD students. However, within a few
months after the start of my study—halfway through the second year
of his master's program—Paul had begun to lose interest in continuing
his graduate education. He saw his own strengths and interests as more
aligned with the type of work he could do in industry than with that
done in academe:

> . . . I think I am not an academic people. Doing re-
> search for me is difficult. Not difficult- I know how
> to work on the project, but the research needs more
> patience [*laughing*] and lots of time you cannot come
> up with any conclusions. For the purpose of writing

> paper, the research is good because you can read some
> corrections you cannot answer now. You present some
> work currently you have. But I think I more like to
> come up with very *completed* conclusions and a solu-
> tion to put it into industry. That's what I'm interested
> in. So [*laughing*] I think that I will not go on to PhD.
> (December 12, 2002)

Paul reiterated this sentiment repeatedly throughout my study.

An additional reason for completing his education at the master's
level was that Paul's research interests no longer seemed to fit with
those of his advisor. He was hesitant, however, to change advisors in
order to work with someone in another area:

> Also, I think that, to say the truth, I don't very like
> the area I'm currently in. I think, I don't know,
> maybe it's difficult or- I don't know. [*laughing*] So, I
> will not go on for the PhD. And I haven't think about
> looking for another advisor, I haven't think about it.
> I just want to finish my master's degree. (December
> 12, 2002)

With or without a PhD, Paul described his long-term goal as working
as a programmer for a computer game company. His true love was
program analysis and experimental work.

Whether or not Paul decided to continue for a PhD, the major requirement for completing his master's degree was to write a master's
thesis. During the first half of my research, the requirements for the
thesis still seemed rather mysterious and vague to Paul, though he believed that his advisor would be playing a prominent role in terms of
giving feedback. By the sixth month of my study, though, Paul had
started becoming nervous about his thesis. He had hoped to conduct
research on the area of inter-network security, but without any promising results in his experiments, he was unable to focus on a specific
topic. Five months later, when his thesis had been completed, Paul had
an increased sense of confidence in writing in English and a sense that
he would be able to tackle whatever future writing tasks he encountered.

Prior to coming to the U.S., Paul had written papers in English
courses, a bachelor's thesis in Chinese, and some internal company

documents in Chinese. He had also translated into English the abstract of his thesis and a peer's short master's thesis. The summer before my research began and at school breaks during the study, Paul worked as an intern at a local computer software company. In this position, he wrote regular progress reports and memos to document his work. At the start of WCGS, Paul described most of his English-language writing as email communication with friends. He explained that he had written homework assignments for classes, but these consisted primarily of algorithms.

Though he wrote a great deal of email—both in English and Chinese—Paul initially told me that he did not like writing very much:

> Because I think reason is I was forced to do so. Writing letters is different. Letters, you are willing to write letters to your friends. Letters is, I think fine, but some formal document is not. (September 3, 2002)

He also described feeling more comfortable with workplace writing than academic writing. He particularly preferred programming documentation (a common form of writing at work), which he described as "very natural" and following a basic format.

After two years of graduate school, Paul felt that his writing had changed, though he found it difficult to identify what the changes were beyond increased confidence. He felt his English-language writing had had been influenced by readings, homework assignments, instructors, collaborative writing, and oral interactions. Despite these influences, however, Paul felt a strong ownership of his writing, and credited his very early days of literacy as contributing most significantly to his current writing style.

Paul's enrollment in WCGS was recommended by his advisor, but Paul felt that it would be helpful to him, especially when writing his thesis. Within the first few weeks of the semester, he explained that he was more accustomed to informal writing than academic writing, and he described his goals for WCGS as learning to format papers and writing them in a way that was "comfortable" for academics.

John

In his rapid, American-style speech, John, a second-year master's student with black hair and small, rectangular glasses, described to me his unique linguistic identity during our first meeting. Twenty-five years of age at the start of my research, John was born in the United States, where he spent his first several years and one year of graduate school. He had spent the rest of his life in South Korea, his parents' home country, where he attended middle school, high school, and undergraduate schooling:

> I think I have two first languages, so basically when I was born and for the first years before preschool, Korean was predominant language, because I would also speak in Korean with my parents. And then after preschool, I spent more time with my peers and spend more time speaking English, so I basically forgot all of my Korean. And then I moved back to Korea. When I moved back to Korea, I didn't have any command of the Korean language. (September 4, 2002)

Out of necessity, John learned Korean quickly. Even after several years living in South Korea, John still felt most comfortable communicating in English. The chance to use English, paired with his feeling that the top electrical engineering schools were located in the U.S., led John to apply to several U.S. graduate programs to continue his education.

John had always been interested in science, but engineering was not in fact his first love:

> Well, I *was* interested in physics. Because when I was a little boy, my, like, dream was to get a Nobel Prize . . . in physics. Because I always loved reading science-related books, or science fiction, fantasy book, even just non-fiction books about science. So, I was just fascinated with physics. And then, after moving to Korea—it's a pretty funny reason—but the college that I wanted to apply to didn't have a physics course separately, but they just lumped all the sciences together. I didn't really like that idea so I chose a different field, which is the closest to physics that I could find, and that was electrical engineering. (September 4, 2002)

Like Paul, John's father was in the field that John himself eventually entered. From the time he began studying in the field of electrical engineering, John's interests had changed from robotics to semi-conductor devices to his current interest in biomedical engineering—more specifically, bio-micro-electrical-mechanical systems, or "bioMEMS." John spoke about his work with passion and intensity:

> I really enjoy helping people. I mean helping people in a direct way. Like, for example, if I were to earn money and become somebody like Bill Gates and then finance all of these things, I probably wouldn't be that happy because that'd be too indirect for me. But if I developed a robotic leg—which I was very interested in robotic prosthesis when I applied to Midwest University—so that I could change somebody's life, even if I didn't know that person personally, I know that the research I did would directly affect somebody in a good way. (September 4, 2002)

At the start of my study, John's goal was to enter a PhD program after completing of his master's degree, and eventually to go on to start his own company. Based on his brief experience in corporate culture prior to his master's degree, John felt that he would be happier starting his own company "where it's more free, and I have associates in that company who agree with what I think" (September 4, 2002). During the first four months of my study, however, John modified these long-term goals. At the end of WCGS, and after submitting applications to five doctoral programs in bioMEMS, John began leaning more toward an academic career, feeling that it would allow him more time for family and other interests.

In our first interview, John told me that he enjoyed writing and that, from elementary school on, it had come fairly naturally to him:

> A lot of my friends suffered through writing, like don't know what to write, but- I don't know about my *form* or anything, but usually I just [*gestures a whirlwind*] go through it, and after recomposing what I wrote, pretty satisfied with what I wrote. (September 4, 2002)

Despite his relative confidence in his writing, John felt that he was somewhat limited to only one "tone of voice," making it difficult to change the style of his writing for different contexts or genres. John, like Paul, felt that his writing style was rooted in his very early writing experiences:

> I think it was the people who influenced my writing, who developed my style of writing. Because it was developed when I was young, and it's more due to *my* reading and the guidance of other people, so I think it was a lot of the English teachers from first through fourth or fifth grade, because they did a lot of creative writing classes, so I think it's different how you learn writing. I mean, your style differs. (May 3, 2003)

While he felt that his early English teachers had influenced his writing in general, John believed that his formal writing had also been influenced by his father, who had taught him how to think like a scientist from very early on.

As a native speaker of both English and Korean, John experienced many differences when writing in the two languages. He felt he was able to write faster in English, but found it difficult to "switch modes" when writing in one language and having a thought in another language. When he first learned to write in Korean—after having already become literate in English—it was initially awkward for him. Over time, however, John felt that "in Korean it started following my English style" (May 3, 2003). John explained that now it was easier for him to write about something in the language through which he had learned the content. He thus tended to use Korean more often for expressing personal experiences, but English for engineering-related work. Because he had chosen the non-thesis track in his master's program, John did not have a close advisor and did not conduct any independent research outside of his disciplinary courses. All of his writing during my study was tied either to coursework or to his applications for doctoral study.

WCGS was John's first writing class in English (beyond his early school years), though he had had some writing instruction in Korean. Despite his very strong English language skills, John was required to take the course because of his score on the Test of Writing English (TWE). Before enrolling in WCGS, John had hoped to improve his English grammar through the course; however, during the summer before WCGS, he reviewed grammar on his own. When WCGS began in the fall, John's new goal was to link the assignments to the writing he would already be doing during the semester, such as his graduate school applications. He also told me that, while he was fairly comfortable with writing in English already, "there will probably be some topics that I'm not familiar with" (September 4, 2002). Despite his high level of English proficiency—much higher than most of the other course participants—John approached the course requirement positively and with clear goals.

Chatri

Chatri, a native of Thailand and in his early 30s, showed an enthusiasm for and positive attitude toward work that seemed to carry over into much that he did. With his straight hair falling in front of his glasses, Chatri spoke quickly and excitedly in our meetings, often laughing as he disparaged his writing and research. As a participant in my study, he eagerly provided me with a great deal of his written work, completed both before and during the time of my research.

A second-year doctoral student in ECE, Chatri was working toward a degree in computer engineering. He had begun studying computer engineering during his master's program in Thailand, though he was unable to pinpoint any particular influences that led him to the field. After completing his master's degree, Chatri worked for four years as a research assistant at a research center in Thailand. He described this work as having different goals than the academic work he was currently involved in:

> At here, the research is about the academic research. I mean, academic research is we don't want our research to be the product, to be the patent. But the job that I worked in Thailand, in that research, we want the *product*, we want something that people can use, people can see. Not the paper. (September 13, 2002)

In our first meeting, Chatri was beginning his fourth semester of doctoral work. At that time, he joked about not being able to pass his qualifier exam the first time he had taken it, and he was studying to re-take the exam in a few months. As a condition of his scholarship for graduate study, Chatri was required to return to Thailand as a professor after completing his doctoral degree.

At Midwest University, Chatri worked in a lab with a group of nine others, including a professor, two postdoctoral researchers, and several other graduate students. In the year before my study, Chatri worked on an interdisciplinary project related to American Sign Language (ASL), in which his role was to develop computer vision for ASL. When the project's funding was not renewed, Chatri joined the others in his lab working on a project funded by a car manufacturing company. Chatri's work in this project focused specifically on the use of robot vision in assembly lines. As an RA, Chatri was required to submit monthly reports to the project supervisor, a postdoctoral student in his lab. Reports from each research team member were then integrated into a monthly report by the project supervisor and sent to the sponsor. During the fifth month of my study, Chatri began looking for a dissertation topic in his lab work. Much of his time during his fifth semester was spent reading research reports and looking for possible approaches to apply to the research problem that he was working on.

Prior to enrolling in WCGS, Chatri had taken only one writing course—an academic writing course that was a component of an English intensive course taken just before coming to the U.S. In this course, he had learned to make rather detailed outlines before writing a complete draft, and he utilized this writing process for several of the writing tasks he engaged in during my study, both in and out of the WCGS classroom. Chatri had also had many professional writing experiences as part of his work in Thailand, co-authoring three papers in English and two in Thai. As he wrote in his first writing assignment for WCGS:

> *I started to use writing in the real world when I worked as a research assistant in a national research center in Thailand. I had to write electronic mail to contact many foreigners. I also wrote three publications in English submitted to international conferences. At that time, I realized that how important of English for my job. At the same time, I also realized how weak my English skill were especially the writing that I felt uncomfortably when I wrote the publication.* (Writer's Autobiography, September 2002)

Perhaps because he had had experience writing professional papers in his native language, Chatri was able to speak quite specifically about differences that he experienced. Though Thai was his first language, he explained that "somehow I think it's more difficult to write in Thai than in English, because sometimes in English, there is only one word or one sentence to explain that idea. But in Thai, there are many" (September 13, 2002). He also felt that Thai tended to be more informal than English. He said he found it easier to write more formally in English, because "you can use another vocabulary to make it more formal" (September 13, 2002).

At the start of the study, he described grammar as posing the most difficulty for him when writing. He felt that he tended to use simple sentences and had difficulty connecting sentences in a meaningful way. He had also received negative feedback from professors of his doctoral courses, particularly about grammar and sentence phrasing. While he hoped to make improvements in his writing during the WCGS course, his expectations were not high. He knew that writing development was a long-term process that took time and practice, but he still seemed quite uncomfortable with his writing. In his Writer's Autobiography assignment for WCGS, he wrote that:

> . . . I still feel very uncomfortably when I have to write no matter it is a short or long paragraph. I know myself that my writing is difficult to understand because I tend to write the awkward sentences. I think that if I do not improve the writing skill, it can cause me trouble when I write the preliminary report and dissertation, and I hope that WCGS will make my writing skill better. (Writer's Autobiography, September 2002)

This discomfort with his writing ability was evident in most of my discussions with Chatri, though over time his conception of writing seemed to shift somewhat. In the later months of my study, Chatri began to speak of writing in a more complex way. He described it as including the articulation of thoughts into sentences, then organizing those sentences into paragraphs, and convincing the reader that the ideas are important; Chatri felt that he was weak in all of these areas.

Yoshi

A first-year master's student in ECE, Yoshi arrived in the U.S. just days before WCGS began. Despite the major adjustments he was making—as a newcomer to the U.S. and to American graduate school education, with his wife and newborn baby back in Japan—he graciously agreed to participate in this study. During our regular discussions, Yoshi spoke slowly and articulately about his writing and his professional experiences in his field.

When asked how his research interests had developed, Yoshi explained that his first experiences using a PC in middle school had sparked his interest in computers. While completing his bachelor's degree in Japan, he decided to study information technology as a mechanical engineering major. He continued directly through school with a master's degree in logical designing and then began working at a major Japanese computer company. In this company, his specialty was design automation development. As part of his work there, he needed to gain additional knowledge in the fields of electromagnetics and optics, which would be his area of focus at Midwest University. Now in his early 30s, Yoshi's long-term goal was to be a general manager at his company, so he saw English as a necessary skill. When I first met Yoshi, he explained, "At this point, I felt it difficult to study or work in English, so I have to practice English speaking and writing skills" (September 11, 2002).

His nine years as an engineer in Japan had lent him the type of valuable experience and knowledge that many graduate students lack. In addition to writing regular experimental reports, a bachelor's thesis, and a master's thesis, Yoshi had written internal research reports, specification documents, project proposals, and patents. Although most of his academic and professional work was conducted in Japanese, he had nevertheless been required to do a fair amount of reading in English. In our first interview and in his Writer's Autobiography for WCGS, Yoshi distinguished between his confidence in writing in academic/professional genres versus "essay" writing, which he found particularly difficult. He owed this to *"shying away from practices about writing an essay in English"* (Writer's Autobiography, September 2002). During my study, however, Yoshi seized opportunities to practice English speaking, reading, or writing. In his second semester of graduate school, Yoshi enrolled in a non-university English speaking course to improve his oral skills, and he began reading English newspapers on a daily basis, checking his comprehension by later referring to the same news reported in Japanese. As a non-thesis student, Yoshi (like John) was not a member of a research group and did not complete any major independent research projects during the study.

At the beginning of my study and the start of WCGS, Yoshi was also trying out a new process for composing, forcing himself to "think in English" when writing, rather than thinking and writing in Japanese and then translating into English. Yoshi also generally made use of multiple dictionaries because of the advice of a previous English teacher who had told him not to trust one single dictionary. In his Writer's Autobiography for WCGS, Yoshi recounted some of the important influences on his writing development to this point:

> *Through research projects at my senior and graduate school years, I published two theses and three papers. In my first research project, I had to read a lot of reference papers, both written in my native language and in English, related to Discrete Fourier Transform algorithms. Through this reading experience, I had gained knowledge of not only the topic but also writing styles for technical papers. Yet once I started to write my Bachelor thesis, I realized the difficulty to express what I meant briefly and concisely. Reviewing and reviewing with my mentor, rewriting and rewriting it, I felt certain that my sentences became brief and concise. What I have learned most through this refining process is to write proper length sentences and to select transitive words logically.*
> (Writer's Autobiography, September 2002)

One of his goals for WCGS was that it would help him write more quickly. He commented also that the class would *require* him to write, giving him practice that he would not otherwise have. During his time at Midwest University, Yoshi noted that he was able to write faster and with greater confidence than he had when he first arrived.

3 Learning through Other People's Words

At advanced levels of academe, classroom writing is, by and large, genred writing. Whether students are writing seminar papers, lab reports, proposals, or critiques, their written texts are guided and evaluated by certain disciplinary expectations. Classrooms therefore become important sites of knowledge building, as it is here that students encounter guidelines, feedback, models, and samples that feed into their developing understanding of writing in general and of genres in particular. Of course, not all classrooms are the same; there are, for instance, considerable differences between a course in biomedical engineering and one in academic writing. Nevertheless, both settings have the *potential* to influence a writer's understanding of writing and of written texts. I will focus on such knowledge building in so-called "disciplinary content classrooms" in later chapters, but first, in chapters 3 and 4, I turn to knowledge building in the writing classroom, a site of particular interest to teachers of writing.

My focus in the next two chapters is on the strategies and resources for genre learning that are available in the writing classroom. Certainly, the stories of the John, Yoshi, Paul, and Chatri are tied to their unique local setting. Nevertheless, their stories provide illustrations of the very specific ways that knowledge building can occur within a writing classroom. When considered alongside related literature on classroom learning, these cases add to a broader theoretical understanding of learning genres outside of the milieu in which they exist more organically.

INTERACTING WITH TEXTS

As I observed students in WCGS, both in the classroom described here and in a prior pilot study, I was struck repeatedly with the ways in which the writers looked to textual samples as important resources for knowledge building within the classroom context. Classroom activities prompted much interaction with texts, but students continued to draw on sample texts as they composed outside of the classroom. While the use of texts as "models" to be analyzed and imitated by students raises concerns of prescriptivism for instructors, students often desire models and tend to make effective use of them. Many studies have shown students to make use of sample or model texts as learning resource in their disciplinary content courses or in workplace or research settings (e.g., Angelova & Riazantseva, 1999; Beaufort, 1999, 2000; Ivanič, 1998; McCarthy, 1987; Riazi, 1997; Shaw, 1991; Smart, 2000; Winsor, 1996), but this area has been less examined within writing classroom contexts. Two studies that have looked at the use of text models as an explicit teaching strategy suggest that exposure to genre exemplars may have a positive influence on student learning.

In an attempt to understand the role of model texts for native English speaking students, Charney and Carlson (1995) studied the effects of exposure to models in a psychology course in which students were learning to write a Methods section for a research paper. The researchers divided 95 students into different groups: (a) no models, (b) three models of Methods sections receiving "A," labeled as such, (c) a model of an "A," "B," and "C" Methods section, labeled with their respective grades, (d) three "A"-graded models with no labels included, and (e) an "A," "B," and "C" model with no labels. Students were then given details related to a particular experiment and asked to compose their own Methods section in a one-hour time period. Exposure to models influenced both the content and the organization of the students' texts in positive ways. Interestingly, there appeared to be no advantage to giving students only "A" models, as opposed to giving them the range of "A," "B," and "C" models. Exposure to models, however, did not seem to help the student-writers discriminate between relevant and irrelevant details; similarly, labeling models (as "A," "B," or "C") also had no affect in this area.

Within the context of a genre-based ESP classroom, Henry and Roseberry (1998) examined the effects of explicit genre analysis of model texts on student writers in a first-year management class in Brunei. As the students learned to write travel brochures, they were divided into two groups: one receiving six hours of genre-based instruction (in which students analyzed model texts) and a second receiving no genre-based instruction. Those students who analyzed model texts had higher "texture" scores (an index designed to measure cohesion and coherence) in a post-test, and their gain scores were significantly higher than the students who had received no genre-based instruction. Like Charney and Carlson's (1995) research, however, this study measures only very short-term benefits of exposure to and analysis of model texts. Also important for instructors is the absence of any consideration of students' application of genre knowledge beyond the immediate classroom context.

If student interactions with texts—whether those texts be "models" or simply "samples"—are so influential in non-writing classroom settings (as these studies, for example, suggest), one might believe that such interactions are also important within the writing classroom. It is, after all, in this space that students are very often given samples and that such samples are explicitly discussed. As I traced student writing in WCGS, it soon became clear that the texts to which they were exposed played a very important role in developing their knowledge of an unfamiliar genre. One such example was the writers' engagement in the writing assignment of a self-promotional genre: a job application cover letter.

Job Application Cover Letters as a Genre

As junior scientific researchers, Chatri, Paul, John, and Yoshi repeatedly spoke of the disciplinary value of remaining objective and impersonal in one's writing. Through years of writing lab reports, research reports, and classroom assignments, they had become accustomed to avoiding any mention of themselves in their writing. Therefore, the job application cover letter assignment in WCGS introduced a fairly new rhetorical purpose to these writers: to promote themselves, rather explicitly, to their readers.

Certainly, scientific texts like research articles do require authors to self-promote or market themselves, persuading readers that they are legitimate and credible members of the discipline (Hyland, 2000). In such texts, writers must illustrate their credibility through relatively subtle means such as displays of disciplinary knowledge or self-citation. Numerous other genres require writers to take more of a "hard-sell" approach, marketing themselves in addition to their work. This class of genres includes, for example, résumés, job application letters, graduate school statements of purpose, or fellowship applications. In composing these sorts of texts, writers need to know how to promote themselves effectively within a specific rhetorical context, balancing the boundary between confidence and arrogance.

Studies of self-promotional genres in general, and job application cover letters in particular, are scarce. Swales and Feak (2000) describe these letters as supporting a research career, "primarily designed to get the 'right' academic people in the 'right' positions" (p. 257). Job application letters are also included in Swales' (1996) list of "occluded genres," which encompass genres that share several characteristics: they are typically formal, kept on file, written for very specific audiences, often highly evaluative, often concerned with promoting the author (and his or her scholarship), and often occluded from the public. While the cover letter meets several of these criteria, it lacks the defining feature of occlusion. Through reference books, career centers, advisors, and, most importantly, the Internet, examples of this genre are readily available—and, as I'll show throughout this chapter, these resources can have a significant impact on writers who are relatively new to the genre.

Bhatia's (1993, 1999) work provides the most extensive discussion of the job application cover letter from a genre perspective. Bhatia (1993) focuses on communicative purpose as the defining element of the cover letter genre, and he analyzes the rhetorical structure of an exemplar, drawing parallels between the job application letter and the sales promotion letter. Bhatia claims that the most important function of this type of letter is to show a favorable and relevant description of the job candidate. In other words, the writer's task is to persuade the readers that he or she is competent and possesses those credentials that are of particular importance to the job at hand.

In his application of generic move analysis to job application letters, Bhatia (1993, p. 62) identifies a typical seven-part structure (see Figure 3.1). He describes "Indicating value of candidature" as the key step, as it is here that the writer attempts to persuade readers that he or she has the relevant experience, qualifications, or background for the position. While Bhatia provides no details regarding the corpus on which this structure is based, he exemplifies it through a letter written for a lectureship in Britain. This generic structure is, however, influenced by socio-cultural factors within any given context. Drawing on a corpus of South Asian scholarship and job application letters, for example, Bhatia (1996) identifies self-degradation as a frequently used strategy in the closing move of a letter.

---

1. Establishing credentials
2. Introducing candidature
a. Offering candidature
b. Essential detailing of candidature
c. Indicating value of candidature
3. Offering incentives
4. Enclosing documents
5. Using pressure tactics
6. Soliciting response
7. Ending politely

Figure 3.1. Move structure of job application letters identified in Bhatia (1993).

Using a corpus of 40 application letters written by native English speakers for a variety of jobs, Henry and Roseberry (2001) identify similar moves to those in Figure 3.1. Their analysis, however, goes further in identifying key lexical phrases common to different promotional strategies. They note, for example, the high frequency of paired nouns, verbs, and adjectives that writers use to describe their relevant skills (e.g., "background and experience" or "assess and implement"). Awareness of common features like these, the authors argue, may help second language writers compose letters that resemble those written by their native-English-speaking peers. While resembling a conventional "native-like" letter may be a goal of many L2 writers, they are also likely to want to assert an individual identity within their letters, standing out as distinct in some ways—and this is, of course, another important goal and rhetorical move of job application letters.

Beyond these studies of generic form, job application letters have not received any significant research attention—a fact that is somewhat surprising given their relative prominence in professional writing course curricula (particularly at the undergraduate level) as well as the weight that these documents often carry in a tight marketplace. Studies of the procedural dimensions of these genres in different domains would be particularly valuable. Outside of the classroom, cover letters, for example, are connected to a whole range of oral and social interactions, ranging from requesting a reference, to contacting potential employers, to more general networking. The genres act as links in a genre chain that might include job advertisements, requests for more information, interviews, thank-you letters, and acceptance and rejection letters. At various stages of this genre chain are nodes to other genres, such as reference letters, employer websites, job search websites, reference books, and online tutorials. There are also the countless social interactions that serve to build writers' repertoires of ideas about what is effective, ineffective, desirable, or discouraged in preparing these documents.

In addition, job application letters are linked to résumés or CVs in an intertextual generic set. Bhatia (1993) describes the letter as the applicant's opportunity to demonstrate his or her qualifications for the job by clarifying the contents of the résumé. In Bhatia's conception, the résumé is dependent on the letter because it cannot persuade the reader on its own; it is the evidence for the claims made in the letter. Furthermore, the letter is often more variable than the résumé, as writers have even more choices about what content they may include or exclude for specific audiences.

This dependence of one genre upon another illustrates the relationship among genres in a genre set. A genre set may, for example, consist of a core genre (or genres) on which other genres are dependent. While the core genre may serve as the primary document of the system, other genres are important in navigating the system and improving the effectiveness of the core genre. I will refer to these supporting genres as *linked genres,* as a way to emphasize their dependence on another genre. Such linked genres require that writers have knowledge of multiple genres (the linked genre and the core genre) within the network. To Bhatia (1993), the cover letter is a core genre and the résumé is a linked genre; as shown later in this chapter, the writers I followed did not always share this relational view.

Previous Knowledge

Chatri, Yoshi, John, and Paul all came to the writing classroom with no previous experience in writing job application cover letters. That said, they did bring different understandings of the genre (along with its linked genre, the résumé) to their first encounters in the writing classroom.

Chatri had neither seen nor written a cover letter prior to the writing course, and in fact said he had not heard the term before. He had written a Thai résumé when applying for the research job he had held in Thailand, and he wrote an English-language résumé when he applied for a position as a research assistant (RA) at Midwest University, but he had not heard of a cover letter accompanying these documents. As a student near the start of a five-year (or longer) doctoral program, Chatri did not appear to see any immediate need for the genre.

Although Yoshi had written his first English-language résumé in cram school in Japan, he did not practice writing cover letters at that time. In contrast to the other writers, however, Yoshi had seen cover letters on Internet websites, and he had written what he described as "a tiny cover letter" (September 23, 2003) when applying to graduate schools. The WCGS assignment was his first real experience writing a job application cover letter. While the other writers seemed quite skeptical about whether or not they would ever write a cover letter, Yoshi believed that if he were to apply for a job in the U.S., he would use a letter similar to what he had written in WCGS. The chances of this happening in the near future, however, were slim, as Yoshi was required to return to his position in Japan upon completion of his master's program.

Like the other writers, John had written his first résumé in English before the WCGS assignment. He found that he needed a résumé to respond to a variety of interactions with his professors:

> . . . every time I went to talk to a professor about any-
> thing, he or she would say, "Do you have a résumé?"
> So I got tired of that, so I just made up a résumé. So
> that was basically what [my original résumé] was for.
> Sometimes I would talk to them about getting an RA
> position or something, so that was probably the main
> reason I made a résumé. (September 20, 2002)

Because he had always given his résumé to others in person, or accompanied them with an application form, John had no prior need to write a cover letter.

Though Paul similarly had no prior cover letter experience, his job application experience in general was broader than the other four writers. Before coming to the U.S., Paul had worked at a "dot.com" company in China where he was at one point responsible for some hiring; he therefore had some insight into an employer's perspective in the job hiring process. In the U.S., Paul had written and used an English-language résumé twice before the WCGS unit: once when applying to graduate school in the U.S. and once when applying for a summer internship during the first year of his master's program. As is typical, these documents were attached to an application form and statement of purpose rather than a letter. Paul had—unsurprisingly—not heard of a cover letter before the WCGS unit. In fact, during the same time as this class unit, Paul also attended a workshop led by a major computer company (referred to here as "Micron") in which professionals spoke to computer science students about résumés and the job application process. Even in this workshop, he was not made aware of the role that cover letters often play in job searching.

The writers' novice background with this genre was typical of the other students in the class and in my experience is also typical for many international graduate students studying in the U.S. One possible reason for this shared lack of experience with cover letters is that genres—that is, the typified response to a recurring rhetorical situation—are realized in different ways in different social and cultural contexts. Some countries, for example, carry out this action (introducing a job application) through other textual means, such as application forms or oral interactions. For students from such countries, the cover letter—including its formal, rhetorical, and process dimensions—will be unfamiliar. A second possible reason that this genre was so new to the writers that I followed could lie in their own histories and trajectories. Even in the U.S., where cover letters are fairly common, college students, graduate students, and first-time job seekers often get by without writing them. Job fairs, on-line job sites, and social networks all provide rhetorical scenes that can make the cover letter an unnecessary genre. In other words, many U.S. graduate students may also have no prior experience writing cover letters, though they would most likely have heard of them before and perhaps even seen them.

COVER LETTERS IN THE WRITING CLASSROOM

In WCGS, the résumé and cover letter were presented as linked genres and were turned in together as one assignment; nevertheless, the procedural or rhetorical relationships between the two texts was never explained or discussed in depth in the classroom. Michele told me that she chose to teach these texts because she felt they were "indicative of the very weird American discourse forms" (August 28, 2002) and provided an opportunity to focus on related grammatical conventions of form like gapping and parallelism. She sequenced this unit after the first course assignment—a writer's autobiography—because she felt it represented a natural progression from a more informal and personal way of writing about oneself to a more formal and public style. In teaching the cover letter, Michele wanted to provide the students with a range of samples written in different contexts and with practice in adapting those samples to their own needs. An additional goal was to help students become more familiar with what Michele called the nuances of language, particularly in relation to describing oneself. She saw this as a difficult rhetorical task which she hoped to help students become more successful in.

The résumé/cover letter unit was covered in 11 class days (see Table 3.1), including one-on-one conferences that took the place of several class sessions. The four writers that I followed attended each class session and both of the conferences in this unit. While Michele made use of many instructional strategies for awareness-raising, typical to genre-based pedagogy, she never used the term *genre* during this unit, nor did she ever explicitly discuss how the awareness-raising strategies might be applied to other genres.

Table 3.1 WCGS schedule for unit on résumés and cover letters.

Day	Date	Topic
1	Sept. 9	CV/résumé contents
2	Sept. 11	CV/résumé contents; gapping
3	Sept. 13	CVs vs. résumés; parallelism; peer editing
4 & 5	Sept. 16 & 17	One-on-one conference with CV/Résumé
6	Sept. 20	Sample cover letters
7	Sept. 23	Cover letter templates; formality and language
8	Sept. 25	Cover letter format and structure in different contexts
9	Sept. 27	Discussion of cover letter samples; peer editing; email requests
10 & 11	Sept. 30 & Oct. 2	One-on-one conference with cover letter

Because few of the students were familiar with cover letters, most of the class sessions on Days 6 through 9 were spent examining and discussing sample letters. By presenting students with a wide range of examples, Michele hoped that they could select what they liked from various letters. Six of these sample texts were job application letters, including three written for jobs in industry, one for a graduate research assistantship, one for a postdoctoral position in molecular biology, and one for an assistant professor position in rhetoric and composition. In addition, Michele provided three cover letters of request asking a professor for a letter of recommendation, and four email request letters, with varying requests. She included these non-job application letters for the benefit of John, who would be writing this type of a "request cover letter" as he prepared applications for PhD programs. To some extent, then, the term "cover letter" was used somewhat ambiguously and its various uses and forms were never fully teased out within the classroom. However, because "the cover letter" was situated within a unit related to job applications, most of the students interpreted the term to be equated with job application letters.

On Day 7 of the unit, Michele distributed two quite different job application letters and asked the students to work in pairs to create a "template for a generic cover letter" (Class notes, September 23, 2002) based on their observations of the samples. Two pairs of students wrote their templates on the board; these are reproduced in Figure 3.2. As the figure shows, both pairs identified a similar basic format of (1) self-introduction/purpose for writing, (2) qualifications and experience, and (3) closing remarks. Their structures generally mirror Bhatia's (1993) moves of establishing credentials, introducing candidature, enclosing documents (found only in John's and Tae's template), and ending politely. They exclude his moves of offering incentives, using pressure tactics, and soliciting response—the first two of which Bhatia claims are less common.

Much classroom discussion also centered on specific sentences in the sample letters and the ways in which they may be interpreted by readers. Michele frequently asked questions that explored relationships between formal and rhetorical features of the genre, such as "What are the differences between the letters for different types of jobs" or "How much of a specialist would you need to be to understand this?" Discussions addressed the formal language style and the connections between style and intended audience. The students generally preferred the shorter letters for more general audiences. In fact, there was strong negative reaction to a sample letter written for an academic position in the humanities. In commenting on this letter, these engineering and science students disliked both the high frequency of jargon and the lengthy prose.

Chatri and Ming-Hua's Template	John and Tae's Template
	Sender info
	Recipient info
	Date
Introduction:	
1.Personal description	Dear _____
2.Qualifications for job	Why I'm writing
Body:	
Experience relevant to the posi-tion	What I've done (qualification)
Conclusion:	
1.Re-stress experience	Closing remarks (enclosures, thank
2.Thank reader	you, etc.)
	Contact information

Figure 3.2. Student-produced templates based on WCGS sample cover letters.

On Days 8 and 9, Michele extended the discussion of cover letters to request letters, including requests for letters of recommendation (attached to a résumé) and email requests. The former were included to address the needs of one student, John, who was hoping to request letters of recommendation from some of his professors. Michele also recognized that requests can be rhetorically challenging, so she incorporated a 20-minute classroom activity in which students examined four email requests that she had received. She asked students to read the emails and try to determine the relationship between the sender and receiver, in terms of familiarity and status, exploring the ways in which social relationships are indexed through texts. Students noted variations in word choice and formality, and asked about how common different phrases were. The inclusion of letters of request may have helped students to draw connections between this genre and the job application letter, but, as I shall show later in this chapter, only John made these connections explicit in discussing the assignment with me.

The WCGS classroom discussions were interesting to observe for several reasons. They showed that the writers did have preferences for some forms over others, despite being unfamiliar with the genre. In some cases, such as the reaction to the lengthy humanities job application letter, these preferences may have been influenced by the discourses of their hard science disciplinary backgrounds. For example, the long sentences and paragraphs of the humanities letter are likely to contrast rather sharply with the hard science preference for more concise text. The classroom discussions also gave students a chance to see how their peers and instructor reacted to the different texts, or even to very specific phrases within those texts. While the students often came to these discussions with preferences, their preferences may also have been shaped in part by the discussions themselves, as they listened to the reactions of others. As I later traced the writers' cover letter practices, the classroom discussion re-emerged in interesting ways through both their texts and their comments, as I shall illustrate in the next section.

Cover Letter Knowledge Building: Four Cases

Each of the four writers experienced the résumé/cover letter assignment uniquely, according to their own prior experience and immediate needs. In order to best capture some of these distinctions, I describe their experiences individually, beginning with Chatri and then Yoshi, the two writers who made no use of the cover letter genre outside of the classroom. Next, I describe John's experience, which included a very immediate need to write a "request cover letter" during the semester he was enrolled in WCGS. Finally, I provide a more detailed description of Paul's experiences, over a six-month period in which the cover letter became an increasingly important and more high-stakes genre for him.

Chatri: Writing Text, Forming Preferences

Of the four writers, Chatri seemed to be the least immediately invested in the cover letter. Because he already held a stable RA position and was obliged to return to a Thai university upon completion of his PhD, he did not foresee any immediate situations in which he would write such a letter. Again, Chatri had not heard of a cover letter before WCGS, but after the class sessions in this unit had finished, he was able to give a very general description of the use and rhetorical goal of the genre, describing it as a letter that covers a résumé and introduces a candidate. He had also developed some understanding of the letter as a linked genre. He distinguished the résumé and cover letter in terms of the work they required of the reader, explaining that the reader must infer meaning from a résumé, but the writer does this task *for* the reader in a cover letter. The letter that Chatri composed for WCGS was written in response to a year-old job posting on Honda's website. In his conference with Michele, he explained that he could not actually apply for the position, and that it was "just for the class" (Conference #3, October 2, 2002).

In the relatively short space of time in which the class focused on cover letters, Chatri developed an awareness of what kind of subject matter should be included and in what order. He described it as something like a template:

> Okay, the format is the first paragraph should be introduce myself, I'm a student, or what I want, why I write the letter. Just only I think three sentence is okay. And then the next paragraph is try to tell about my experience or tell that why my qualification is okay for this position. Actually, this can try from the CV, but I think just write only short paragraph to tell about me. And then the ending paragraph is just, I think it's typical that, "Okay, I feel that your company is really good. I hope that you will accept me." Or something like that. (October 2, 2002)

After writing his first draft, but before receiving feedback on it, Chatri was still unsure about some of the genre's conventions of form. For example, he didn't know the meaning of "enclosure" written at the bottom of the page or whether he should include his signature in the space between "Yours sincerely" and his printed name. Chatri also did not know whether to introduce himself by name in the first sentence. With this issue he differentiated between a paper-based cover letter, in which he thought it was appropriate to begin by stating his name, and an electronic cover letter, in which he thought he should not include this information. Chatri's questions here give a sense that he is still trying to make sense of the genre as it is used for real purposes. Without any experience reading or writing cover letters to actually obtain a job, he can only make guesses at this point about the appropriacy of various formal conventions.

In discussing some of the sample texts distributed in WCGS, Chatri illustrated his emerging rhetorical understanding, including the roles that readers and writers may play when encountering the genre. For example, he commented on one sentence from a sample cover letter that he felt was inappropriate and may anger the reader: *I will follow up next week by phone to see if we can set up an interview.*

> Chatri: I don't think it's suitable. I think that he [is trying to] convince someone to meet this guy, "Okay, I will call you to ask about the result of my application." Because I think it's- [if] someone don't interest this guy, he just ignore, not contact, and that's it.
>
> Chris: So you wouldn't do that?
>
> Chatri: I will not do it! [*laughing*] Sometime I think it will make this guy angry, I think. (October 10, 2002)

He also ventured some guesses regarding the reading practices surrounding the genre. He felt that as an employer, he would likely read only the first paragraph of the letter to look for key information:

> Everyone knows that the [cover letter] is just an introduction, and what's important is CV. Because it's easier to look in the CV. We don't have to read the sentence, just, "Okay, PhD, okay, from this school, master from this school. What's the work experience? And how many publications, and which publications?" And for my case, I would read only this. (October 2, 2002)

Chatri's reading practices, as he described them to me, may not be typical. In some contexts—such as academic job searches—the cover letter may be quite important to readers; however, what Chatri illustrates here is a growing awareness of how the CV and cover letter genres work together and how they may be read for a given purpose. His description above also reflects some of his own values about what is important in judging a candidate's qualifications. For example, it may be notable that Chatri did *not* refer to the cover letter's role as a writing sample or a glimpse into the character of the job candidate. At this point, he seemed to view the cover letter primarily as a functional document that helped guide the reader through the CV.

During the three-week class unit on résumés and cover letters, then, Chatri was just beginning to form an understanding of the genre. He had developed a template-like awareness of the form and content, preferences for some forms over others, and some nascent knowledge of the procedural practices around the genre. However, he focused very little on rhetorical context when discussing the cover letter with me or Michele, and he did not distinguish between academic and business cover letters as he had with the CV/résumé. Neither did he focus heavily on the intended action of the cover letter—that is, self-promotion. While Chatri seemed to have this overarching purpose in mind, he lacked an urgent need to shape his letter to a specific audience for a specific position. Because this assignment constituted Chatri's first exposure to the genre, it is likely that he would extend his knowledge through subsequent exposures and practices.

As Chatri developed his understanding of cover letters, classroom activities in WCGS played an important role. Because he had not encountered cover letters previously and did not seek information about them outside of class, the discussions and texts from WCGS served as his primary resource for knowledge development of this genre. Although some of this knowledge may have been developed by applying his knowledge of other genres (like résumés), WCGS provided an opportunity for him to make these connections. Through classroom discussion and activities, Chatri learned a basic structure for a cover letter and developed a sense of readers' reactions to different writing styles and approaches to the genre, thus helping him to develop some knowledge of the genre's form, rhetorical strategies, content, and procedural practices.

By far Chatri's most important strategy for learning about cover letters, though, was the use of sample texts. Chatri explained that he referred to the samples from class to determine the format of his first draft. He said the most difficult parts to write were the opening and closing paragraphs; to facilitate this challenge, he referred to two sample letters, borrowing their discursive structures as well as specific textual fragments. Figure 3.3 illustrates the extent of Chatri's textual borrowing in his opening paragraph, with the underlined sentences adapted from a sample cover letter for a job in industry. The overall structure of the two texts is identical, and many of Chatri's sentences can be traced directly to the sample letter.

Sample Cover Letter from WCGS	Chatri's First Draft Cover Letter
I am <u>a PhD candidate in Biomedical Engineering</u> (degree anticipated June 1999). <u>I am writing in response to</u> the Biomaterials Engineering position posted on your company's web site. <u>I understand that you seek a candidate who has experience</u> prototyping of an implantable drug delivery device, as well as with biomaterials, tissue interactions, and impurity identification. <u>I hope</u> you will agree <u>that my qualifications</u> and experience <u>meet your</u> needs.	My name is Chatri Boonmee, <u>a PhD student in school of Electrical and Computer Engineering</u>, Midwest University. <u>I am writing in response to</u> your advertisement in 'Research Internship Positions at Honda R&D Fundamental Research Labs.' <u>I understand that you</u> are <u>seek</u>ing <u>a candidate who has</u> research <u>ex</u>perience in Computer Vision area. <u>I hope that my qualifications</u> will <u>meet your</u> requirement.

Figure 3.3. Opening paragraphs from industry cover letter and Chatri's WCGS cover letter. Shared words are underlined.

Chatri also borrowed structures and text fragments from multiple samples when composing the closing paragraph. Several of the WCGS samples, for example, referred to the writer's interest in the company in or near the final paragraph. Chatri adopted this same structure and integrated it with the final paragraph of a second sample letter written for a post-doctoral position in science. Figure 3.4 illustrates Chatri's creative use of this sample letter and later revisions between his first and second drafts.

Sample Cover Letter from WCGS	Chatri's First Draft Cover Letter	Chatri's Second Draft Cover Letter
<u>I have enclosed a copy of my curriculum vitae,</u> together with the three manuscripts and have arranged for three letters of reference to be forwarded to you. <u>I look forward to hearing from you soon</u>. <u>If you require any further information please</u> write, call or <u>contact me by e-mail on:</u> johnsonmh@musc.edu.	*I feel that many of your company research topics are very interesting. And, I think that if I will be able to expand my research skill with your company I will also be able to use the knowledge that I will obtain there to improve the quality of my PhD research.* <u>I</u> also <u>have enclosed a copy of my curriculum vitae. If you require any</u> more <u>information please</u> feel free to <u>contact me by e-mail on:</u> name@Midwest.edu. <u>I look forward to hearing from you soon.</u>	*I feel that many of your company research ar-eas are very interesting* especially the topic about vision system for humanoid robot which I think that my current research topic can be applied to de-velop more robust algo-rithms for this project. Additionally, *I think that if I will be able to expand my research skill with your company, I will also be able to use the knowledge that I will obtain there to improve the quality of my PhD research.* <u>I</u> also <u>have enclosed a copy of my curriculum vitae. If you require any</u> more <u>information please</u> feel free to <u>contact me by e-mail on:</u> name@Midwest. edu. <u>I look forward to hearing from you soon.</u>

Figure 3.4. Closing paragraphs from post-doc sample cover letter (left column) and Chatri's first draft (right column). Words borrowed from the sample cover letter are underlined. Words shared in both drafts one and two are italicized.

While much of Chatri's writing here is borrowed from the closing paragraph of the sample letter, part of it is also borrowed from the *opening* paragraph of the same sample:

> *I have found your studies on viral proteases to be fasci-nating and I feel that while I will be able to contribute expertise to your project I will also be able to develop*

and expand my understanding of inhibitor function.
(Sample letter)

*And, I think that if I will be able to expand my research
skill with your company I will also be able to use the
knowledge that I will obtain there to improve the quality of my PhD research.* (Chatri's letter, first draft)

After writing this initial draft, however, Chatri remained uncertain
about the effectiveness of this sentence, so he asked Michele about it in
their one-on-one conference. Their discussion, as the excerpt here illustrates, gave him more confidence in retaining the sentence but also
prompted him to expand this closing paragraph in additional ways:

Chatri: Do you like this sentence [*And, I think that if
I will be able to expand . . .*] or not? Because,
actually, I saw from the example that you gave
me, but I think that because the intern position
normally we don't make some contribution so
much to the company, just practice the skill or
something—

Michele: -yeah, so they're hoping to *nurture* future researchers.

Chatri: -then, I come up with some sentence that "*I think
that if I will be able to-*"

Michele: Yeah, I like that. Like I say, I think it's good that
it's all there. I just think you need, um, maybe
here where you say, "*Many of your company's research areas very interesting,*" like specifically *what*
about them do you find interesting?

Chatri: I see.

Michele: That might give them more of a sense of how
you're going to contribute.

Chatri: Oh.

Michele: Because I think you're right. For a lot of these
internship positions, it seems to me they don't really expect you to be totally contributing to the
company, because otherwise they just give you a
job instead of an internship. But you'd still want
to know—

> Chatri: I see, so some specific topic or project—
> Michele: that they're working on. *If* you know of any. I
> mean, since this is all hypothetical, you might
> not know. (Conference, October 2, 2002)

The final version of Chatri's closing paragraph, then, is a coordinated mixing of two sample letters and oral feedback from Michele, as well as his own preferences and goals.

The borrowing of words and phrases from the sample letters is found most commonly with what might be considered to be formulaic or conventionalized phrases. Many of these phrases were new to Chatri, and the samples provided him with a kind of scaffolding for composing his letter:

> I don't know what kind of meaning of some sentences, and I have to look to copy something. *"I'm writing in response to your advertisement."* I use this kind of sentence in my cover letter. And I think *"In response to you..."* Actually, if I didn't see the example of this, I will not write this sentence because I don't know what the meaning of this. And also in the final paragraph, I also have to see from the example. For the second paragraph, it just tell about me. It's not too difficult. (October 2, 2002)

Chatri went so far as to say that without the formulaic phrase *"I'm writing in response to..."* he would not know how to begin the letter. Textual fragments like these guided him through the rhetorical maneuvering of the opening and closing of the letter—moves that seemed to pose particular challenges for Chatri as a novice to the genre.

Chatri's primary strategy for learning this new genre became mining sample texts for conventional phrases and discursive structures. By reading a variety of samples, he developed a preference for some styles over others, and he was able to adapt the samples' generic structures and actual words creatively in composing a text that matched his own sense of the genre. In the subsequent year and a half, Chatri did not have any opportunities to write a cover letter, so one can only guess what he retained from the assignment and the practice. Nevertheless, at the completion of the WCGS course, Chatri commented that the cover letter assignment was useful because, in his words, "we have to show some writing skill" (December 2, 2002).

Yoshi: Borrowing Identities

Unlike the other writers, Yoshi had seen examples of cover letters through websites and electronic mailing lists that he belonged to, yet he had never written a cover letter himself. Although this was a relatively new genre for him, he found it somewhat similar to another self-promotional genre—the graduate school statement-of-purpose essay:

> I think [the statement of purpose is a kind of cover letter, but statement of purpose is too long, so I have to write [this] using letter style and too short one. Statement of purpose is also too difficult to organize. (September 23, 2002)

Despite this past experience with U.S.-style self-promotional genres, Yoshi was indeed a novice to this type of writing, and he began the WCGS unit with more questions than answers.

When planning his cover letter for WCGS, Yoshi told me that he would first choose a "virtual" target audience, writing his letter to apply for an advertised job. After having written his first draft, Yoshi illustrated his growing understanding of the genre, describing his letter as follows:

> Cover letter is to apply academic job or industry job. Introduce oneself and . . . generally, the cover letter is attached to the documents, and give brief introduction and background. And this time, the object of the cover letter is to apply academic or industry job, so I wrote my brief- where I note the information and my background and descriptions. Then and finally my contact information. (October 16, 2002)

With the exception of the second sentence of his letter, Yoshi's first draft generally follows the template presented by John and Tae in class (see Figure 3.5), which was (1) explain the purpose for writing, (2) explain your qualifications, (3) closing remarks, and (4) contact information. A revised second draft was unchanged except for the addition of a third paragraph that described Yoshi's prior work experience in more specific detail. Yoshi's letter in fact closely resembles the seven-part move structure outlined by Bhatia (1993), most particularly in the last three moves: using pressure tactics, soliciting response, and ending politely.

Bhatia's (1993) Moves	Yoshi's Letter, First Draft	John and Tae's Template
	Dear Mr. Greim,	
Offering candidature	I am writing in response to the Simulation Engineer position posted on the High Frequency Measurements web site. Having been employed with Hitachi Ltd. previously, I know firsthand that your corporation is a strong and growing organization in which I could meaningfully contribute the engineering and management experience I've gained through both education and experience.	Purpose for writing
Essential detailing of candidature	My academic career, work experience, and knowledge of simulation engineering have prepared me well for this position. I have studied electromagnetic field theory, transmission line theory, methods and tools for analyzing designs through academic and work experience.	Background and qualifica-tions
Using pressure tactics	I am confident that we would find it mutually beneficial to discuss my qualifications face-to-face. I will phone your office at the	
Soliciting response	end of next week to arrange an appointment. You are also welcome to contact me at the numbers on this letterhead. I	Contact information
Ending politely	look forward to meeting with you. Thank you for your time and consideration.	Thanking

Figure 3.5. Yoshi's first draft cover letter in WCGS.

The second sentence of the letter ("*Having been employed . . .*") is especially noticeable because it makes an interesting rhetorical move that was not discussed in class. Here, Yoshi attempts to align his own experience with the company's profile, revealing an awareness of the genre's overarching purpose of self-promotion. In her writing conference with him, Michele commented that she found this sentence particularly effective. Yoshi explained to me that the sentence was in fact an excerpt borrowed from an Internet site that he had used as a resource:

> I believe this is the truth, and I used the truth from their computer is good company, and so I use the fact. And I was looking for the perfect sentence to describe that one, and I found this sentence. And using- starting from "Having been . . . ," not always starting the "I" or "You." But I think this is more elegant than what I usually write. (October 16, 2002)

Yoshi also makes use of the lexical pattern of paired phrases found in Henry and Roseberry's (2001) corpus of cover letters—for instance, "*engineering and management experience*" and "*education and experience*." Use of such paired phrases may help emphasize an applicant's attributes, but Yoshi's use of these pairs appears to be more motivated by borrowing from sample letters that contained these phrases, as I'll explain below.

One particularly interesting feature of Yoshi's cover letter is the final paragraph in which he uses the "pressure tactics" described by Bhatia (1993). Yoshi explained to me that he liked the final paragraph of his cover letter, but he admitted that this was not the Japanese writing style that he was accustomed to:

> I [would] never say this in Japanese [*laughing*], but if I- I felt this is a *English* cover letter, even [though] I don't think this, but I'd better advocate like this. (October 16, 2002)

In fact, Yoshi commented rather extensively on the difficulty of promoting himself in an U.S.-style cover letter. He believed that the hardest part of writing such a document was "to describe myself objectively" (October 16, 2002) and to not come across as arrogant. He contrasted the Japanese style of self-promotion with the U.S. style, and he admitted that he felt awkward writing in the more aggressive U.S. style:

> Japanese tend to write modestly [about] myself. But to write in English, you tend to write more aggressive- you'd better write aggressive. So I am not accustomed to write that way, so it is- I feel strange still. (October 16, 2002)

Specifically, he felt that the frequent use of "I" would sound selfish or arrogant in Japanese and would thus be avoided as much as possible in a Japanese letter.

This conflict in his own positioning as a writer seemed to pose the biggest challenge for Yoshi in writing the cover letter. Although he was aware of the conventions and expectations of the U.S.-style cover letter and was willing to adopt these conventions, he felt awkward in doing so. In the end, Yoshi's understanding of the differences between the Japanese and English rhetorical writing styles in this genre may have led him to overcompensate in the final paragraph, which may strike many readers as overly confident. It may be that Yoshi was unaware of the tone established in this paragraph, or that he simply adopted another discursive identity when writing in English, at least for this particular task. The borrowing of others' words became, in essence, the borrowing of an alternate identity.

After he had revised and turned in the final draft of his cover letter, Yoshi explained, "Through this experience, I learnt it is important to write a distinctive letter to get a job. Do you think that is right?" (October 16, 2002). He expressed knowledge of the larger application process in which a cover letter existed, saying that he believed the cover letter was a key to impressing the employee, which may then help the candidate secure an interview. When asked what he thought made a letter distinctive, Yoshi astutely responded, "one's experience and the rhetoric to describe this more like the fact" (October 16, 2002). In Japan, on the other hand, he felt that issues such as pedigree, experience, and age would make a candidate stand out to employers.

One interesting rhetorical omission from Yoshi's letter is any attempt to adapt it to the particular position that he is applying to. While he does describe his qualifications and relevant experience, he fails to make the key move of connecting those attributes directly to the needs of the employer. And despite the nod to the company in the opening paragraph (" . . . *I know firsthand that your corporation is a strong and growing organization* . . ."), his letter does not include any convincing evidence that he is indeed familiar with the company or its needs. Nevertheless, this omission went relatively unnoticed by Michele in her feedback conference with Yoshi, perhaps because she was impressed with his writing style overall. Another notable feature of Yoshi's cover letter at this point was the lack of connection between the cover letter and résumé. His letter made no reference to his résumé other than the use of the conventional form *"Enclosure: resume"* at the bottom of the page. Although he knew that the job application cover letter attached documents, he treated these largely as separate documents as he worked through the WCGS assignments.

Despite Yoshi's limited experience with the cover letter genre, then, he did develop particular elements of genre knowledge during this short time period. He began to understand more about the letter's form, including a typical move structure, content that might serve to promote the writer, and conventionalized phrases of the genre. He also gained some sense of the procedural practices surrounding cover letters, understanding that the letter may play an important role in attracting a reader's attention to the job candidate. And he recognized differences in the Japanese and U.S. contexts for reading and writing cover letters. When writing a U.S.-style cover letter, Yoshi consciously attempted to position himself as he believed that a U.S. writer would—that is, with confidence that may be construed as arrogance in his own country. More experience with this genre might lead to an increased awareness of the ways in which writers can position themselves as competent and distinctive without appearing overly confident, or how to adapt a letter for a very specific position.

The resources that aided Chatri—classroom activities and interactions with genre samples—similarly helped Yoshi. Classroom activities exposed him to a variety of reactions to various cover letter writing styles, while discussions of the sample texts gave him practice in analyzing generic structures, linguistic formality, and the use of technical language. He referred to all of these elements as he described the genre to me, and an awareness of these elements is also evident in his writing, as shown here. But for Yoshi, classroom activities seemed to have much less of an impact than his own self-instructional activity of locating sample texts outside of class.

Prior to WCGS, he had seen sample cover letters on websites and mailing lists, gaining an implicit understanding of the genre's purpose and form; the samples provided in WCGS helped Yoshi extend this knowledge. Through many of these samples, Yoshi learned what he did *not* like in cover letters, such as unusually long sentences or overly technical language. Like the other learners, Yoshi borrowed extensively from other texts; what made his borrowing unique was his more proactive and self-directed approach to seeking out sample texts on his own. In writing his own cover letter, Yoshi drew upon a template that he found outside of class on the Internet. The letter that Yoshi wrote and turned in for class was in fact patched together from multiple excerpts provided in what I later traced back to an on-line tutorial for writing cover letters. His overall letter structure matched both the structure outlined in WCGS (as shown earlier in Figure 3.1) and in the tutorial. Working within this structure, Yoshi selectively integrated texts and examples from this tutorial in order to maneuver the rhetoric that contradicted what he was more accustomed to (Figure 3.6).

It may be easy to view Yoshi's writing in this instance as mere plagiarism, as few changes were made to the original texts. The verb "copy" may indeed be a more accurate descriptor of his practice than the word "borrow," but a closer look at what's going on here reveals at least a very deliberate and informed approach to the use of other texts. As I made my way through the on-line tutorial (a site I admittedly stumbled upon by Googling some of the more "non-Yoshi" sounding phrases from his letter), I realized that Yoshi would have to read through a quite extensive tutorial—made up of nearly 60 different pages and at least that many sample letters and paragraphs—in order to locate the passages that he used in his own letter. For both the opening and closing paragraphs, nearly a dozen examples were provided; Yoshi clearly made decisions on which examples to use and which to reject.

In addition to the numerous samples included in the tutorial were many pieces of advice on writing a "dynamic" cover letter. These included using an attention-grabbing opener and closing the letter proactively by asking directly for an interview. As an interesting side note, one sample cover letter from WCGS contained one of these "proactive" closers ("*I will follow up next week by phone to see if we can set up an interview*"), which two students described as "pushy" during class discussion. Although Yoshi too found the closer to be a bit "arrogant," these reactions did not seem to dissuade him from following the advice of the on-line tutorial and incorporating this move. Still, there were other sections of the tutorial that Yoshi apparently made less use of. For example, later sections advised letter writers to adapt their letters specifically to the job they are seeking and to find ways to show a "window" into their personalities. Both of these features, which could have strengthened Yoshi's letter, were absent from each of his drafts.

The on-line tutorial was clearly very influential in developing Yoshi's understanding of the genre, and although he made reference

Dear Mr. Greim,

I am writing in response to the Simulation Engineer position posted on the High Frequency Measurements web site. Having been employed with Takada Ltd. previously, I know firsthand that your corporation is a strong and growing organization in which I could meaningfully contribute the engineering and management experience I've gained through both education and experience.

My academic career, work experience, and knowledge of simulation engineering have prepared me well for this position. I have studied electromagnetic field theory, transmission line theory, methods and tools for analyzing designs through academic and work experience.

Most recently, at Enterprise Server Division of Takada Ltd., I served as an assistant chief engineer and managed a ten-person project team to establish a printed circuit board design automation system for a cooperative product development alliance with IBM Corp. In this project, I realized a high accuracy cross-talk noise and timing check system, which is essential to design a cutting-edge computer product.

I am confident that we would find it mutually beneficial to discuss my qualifications face-to-face. I will phone your office at the end of next week to arrange an appointment. You are also welcome to contact me at the numbers on this letterhead. I look forward to meeting with you. Thank you for your time and consideration.

Sincerely yours,
Yoshi Tanaka

Enclosure: resume

Dear Mr. Cutts:
Having been employed with Hawaiian Tropic previously, I know firsthand that your corporation is a strong and growing organization in which I could meaningfully contribute the management and marketing experience I've gained through both education and experience.

I am confident that we would find it mutually beneficial to discuss my qualifications face-to-face. I will phone your secretary at the end of next week to arrange an appointment. You are also welcome to contact me at 212/555-8283. I very much appreciate your consideration.

I am writing in response to your ad in Sunday's *Sentinel* for a medical

My academic career, work experience, and knowledge of photography have prepared me well for this position. I have studied retail sales, ...

In my most recent experience, I took on a leadership position....

Figure 3.6. Yoshi's final cover letter from WCGS, along with influential excerpts from an on-line cover letter tutorial.

to finding other examples of cover letters he did not describe this site specifically as we discussed his composing process; it's unclear to me whether or not he saw his use of the site as something he should conceal. He spoke more openly, however, about his borrowing practices in writing his résumé, saying:

> I used some template which I liked. [. . .] Quite useful.
> I have less time to try for originality. It is suspicious,
> but time-saving [*laughing*]. (September 23, 2002)

John: Integrating Practice and Instruction

John's experience with the cover letter assignment differed somewhat from the other writers. During the semester, John was beginning the process of applying to PhD programs, and at the time of the cover letter assignment, he was starting to think about how to ask his professors whether they would be willing to write letters of recommendation for his applications. He wanted to write each professor a note to ask if they would be willing to write such a letter, so Michele encouraged him to modify the WCGS course assignment to suit these needs, composing a "cover letter of request" instead of a job application letter. John's intention was to first ask each professor orally whether or not he (all were men) would be willing to write a recommendation letter. If the professor agreed, John would then provide a more detailed cover letter requesting the recommendation along with an attached résumé. Because John was actually carrying out a different task than that required by a job application letter (and engaging in a different genre), tracing his processes with this assignment provides insight into the ways in which he extended discussions about job application letters to "cover letters of request." Rather than focusing on the cover letter as a self-promotional letter, then, John seemed to develop an understanding of the label "cover letter" as a broad term that included job application letters as well as a range of other letter types, as I shall show below.

At the start of the WCGS unit, John told me he was unfamiliar with the genre of a "cover letter" prior to this class, and that he had previously believed that it was an outdated form of communication:

> I actually thought cover letters were pretty much
> like dinosaurs from the past, where you had to send
> a cover letter because you're faxing it, so the people

> needed a cover letter because that's the first thing to pop out of the fax, so to know what the document was. And I think that was why people needed cover letters. I'm not really sure about this, but I think I read it somewhere or I came upon it on the Web when I was looking about what was a cover letter. (September 20, 2002)

Like Chatri, John drew distinctions between different modalities for the job application cover letter, saying that he personally would use an electronic cover letter but not a paper cover letter:

> I thought if I needed to do anything like that, today it's email, so my email would act as a cover letter. And, I don't really know what a cover letter format should be, but I know I'd just send an email instead. To make it professional-looking, it would probably look more like a cover letter. I'd have the person's name, address in the front, and then have "Dear Whatever," colon, and then have the letter. (September 20, 2002).

After several WCGS class sessions focusing on job application letters, however, John developed a different sense of the format and purpose of such letters. John extended his understanding of the job application letter when writing his own letters of request, by adopting some of the same rhetorical moves. John wrote two versions of his letters of request (because he initially misplaced one version, though he later located it and merged the two versions together). Although his two versions differed somewhat in their level of formality, they adopted the same basic move structure: describing his experience as a TA in Professor X's department; requesting a letter of reference; asking for a response to the request; referring to the attached résumé. These moves correspond roughly to Bhatia's (1993) moves in job application letters (Figure 3.1) of establishing credentials, introducing candidature, soliciting response, and soliciting response; the moves are also similar to the more general student templates of job application letters (Figure 3.2).

John's decision to begin his letter by reminding the addressee of his experience was quite intentional. During in-class peer editing, John's classmate recommended that he flip the order of the first two moves, but John disagreed and kept his original organization. He justified this decision, saying:

> Personally, I think what I've *done* should go first be-
> cause that would remind who I am. If I just start out
> with "I will be graduating next semester" or "I need
> this," I don't think that's a good idea. (October 10,
> 2002)

His reasoning behind his organization illustrates his effort at under-standing the text rhetorically, from the perspective of the reader.

While composing his letter, John noticed its resemblance not just to the job application letter but also to other letter genres with which he was familiar. He explained that, although he did not know what a cover letter was prior to WCGS, he now realized that it was similar to some letters he had written during the six months he had worked in industry. Both types of writing followed the same business letter layout, then began with a reminder of who the writer is, followed by the request, and then a formal, standardized closing. In other words, John noted similarities among genres that carried out the rhetorical function of *request* (rather than self-promotion), revealing his under-standing of the term "cover letter" as somewhat of an umbrella term for letters and requests that included an attachment.

One textual dimension of the cover letter that John struggled with was achieving an appropriate level of formality. He felt that his two versions differed primarily in terms of formality, with the first being relatively formal and the second more informal. John preferred the sec-ond because it sounded "less distant" (October 10, 2002) but wanted in the end to use some aspects of each. A second element of the letter's form that proved difficult for John was the decision of how to obtain a *strong* letter of recommendation. Specifically, John faced the question of how to let the professors know that if they could not write him a strong letter, they did not need to write a letter at all. In considering his various options, John illustrated an understanding of how this genre is integrated with various procedural practices:

> I asked a [department] secretary a couple of questions
> about recommendation letters and she said "Just ask
> the professors if they'll write you an excellent letter of
> recommendation because that's the only way you can

make sure that you get a good letter of recommendation." But that kind of seemed too awkward for me,
so I'm probably not gonna ask them right out there if
they can write me an excellent letter of recommendation. (October 10, 2002)

When making such a request, John preferred to give his professors an
"out" (a term used and described in WCGS when discussing letters of
request), so he decided that instead of asking the professor outright,
he would simply explain the context to the professor orally and then
make the actual request in the letter. As shown in Figure 3.7, both versions of John's request are couched in almost excessive hedging, index-
ing John's concern about appearing too bold or presumptuous.

Finally, John was quite concerned about what he called the "tone"
of his letter, considering carefully how it might be read by the different readers. He had planned to write a different version of the letter for

Excerpt from John's First Cover Letter	Excerpt from John's Second Cover Letter
I will be graduating next semester, and I will be applying to PhD programs at several universities. Since you are more familiar with my work background than anyone else, it would be an honor if you would write me letters of recommendation to use on my applications.	I will be graduating in May next year, and I will be applying to several graduate programs. It would be an honor if you could write me a letter of recommendation. If you feel comfortable doing so, and if you have the time to do so, I was hoping if you could write about my teaching abilities.
I would appreciate it very much if you would let me know if you are comfortable writing me letters of recommendation and have the time to do so. I have enclosed all the material needed in case you decide to write the letters of recommendation. Thank you for your time.	A resume is enclosed in case you decide to write me a letter of recommendation. I thank you for all you help and your time. I hope to hear from you soon. You can e-mail me at name@midwest.edu.
Sincerely,	Thanks again.

Figure 3.7. John's requests in his two cover letters written in WCGS.

each professor because "what I did [for them] was different, and what I'm asking them is gonna be different" (October 10, 2002). He was particularly worried about self-representation and appearing arrogant in his letter. He had read somewhere that arrogance generally did not sway academic readers positively or negatively, but John himself felt strongly about resisting this sort of identity in his writing:

> I just don't like arrogant sounding paragraphs and phrases. Even if- personally, if I were a professor and somebody wrote me this really arrogant thing, even if he was really good, you know, I just wouldn't feel like writing. (October 10, 2002)

By entirely omitting any self-praise and focusing instead on the work he had done, John hoped to avoid appearing arrogant. He said that the professors would write him a strong letter if they liked his work; if they did not feel his work was strong, John felt that he did not deserve a good letter of recommendation.

While at the start of the WCGS cover letter unit, John saw "cover letters" as archaic relics from the past, he later saw them as useful documents used to accomplish difficult and delicate rhetorical tasks of request or persuasion. His concern with the procedural practices that might best serve his goals was evident in his discussions with both me and Michele, during which time he asked many questions about such conventions within U.S. higher education. Keenly aware of the importance of the social relations surrounding these tasks, John focused much of his attention on issues of identity, formality, and tone as he wrote his letters. Even his decision to use a cover letter when contacting potential doctoral advisors illustrates a shift in his understanding of this new genre.

What led John to move from seeing cover letters as "dinosaurs" to seeing them as rhetorically useful documents? Although classroom activities and sample texts both proved influential to John's knowledge development, his more proactive approach to seeking out knowledge was, in the end, the most dominant strategy on which he relied. John sought out information about the rhetorical and procedural dimensions of the genre, asking me, Michele, and a secretary in his department about appropriate ways to ask professors for letters of reference. He also mined the Internet, hoping to learn more about both cover letters and the application process for graduate schools, from the perspective of those selecting candidates. John knew that learning the genre, in this case, went far beyond learning a conventional form. He wanted to know the ins and outs of how, when, and who to talk to about what, and he looked to as many resources as he could to find this information. His understanding of a cover letter as just one part of a much larger network of genres involved in the graduate school application process shows either a relatively sophisticated awareness of writing as socially contextualized and/or a relative confidence with his linguistic abilities, allowing him to consider the big picture rather than focus exclusively on text form. In John's case, of course, the letter writing task was authentic. He was not writing it simply to fulfill a course requirement—as was the case for Chatri, John, and Paul—but instead to give to real people for real purposes, on which important outcomes were riding. It seems quite likely that the real, rather than hypothetical, nature of the task led John to look beyond the formal dimensions of cover letters and to build a more sophisticated understanding of this text's role within a larger context.

In addition to seeking out information from people and on-line sites, John used sample texts from WCGS to learn how to organize his letters. In selecting from the samples, John clearly distinguished between job application cover letters and letters of request. Because the latter were aligned with his own purposes, it was these that he seemed to draw upon in composing his own texts. In fact, John's first cover letter adopts the same general length and rhetorical structure as one of the WCGS sample letters, also written to request a letter of recommendation; John's letter also includes two small fragments from the sample text. His second WCGS letter, written after he thought he had lost the first version, seemed to be composed without looking explicitly at the WCGS sample, as there are no direct borrowings. Nevertheless, a comparison of the texts (see Figures 3.8a and 3.8b) shows that the classroom sample and John's first letter work their way into this later text, with all three sharing similar rhetorical structures. In other words, while John developed his own words in this later text, he fit them into the familiar structure of the sample. In addition to drawing on the WCGS samples, the classroom also helped to build John's understanding of the pragmatics of requests in English. Specifically, John remembered Michele's suggestion during class to give the addressee "an out" when making a request, and he incorporated this strategy in both of his letter versions.

Sample Letter from WCGS

Dear Mr. Olson:

For the past three summers, I have been employed by MarkHon Industries in departments ranging from maintenance to mechanical assembly. I enjoyed working at MarkHon and learned a great deal about industrial organization.

I am now a senior at Midwest University, majoring in industrial management, and will soon start working for a position in industry. <u>Since you are more familiar with my work background than anyone else,</u> I would like to use your name as a reference on my job applications and at the Midwest University Placement Center.

<u>I'd appreciate it very much if you would let me know if</u> I can list you as a reference. Will you please return the enclosed post card to meet at your earliest convenience? Again, thanks for giving me the chance to work and learn at MarkHon.

Sincerely,

Figure 3.8a. Sample WCGS "request cover letter." Phrases borrowed by John in his own writing are underlined (see Figure 3.8b).

In the end, notably, John did not use either of his WCGS cover letters at all, opting instead to ask his professors for the reference letter orally. However, a few months later, John did write a cover letter similar to the job application letters discussed in WCGS, contacting professors with whom he hoped to work as a doctoral student (see Figure 3.9).

John's First WCGS Letter	John's Second WCGS Letter
Dear Professor ?:	Dear Professor S:
I have been working at Midwest University as a TA for more than a year. I have been a TA for EE 201 and EE 305 for 4 semesters. During this time, I have done many duties including having office hours, maintaining the web page, having help sessions, and grading homework and exams. It has been a pleasure working with you this semester assisting students and helping administer the EE 305 course.	I have been a TA for the EE department for 4 semesters. I have maintained the web page, graded exams, held help sessions, and held office hours for EE 201 and EE 305. t has been a pleasure working with you for the EE 305 course this semester.
I will be graduating next semester, and I will be applying to Ph.D. programs at several universities. <u>Since you are more familiar with my work background than anyone else</u>, it would be an honor if you would write me a letter of recommendation to use on my applications.	I will be graduating in May next year, and I will be applying to several graduate programs. It would be an honor if you could write me a letter of recommendation. If you feel comfortable doing so, and if you have the time to do so, I was hoping if you could write about my teaching abilities.
<u>I would appreciate it very much if you would let me know if</u> you are comfortable writing me letters of recommendation and have the time to do so. I have enclosed all the material needed in case you decide to write the letters of recommendation. Thank you for your time.	A resume is enclosed in case you decide to write me a letter of recommendation. I thank you for all your help and your time. I hope to hear from you soon. You can e-mail me at jkim@ecn.midwest.edu.
Sincerely, John Kim	Thanks again. -John Kim

Figure 3.8b. John's two letters written for WCGS. Phrases borrowed from a sample text are underlined (see Figure 3.8a).

John Kim
School of Electrical and Computer Engineering
Midwest University

Private University
Department of Electrical Engineering
Center for Integrated Systems

Dear Professor X:

I am a student in the M.S. program at Midwest University. I will be
graduating in May 2003. I plan on applying to Stanford for the fall
semester. At the suggestion of professor Y, I am writing to inquire
about the possibility of conducting research under your supervision.
Your textbook is used as the main textbook in the bioMEMS course
taught by professor Y, and your paper on the bulk micromachining
of silicon was the first paper given as a reading assignment in that
course. After reading this material, I have been fascinated by the field
of MEMS. I am interested in nanofabrication techniques, biomedical
MEMS applications, and nano-scale actuators, sensors and electrodes.

I will have completed all the necessary coursework for a M.S. degree
in both the solid state and biomedical fields. I am currently a TA for
the solid state devices course, and I have completed the IC fabrica-
tions course. For my undergraduate thesis research, I worked on the
simulation of a 36 DOF humanoid biped robot using Visual C++ and
OpenGL. I have taken courses relating to mechanics, semiconductor
physics, and biomedical topics. I have learned about the importance
of teamwork and good communication from working as a programmer in a software company.

My resume is enclosed for your review. I appreciate your time and
look forward to hearing from you soon. If you require any further information please e-mail me at jkim@ecn.midwest.edu
Thank you very much.

Yours sincerely,

John Kim

Figure 3.9. An RA application cover letter John sent two months after
the WCGS course assignment.

John's cover letter written for this new purpose—essentially an RA application letter—closely followed the template he had created in a classroom activity in WCGS (shown earlier in Figure 3.1); it also adopted the same three-paragraph structure as his WCGS letters of request, though modified for the new audience and purpose. In fact, the final paragraph of John's RA application letter, shown in Figure 3.10, was nearly identical in structure to his request letter, though written in a more formal style. At this later stage, John seems to have taken new ownership over the texts that had originally stemmed from WCGS, manipulating them to serve his own later purposes and instilling them with his own style. He also illustrates through these letters an ability to extend his knowledge of letter writing to various contexts and purposes, going beyond simple imitation of template-like forms.

John's "Request Cover Letter"	John's "Job Application Cover Letter"
A resume is enclosed in case you decide to write me a letter of recommendation. I thank you for all you help and your time. I hope to hear from you soon. You can e-mail me at jkim@ecn.midwest. edu	My resume is enclosed for your review. I appreciate your time and look forward to hearing from you soon. If you require any further information please e-mail me at jkim@ecn.midwest.edu. Thank you very much.
Thanks again.	Yours sincerely,

Figure 3.10. Closing paragraphs in John's request cover letter written during WCGS (left) and job application cover letter written two months later (right).

Importantly, in his letter writing tasks completed for and after WCGS, John developed his understanding of the genres through a range of resources, prompted by the very real nature of his tasks. Specifically, the exigencies of the task—the need to obtain reference letters fairly quickly and, later, the need to contact professors with whom he truly hoped to work—required him to learn about the procedural and rhetorical elements of the genre in combination with the formal dimensions. Because the WCGS assignment coincided with John's immediate needs, and because Michele was happy to let him modify the assignment to meet these needs, John was able to integrate the two domains of real-world demands and writing instruction in order to develop a more sophisticated view of cover letter genres.

Paul: Appropriating Prior Texts

Of the four writers, Paul was the most active user of job application cover letters during the time of my research. Like the others, Paul had neither written nor seen a cover letter prior to WCGS and initially believed that this genre was fairly uncommon in his field. This belief was reinforced by the fact that a departmental job search workshop that he attended, run by a major computer company, did not address the use of cover letters in job applications at all. Yet, rather unpredictably, Paul re-encountered this type of writing at a few points subsequent to the WCGS assignment, and these later encounters illustrate an interesting development in Paul's understanding of the genre.

In writing his cover letter for WCGS, Paul imagined a fictitious position to guide his letter writing. He chose the type of work that he was very interested in but that he was unlikely to obtain at this point. When we first discussed the cover letter, Paul described it in very general terms but expressed some uncertainty as to its rhetorical purpose:

> I think a cover letter is a formal way to introduce myself to the company and state the reason I write the résumé or why I apply for a job. It's a formal way to write. I don't know if it's required in current- in my area. Because I always send the résumé not with a cover letter. I always send the résumé alone. I don't know- I'm confused [*laughing*] why we need a cover letter. (October 15, 2002)

In fact, Paul went on to explain that he had asked a peer if cover letters were necessary and was told that they were not.

At this early point in time, Paul—like Chatri—viewed cover letters as much less important than résumés. Employers, he said, had very little time to look through applications, and the résumé would be more helpful in allowing them to focus on the candidate's most relevant qualifications. He felt that the cover letter might be best used to provide follow-up information to employers who had already expressed an interest in a candidate after seeing a résumé. He suggested that the letter could simply be brought to an interview (rather than mailed ahead of time), where employers may be able to spend more time reading it. Although he had not written a cover letter himself, Paul (like Yoshi) compared it to the statement of purpose he had written when applying to graduate school, perhaps because it shared the same general purpose that he states above (that is, to introduce oneself and explain the reason for the application).

The structure of Paul's first draft letter illustrates that he had built some knowledge of the genre's typical move structure early on:

1. Establishing credentials
2. Introducing candidature
   a. Offering candidature
   b. Essential detailing of candidature
3. Ending politely
4. Soliciting response

One notable exclusion from Paul's letter, however, is a reference to his résumé, even in the form of an *"Enclosures"* postscript, suggesting that he did not immediately see these genres as interrelated.

Paul, like the other writers, felt that the opening and closing paragraphs of cover letters did not vary too much for each writer and that these paragraphs should be relatively brief. The middle paragraphs, however, were more complex and required him to write largely from his own experience rather than by referring to samples:

> . . . in the middle, the content should be relevant to my background. I think there's little I can borrow from [the samples]. I have my own experience and I should organize *my* opinion. I think this way we can express our characteristic, but for the first and last one, that's required by the format. (October 15, 2002)

This understanding of conventionalized form, in fact, echoed a statement made by Michele during WCGS, when she stated that the first and last paragraphs of the cover letter are "very standard" but that the middle part is more complicated.

In his early encounters with the genre, Paul also emphasized that one key to a good cover letter was writing in a formal style. When asked about which phrases in his cover letter he thought were most effective, Paul pointed out two sentences near the end of his own letter:

> *I continue to work on using software engineering theories in real development processes, and I have obtained significant experiences through these practices.*
>
> *I am attracted to your company because of the great chance for me to implement an innovative project, and lead hundreds of well-trained developers to team work together.*

His reasons for selecting these sentences stemmed from his developing understanding of the purpose and audience of his text. He felt that the sentences expressed his ambitions well, and he said that "it's important to impress someone who will review the cover letter. I hope they will [be] *impressed*" (October 15, 2002).

Paul was also reasonably happy with his third paragraph, in which he described some of his experiences in program development:

> I think this paragraph I feel is good. Because I tried to *convince* somebody that I'm *really* interested in software engineering, so I want to express my emotion to use the knowledge in the real practice, in the practice. So, I write in this way. I think it's . . . I don't know, I'm not sure if it's not a good way to write. (October 15, 2002).

Here again, Paul demonstrates an understanding of the rhetorical importance of leaving a strong impression on the reader by finding some way to show his enthusiasm for relevant work.

Approximately one week after completing his WCGS assignment, graduate students in the Computer Sciences department were encouraged to email their résumés to "DigiTech" (a pseudonym for another prominent technology company) in preparation for the company's upcoming visit to the department. The cover letter that Paul sent to DigiTech was a much truncated version of his WCGS letter. He explained that he still felt that a cover letter was usually unnecessary in his field, but that that he had to include *some* text in the body of his email:

> In the main body of the email, I picked some sentence
> here because I think if I only attached the résumé as
> an attachment, and the body of the email is empty,
> it seems weird. I think I need to write something, so
> I just say I'm a master student and why I apply the
> job. I think it looks more natural. But I do not think
> I need to write the whole thing- or need to put the
> *whole* thing, so I just pick some sentence from here.
> (October 15, 2002)

In fact, Paul's entire cover letter consisted of only three short sentences
(see Figure 3.11), and only the first sentence bears any resemblance
to his WCGS cover letter. In contrast to his WCGS letter, this letter
contains only three moves:

1. Establishing credentials
2. Enclosing documents
3. Ending politely

Dear Sir/Madam,

I am a MS. degree candidate of CS department, Midwest University.
The attachment is my resume. Thank you for your attention.

Regards

Paul Shi
Dept. of Computer Sciences
Midwest University

Figure 3.11. Paul's email letter to DigiTech on 10/13/02.

The most notable exclusion is the detailing of his relevant experience. Paul felt that he could not recycle this section from his WCGS
letter because it was irrelevant to DigiTech. He explained that he
wrote the paragraphs originally "only for the purpose of the assignment" (October 15, 2002) and that they did not apply to this position.
However, the complete omission of this content alters the rhetorical
purpose of the cover letter itself; the letter sent to DigiTech functions
exclusively as an introduction to the résumé rather than as a self-promotional text in its own right.

At this point in time, Paul's knowledge of the cover letter genre embodied contradictions and uncertainties. In class, he was able to write a cover letter that bore close resemblance to a prototype of the genre; however, when he faced a situation in which he might actually utilize this letter, he opted instead to write only a very skeletal version of it, even a different genre from that which he had written in class. In general, Paul's understanding of the procedural practices surrounding cover letters were also limited at this point. He was aware that employers had very little time to read applications, but he overgeneralized this knowledge to mean that a prose letter was a largely unnecessary step in finding a suitable candidate.

Six months later, however, Paul took a radically different approach to writing a cover letter. Faced with a more immediate need for a job, Paul revised his WCGS letter, creating three new versions for applications to jobs in the computer industry. He wrote a basic letter for jobs in handheld devices, general software development, and game development; for each company he applied to, he could then modify from his most appropriate version and adapt it further toward the requirements of the specific position.

Appendix E compares Paul's WCGS version and two of these later versions written and mailed to companies in the U.S. Although all three versions in Appendix E follow the same structural pattern, those written in response to actual positions provide much more detailed and tailored descriptions of Paul's experience. His subsequent letters also include references to his Internet homepage, where he invites readers to view his programming development work. These subsequent letters demonstrate his ability to anticipate a company's needs, to promote his own qualifications and interests relevant to those needs, and to link the cover letter to other genres like a webpage to enhance his opportunities for showcasing relevant information about his work.

I was particularly interested in Paul's change of attitude about cover letters, as he had previously told me that he thought such letters were unnecessary in his field. His decision to use a cover letter in his own job hunt seemed to be related to his impression that such a letter might give him an edge in a very tight job market:

> Because when I apply jobs on-line, I think if I just at-
> tach a résumé, I think due to the large volume of the
> applicants, that company may not go through your

> résumé carefully. They may not notice you. So, if I
> write a cover letter introducing myself, maybe that
> may help me to have better chance. (June 26, 2003)

Of the different versions that he had written, Paul said he most liked the game development letter, primarily because he was really interested in this type of position. In fact, he did receive a telephone interview in response to his game development letter in Appendix E but did not receive an offer.

As his texts and comments show, Paul's change in genre knowledge was marked. He had moved from a very uncertain view of the purpose of cover letters and the procedures surrounding their use to a more informed understanding of how such a text might be used to persuade readers of the strengths of an applicant. In the early stages of learning about this new genre, Paul developed some formal knowledge through Michele's feedback in a writing conference. All of Paul's revisions to his first draft were prompted by Michele's oral feedback in conference. Other than minor grammatical issues, Michele was impressed with his letter. She particularly liked his non-repetitive sentence structure and told him that the letter was fine as it stood. This positive feedback may have served as reinforcement to Paul, indicating that he had created a letter that resembled the genre at least to a reasonable level.

While Michele's feedback did play a role for Paul, he—like the other writers—turned to other texts as a primary resource for learning more about cover letters. In initially writing his WCGS letter, he borrowed the overall structure and some direct phrases from the opening and closing paragraphs of one sample letter from class. Paul explained that he referred to the sample that he found easiest to read. Because that letter was written for a job in industry, it was also a close match for Paul in terms of context. While his closing paragraph was a somewhat modified version of the original sample, Paul's opening paragraph was nearly identical to it (see Figure 3.12). He explained that he found these framing paragraphs to be somewhat conventional and therefore less individualized:

> You can see the sentence[s] I used is very close . . . The
> *structure* and the first paragraph and the last para-
> graph. The two paragraphs in the middle, I wrote
> by my own. But the first paragraph, the structure,
> I think is similar. [. . .] Because in the middle the

content should be relevant to my background, I think
there's little I can borrow from this [sample]. I have
my own experience and I should organize in *my* opin-
ion. I think this way we can express our characteristic, but for the first and last one, that's required by the
format. I think that's the reason. (October 15, 2002)

Like the other writers, Paul had learned—through exposure to multiple samples and discussion in the classroom—what the more standardized parts of the cover letter are and also where writers are less able
to rely on formulaic structures and phrases.

Sample Letter from WCGS

Dear Mr. Duggan:

I am a Ph.D. Candidate in Biomedical Engineering (degree anticipated
June 1999). I am writing in response to the Biomaterials Engineer position posted on your company's web site. I understand that you seek a
candidate who has experience prototyping of an implantable drug deliv-
ery device, as well as with biomaterials, tissue interactions, and impurity
identification. I hope you will agree that my qualifications and experience
meet your needs.

In collaboration with the Orthopedic Implant Group at MGH. I have
developed a prototype of an orthopedic implant using biomaterials. In
addition, I am experienced in [. . .]

Throughout my research project I have cooperated with professors
in Department of Materials Science and Engineering, and the Biology
Department. [. . .]

I am attracted to your company because of its innovation in biomaterials
and its motivation to turn ideas into safe medical products. Thank you
for your attention. I will follow up next week by phone to see if we can
set up an interview.

Paul's WCGS Letter

Dear Mr./Mrs. Someone:

I am a MS. <u>degree candidate in</u> Computer Sciences <u>(degree anticipated June 2003). I am writing in response to the</u> Chief Software Engineer <u>position posted on your company's web site. I understand that you seek a candidate who has experience</u> in leading a large team to develop professional software. <u>I hope you will agree that my qualifications and experience meet your needs.</u>

Since the early 1990's, I have begun to develop software for companies as my part time job. Some of the products were recognized among the best of other similar products. [. . .]

I continue to work on using software engineering theories in real development processes, and I have obtained significant experiences through these practices. [. . .]

<u>I am attracted to your company because of</u> the great chance for me to implement an innovative project, and lead hundreds of well-trained developers to team work together. I am looking forward to your reply to arrange an interview.

Figure 3.12. A sample cover letter distributed in WCGS (previous page) and Paul's WCGS cover letter (this page). Share words are underlined.

While WCGS sample texts were important for Paul in composing his first cover letter, he turned to his own texts when composing subsequent letters months later. In other words, rather than referring back to the original sample letters and modifying them for his new purposes, Paul revised the letter that he had written in WCGS. As his purposes and exigencies changed, we can see changes in the letters' content and sub-moves, as Paul tailored these later letters to specific employers. The excerpts below, for example, show how Paul's closing paragraph evolved from the WCGS sample text to subsequent versions sent to three different companies. (Underlined words indicate shared words stemming from the WCGS sample, italicized words indicate shared words stemming from Paul's WCGS letter, and bolded words

indicate shared words stemming from Paul's first version of his cover
letter written six months after WCGS.)

> <u>I am attracted to your company because of</u> its innova-
> tion in biomaterials and its motivation to turn ideas
> into safe medical products. Thank you for your at-
> tention. I will follow up next week by phone to see if
> we can set up <u>an interview</u>. (WCGS sample letter)

> <u>I am attracted to your company because of</u> *the great
> chance for me to* implement an innovative project,
> and lead hundreds of well-trained developers to team
> work together. *I am looking forward to your reply to
> arrange* <u>an interview</u>. (Paul's WCGS letter)

> <u>I am attracted to</u> [company name] <u>because of</u> *the great
> chance for me to* **work with leading edge technolo-
> gies, and enhance my technical skills**. *I am looking
> forward to your reply to arrange* <u>an interview</u>. (Paul's
> actual job application letter, version one)

> <u>I am attracted to your company because of</u> *the great
> chance for me to* **work with leading edge technolo-
> gies**, learn from other outstanding colleagues **and en-
> hance my technical skills** *and leadership skills. I am
> looking forward to your reply to arrange* <u>an interview</u>.
> (Paul's actual job application letter, version two)

> <u>I am attracted to your company</u> not only <u>because of</u>
> *the great chance for me to* **work with leading edge
> technologies, and enhance my technical skills**, but
> also the chance to be really involved in developing a
> award-winning sports game. *I am looking forward to
> your reply to arrange* <u>an interview</u>. (Paul's actual job
> application letter, version three)

Paul's evolving manipulation of texts reflects an increased sense
of ownership and ability to control the genre. In part, this increased
ownership seemed to stem from his accumulation of experience (albeit

slight) with the genre and from the much higher stakes involved in the later letter-writing tasks, as obtaining a job became a real and pressing need. At this stage, Paul's entire attitude about the genre changed, as he began to see it as playing a much more important role in the application process. Paul's practice in WCGS, then, served as a foundation or scaffold, building his general knowledge of the genre and its conventionalized forms. His subsequent practice, situated within the context of his own work, provided an opportunity for him to build more understanding of the procedural and rhetorical dimensions of the genre within his own local context and needs.

LEARNING THROUGH TEXTUAL INTERACTIONS

During the time that I followed their writing, the four writers displayed—to varying extents—formal, rhetorical, and process knowledge of job application cover letters. Because the writers were largely unfamiliar with cover letters at the start of this WCGS unit, their genre knowledge development was relatively visible and easy to trace. Their individual paths to learning point to several important conclusions that might contribute to a theory of second language genre learning.

First, when learning new genres in the writing classroom, learners may most easily build knowledge of genre form. Through instruction and textual borrowing of sample texts, all of the writers here built awareness of the structure, contents, conventional phrases, and formal language typical to the genre; their letters written for WCGS were clearly identifiable as cover letters. It is also important to note that much instructional time in WCGS was spent analyzing texts and discussing text form, albeit often in connection to audience and context. Students therefore may have tacitly developed skills of text analysis in class and continued to apply those skills outside of class, similarly building their formal knowledge. While Chatri and Yoshi developed some rhetorical knowledge of the genre, it was general and hypothetical. Paul and John, on the other hand, developed more context-specific rhetorical and process knowledge of cover letters as they engaged in tasks that were important in advancing their own careers. Furthermore, the writers' multilingualism and experiences with related genres in other languages and contexts seemed to benefit them, helping to note specific features of the genres that contrasted with what they were accustomed to, such as the heavy use of first person or the inclusion or exclusion of certain information.

Additionally, non-classroom genre encounters may differ considerably from classroom encounters, yet both contexts can play important roles in genre learning. Although Chatri and Yoshi did not re-encounter cover letters in the year and a half after the WCGS task, both Paul and John did. Their more sophisticated—and particularly, more rhetorical—view of the genre in these later tasks is evident as they made serious attempts to address their audiences in persuasive and effective ways. Aside from the obvious reality and urgency of the context in these later tasks, what else differed? Figure 3.13 attempts to capture some of the distinctions between Paul's classroom and non-classroom cover letter tasks. As the figure illustrates, Paul's actual job application included a more complex network of genres, so that the cover letter was integrated with a variety of other genre-texts, like Paul's homepage, and the employers' websites. As he engaged with this intertextual web, Paul then learned—consciously or unconsciously—about the procedural elements of the genre and how it fits with other related genres as it is used to carry out social action. At the same time, it is notable that Paul's classroom task afforded him multiple resources for learning, including sample letters, instructional discussions, and instructor feedback. There is, of course, no evidence that Paul's tasks in these different domains are typical, but this comparison does suggest one potential benefit of classroom contexts: tasks in these contexts can provide learners with important meta-generic discussions and analysis that may well be absent from non-classroom contexts. If later encounters are largely devoid of such resources—as was the case with Paul— the classroom tasks offer an important learning foundation, eventually becoming a part of students' prior experience.

In addition to following different trajectories after leaving WCGS, the writers also adopted somewhat unique approaches to learning about the genre more generally, the most obvious case being John's well used strategy of seeking out rhetorical information. By following a peer as he applied for jobs, asking non-experts for advice, and searching Web sites, John learned not only what a text looks like, but also how it operates within specific groups for specific purposes. Overall, John focused more on rhetorical and procedural elements and less on formal elements than did the other participants. As a native speaker of English, perhaps he was less concerned than the others with his

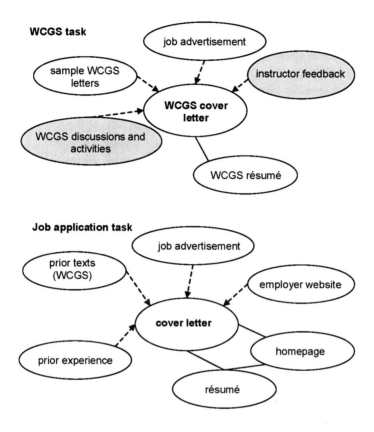

Figure 3.13. Genre networks in Paul's cover letter tasks. Oral interactions are indicated by shading.

ability to write grammatically and appropriately in a given genre and thus shifted his attention to the genre dimensions that seemed more mysterious to him.

Despite some individual preferences for some learning strategies over others, interactions with other texts provide writers with a major resource for shaping and extending their understanding of a new genre. Without prior experience to draw upon, texts provided these writers with scaffolding for completing the WCGS task with more confidence. As illustrated throughout this chapter, all four writers relied quite heavily on sample texts to learn about lexical and discourse conventions and generic structures (discursive borrowing), and they all borrowed exact textual fragments (textual borrowing). Interestingly, this use of exact words was employed for the generic moves that the writers felt were most difficult, such as the opening and closing paragraphs of the cover letter. These borrowed fragments were most commonly what the writers had learned to recognize as conventionalized phrases—phrases that might be easily identifiable to native-speakers but are perhaps less so to non-native speakers.

These writers' propensity for textual and discursive borrowing is not unique, but instead is an important learning strategy for writers more generally. In essence, they engaged in what Howard (1995) refers to as *patchwriting*, defined as "writing passages that are not copied exactly but that have nevertheless been borrowed from another source, with some changes" (p. 799). As Howard (1995, 1999) and Currie (1998) maintain, writers often use patchwriting when they are unfamiliar with the language they are reading and/or writing. Textual and discursive borrowing need to be recognized then as legitimate—and valuable—strategies for language learning in general and for genre learning in particular. If genres are considered to be *typified responses to recurring rhetorical situations,* as they are often defined, novice genre users need to learn what is "typical"; their use of borrowed phrases and structures illustrates an attempt to identify what is typical and to incorporate that into their own writing. One has only to imagine the task of writing any self-promotional genre in another language and culture to realize how much more complicated the task becomes in a second language. Even if they have not written a cover letter before, native English speakers are likely to approach the task with *some* formal, rhetorical, and process knowledge, however tacit and implicit that knowledge may be. Explicitly borrowing from samples can help assure the second language writer that his or her written product will at least fall within the conventionalized expectations of form, if that is indeed the writer's goal. This borrowing strategy is also important because it is one that writers can—and do—use in multiple domains: writing classrooms, disciplinary classrooms, workplaces, and academic research settings.

The use of patchwriting here, of course, differs somewhat from the process found in much academic writing—that is, the integration of unattributed and unchanged source texts to create a research summary or literature review (e.g., Pecorari, 2003; Shi, 2004). Here, the writers patched together bits of an already quite conventionalized genre in order to create their own text. This type of borrowing would seem to be less prone to accusations of plagiarism; after all, it is difficult to imagine a job application cover letter that does not contain traces of other texts. The challenge for second language writers approaching this genre for the first time is to strike the appropriate balance between writing within the conventionalized expectations while also promoting themselves as an individual who is uniquely suited to the job at hand.

One point worth emphasizing, then, is that even when borrowing textual fragments, writers can draw upon texts as a creative and productive strategy rather than as mimicry. When exposed to numerous samples, they often select from those that most suit their needs and preferences; in other words, they make choices, aligning themselves with particular styles and not with others. Indeed, Chatri, Yoshi, John, and Paul used textual borrowing as a strategy for shaping their textual identity, displaying an image of the writer to be "marketed" to the reader. Although each writer was exposed to roughly the same sample texts, their opening paragraphs are not carbon copies of one another; instead, they reflect, in various ways, each author's choices for how to present himself to his audience (see Figure 3.14).

Paul's Letter, May 2003 (sent to a company)	Yoshi's Letter, October 2002 (for WCGS)
I am a MS. degree candidate in Computer Sciences (degree anticipated Aug. 2003). I am writing in response to the position posted on Monster's web site. I understand that you seek a candidate who has strong computer science background and lot of experiences in developing professional software, games and most important, has deep love for game development. I hope you will agree that my qualifications and experience meet your needs.	I am writing in response to the Simulation Engineer position posted on the High Frequency Measurements web site. Having been employed with Hitachi Ltd. previously, I know firsthand that your corporation is a strong and growing organization in which I could meaningfully contribute the engineering and management experience I've gained through both education and experience.

John's Letter, December 2002 (sent to a professor)	Chatri's Letter, October 2002 (for WCGS)
I am a student in the M.S. program at Midwest University. I will be graduating in May 2003. I plan on applying to Stanford for the fall semester. At the suggestion of professor Y, I am writing to inquire about the possibility of conducting research under your supervision. Your textbook is used as the main textbook in the bioMEMS course taught by professor Y, and your paper on the bulk micromachining of silicon was the first paper given as a reading assignment in that course. After reading this material, I have been fascinated by the field of MEMS. I am interested in nanofabrication techniques, biomedical MEMS applications, and nano-scale actuators, sensors and electrodes.	My name is Chatri Boonmee, a Ph.D. student in school of Electrical and Computer Engineering, Midwest University. I am writing in response to your advertisement in 'Research Internship Positions at Honda R&D Fundamental Research Labs.' I understand that you are seeking a candidate who has research experience in Computer Vision area. I hope that my qualifications and experience will meet your requirement.

Figure 3.14. Opening paragraphs from the final letters written during the time of the study by each writer.

Ivanič (1998) recognizes the competing ways in which patchwriting, or intertextuality, contributes to writer identity: writers' identities are constituted by the discourses adopted, yet they are also shaped by the unique ways in which individuals draw upon and combine these discourses. As a result, even when writers rely heavily on the words of others, they can maintain a sense of ownership over their texts. They manipulate phrases, infusing them with their own voices. Paul, for example, described to me this balance between other voices and his own, illustrating a profound sense of ownership over his writing:

> For me, I *still* think that my writing style is more based on my thought, not the language, and it's not based on what I learned from *others* in English. It's based on my experience from the first day I was literate, the first day I went to school. I was cultured- the

writing style was formed from that day. The way I was trained to write. It's in *my* logic. Although I may borrow some sentence when I write in English, I may borrow sentence from what I learned from others, they serve the purpose of my logic. I will not borrow the *whole* thing. (August 4, 2003)

If learning a genre is a process of becoming familiar with—and eventually able to control and integrate—all dimensions of that genre, this process can pose a greater challenge for writers who are contending with linguistic and sociocultural difference. Interacting with text examples of the genre builds learners' familiarity with the genre and exposes them to alternate ways of carrying out the task. Much genre learning is a process of initially borrowing from and then eventually taking ownership of the texts around us. Teachers of second language writing—particularly in English for Specific Purposes or writing in the discipline settings—are right to see their classrooms as providing tremendous opportunities for honing writers' borrowing skills, helping them learn to appropriate other texts in both sound and effective ways as they begin to explore new genres.

4 Genre Analysis in the Writing Classroom

As I watched the students of WCGS analyze the unfamiliar genre of a job application letter, I was impressed with their analytic skills as well as their abilities to apply knowledge from their analyses in dynamic and individual ways. I was optimistic that Michele's final course assignment—a genre analysis of a text of each student's choice—would allow them to take these skills a step further, building an understanding of generic texts as contextualized social action and developing a writing strategy that they could apply beyond the classroom walls. My optimism was somewhat misplaced, however, as I had overlooked the central importance of *task* in the learning process—that is, how a classroom (or non-classroom) task is presented to and perceived by learners, and how that task fits into the larger pressures and constraints of students' academic lives.

Though it hasn't been a major area of study within research of writing classrooms, *task* plays a central role in Swales' (1990) model of genre-based pedagogy. In Swales' definition, described in chapter 1, tasks have communicative outcomes and are situated within sociorhetorical settings; a task-driven pedagogy, then, foregrounds rhetorical action and communicative effectiveness. Students' perceptions of a task—including its purpose and applicability to their own goals—can also be an important influence on task effectiveness. For example, if students perceive a task to be of limited use in meeting their writing needs, they may invest minimally in it. Parks (2000b), for example, observed three students in an ESP tourism course as they completed a video project. One student in her study saw little use for this classroom task, believing that she could only truly improve her English skills through real world activities and interactions. With this orientation, the student treated the video task purely as a course requirement, focusing on completing the task efficiently.

It may be unsurprising for learners to view a classroom task as less useful when it is relatively removed from "real world" domains, yet similar perceptions can occur even when classroom tasks closely replicate—and are in close proximity to—the target real world setting. For example, Hansen (2000) studied an international graduate student ("Mei-Huei") who was concurrently enrolled in an advanced writing course and courses in her discipline. Such a setting would seem to provide optimal opportunity for student writers, who may be able to immediately apply learning from one domain to the other; yet, Mei-Huei experienced a great deal of conflict in carrying out the tasks of the writing course. The classroom tasks asked students to take an authoritative stance in their writing by assuming an audience of field specialists, but doing so proved to be difficult to Mei-Huei. While most graduate students find it challenging to write for a specialist audience at the early stages of graduate school, Hansen believes that the difficulties that Mei-Huei faced were a result of the conflicts of audience, purpose, and subject-matter knowledge, as Mei-Huei perceived these within the writing tasks. Her own task perceptions (which may or may not have been influenced by the ways in which the task was presented) left her unable to see the relevance of the course to her own disciplinary writing. This outcome is consistent with James's (2008) conclusion from a quantitative study that it is students' *perceptions* of task similarity and differences that seem to be crucial in influencing learning transfer.

Of course, classroom tasks are not inherently doomed to failure. Several studies of genre-based instruction suggest that classroom tasks can serve to motivate students (Carter, Ferzli, & Wiebe, 2004; Henry & Roseberry, 1998; Hyon, 2001) and to aid students in developing a meta-language for talking about writing (Gosden, 1998; Hammond & Macken-Horarik, 1999; Reppen, 1994). Awareness-raising tasks may also help build learners' understanding of texts' rhetorical features (Hyon, 2002; Sengupta, 1999; Swales, 1990). The extent to which any one task facilitates learning for an individual student depends, to at least some extent, on the task's perceived authenticity or value and the student's motivation in the task.

As students in WCGS approached the genre job application cover letters, sample texts and class discussions of those texts helped them gain insight into this new and unfamiliar genre. The tasks that Michele used to teach the cover letter—discussion of common moves, conventional phrases, and structural variations based on audience—were typical of the kind of genre-based pedagogy tasks that Swales and Feak (1994a, 2000) implement. However, during that unit, Michele never used the term "genre," nor had she drawn explicit attention to the strategy of analyzing a genre's rhetorical structures. The pedagogical approach, then, might be best characterized as a very *implicit* analysis of genre. In the final course assignment, Michele introduced her WCGS students to two more systematic frameworks for genre analysis, including the meta-language used to discuss texts as socially situated, typified responses. In this chapter, I examine the way in which this framework was presented, applied, and taken up by John, Yoshi, Chatri, and Paul. In following the writers through this final assignment, two interrelated elements of the learning environment became increasingly salient to me: first, the writers' perceived exigence of the writing task, and second, their understanding of the goals and use of classroom activities and approaches.

Principles of Genre-Based Pedagogy

One of the most important beliefs underlying many genre-based approaches is that an explicit knowledge of a genre's linguistic and rhetorical conventions will facilitate the process of learning to write effectively in that genre. John Swales acknowledges that this idea did not originate with his examples found in *Genre Analysis* (Swales, 1990), but his work can certainly be credited for shaping much pedagogical practice in today's EAP and ESP classrooms. In his early work, Swales defines a genre-centered approach as "likely to focus student attention on rhetorical action and on the organizational and linguistic means of its accomplishment" (1990, p. 82). A key element of his pedagogic work has been that of rhetorical consciousness-raising. Through activities that ask students to explicitly describe, analyze, or compare generic conventions of multiple samples, it is hoped that students will take on a better understanding of the linguistic and sociorhetorical dimensions of those genres. Interestingly, Swales' early work describes the importance of this process in somewhat tentative terms, stating only that "there may be pedagogical value in sensitizing students to rhetorical effects, and to the rhetorical structures that tend to recur in genre-specific texts" (1990, p. 213). Still, he outlines several advantages of such consciousness-raising:

1. The problem of heterogeneous content interests in the class (medics and economics) is partially if temporarily sidestepped.

2. Insight into rhetorical structure is useful for both the reading and the writing of research.

3. General features are examined before specific details.

4. Discussion of rhetorical structure usefully develops in participants an increasing control of the meta-language (negotiation of knowledge claims, self-citation, metadiscourse, etc.) which, in turn, provides a perspective for critiquing their own writing and that of others.

5. Rhetorical structure may have 'novelty' value, and may thus identify the class as being different from others that participants have experienced.

6. The rhetorical element is likely to present the instructor as having something to contribute over and above methodology.

(Swales, 1990, p. 215)

In later work, Swales is less cautious in praising the pedagogical value of consciousness-raising. In a paper given at the Symposium on Second Language Writing in 2000, for example, he emphasized the value of student *analysis* of generic structures, in contrast to the learning of static models. He noted that "non-normative depiction and discussion of generic structures provides a locus for enhanced meta-linguistic awareness on the part of the participants and for further adjustment and enlightenment on the part of the instructors" (Swales, 2000, p. 17). Such analytical activities, not coincidentally, form the basis of the textbook materials created by Swales and Feak (1994a; 2000), written originally for their international graduate students at the University of Michigan but used now in many EFL contexts as well. This kind of focus on consciousness-raising through analytical tasks is now also reflected in numerous descriptions of genre-based teaching, usually presented as a standard activity type in such an approach (see, for example, Casanave, 2003; Hyland, 2003, 2004; Paltridge, 2001).

Genre, and consciousness-raising activities in particular, has unquestionably been central to advanced academic writing instruction, but its role in more generalized academic writing classrooms, such as undergraduate academic writing, has been somewhat less prominent. Here, Ann Johns's work is of key importance, especially for teachers of multilingual undergraduates. Johns has long advocated giving genre a central role in the writing classroom, whether that classroom be a first-year composition course, a writing-in-the-disciplines course, or an EAP/ESP course in an EFL context. Johns (1997) has described various examples of what she calls a "socioliterate classroom"—that is, a classroom in which students develop skills for reading, writing, and exploiting the texts that they encounter in a given social context. She asks students to collect genre exemplars, to locate textual similarities and differences, to study the sociocultural influences that act upon texts, to examine the ways in which readers process texts, and to leave the classroom to study the texts and textual practices of disciplinary experts. Her approach suggests particular value for teaching writing in the disciplines but is applicable to a wide range of classroom contexts.

While genre has become an important concept in the teaching of first-year writing in the United States, it is less commonly taken up as an organizing principle to course design or task development in the same way that it has been in EAP/ESP[3]. In his analysis of current approaches to teaching composition in the U.S., Fulkerson (2005) situates genre-based teaching under the umbrella of "rhetorical approaches" to writing pedagogy, which he contrasts with "critical/cultural studies approaches." He claims that "outside of ESL contexts, genre-based composition is likely to be found either in courses devoted to argument genres or in technical writing, where the idea of learning quite specific genres has been entrenched and is largely without controversy" (p. 676). Recent exceptions include approaches described by Devitt (2004) and Bawarshi (2003) and applied in textbook form by Devitt, Reiff, and Bawarshi (2003b). Focusing on the first-year composition classroom, these scholars emphasize awareness-raising, albeit through somewhat different terminology from that typically used in ESL or applied linguistics contexts. Curiously, first language (L1) composition approaches to genre seem to have developed fairly independently of the earlier work of Swales and Johns, though general similarities in approach and theory are fairly clear.[4]

In *Genre and the Invention of the Writer,* Bawarshi (2003) describes a genre-based writing approach to first-year composition, and while his theoretical basis (and thus terminological style) is drawn from classical rhetoric and more contemporary social theory, his goals echo those of Swales and Johns:

> I argue that teachers can and should teach students how to identify and analyze genred positions of articulation so that students can locate themselves and begin to participate within these positions more meaningfully, critically, and dexterously. Genre analysis can make visible to students the desires embedded within genres; and by giving students access to these desires, we enable them to interrogate, enact, and reflect on the relations, subjectivities, and practices these desires underwrite. (p. 146).

Bawarshi teaches his first-year university students to analyze genres by asking the rhetorical question of why certain genres use the conventions that they do. In doing so, he hopes to demystify the project of writing in academic settings and also hopes that students will gain a more nuanced view of both how writers position themselves within genred spaces and how those genres position them. There is less emphasis on form in Bawarshi's approach in comparison with Swales's or Johns's work, though this dimension is still present.

Drawing on similar pedagogical and theoretical principles, Devitt (2004) argues for teaching genre awareness, "a critical awareness of how genres operate so that [students] could learn the new genres they encounter with rhetorical and ideological understanding" (p. 194). Adopting such an approach, Devitt says, requires an integration of textual form and context, helping students see how forms fit within and are shaped by particular social contexts. Like Johns (1997), she recommends beginning with genres with which students are already familiar—syllabi, wedding announcements, letters, and so on. Students are asked to collect examples and explicitly analyze these samples using questions that will lead them toward a more critical consciousness of genres as dynamic, social, and intertextual.

The analytical framework advocated by both Bawarshi and Devitt forms the basis of their composition textbook, co-authored with Mary Jo Reiff, *Scenes of Writing* (Devitt, Reiff, & Bawarshi, 2003b).

Throughout the text, students work through a process of genre analysis that again resembles EAP/ESP genre-based pedagogy: collect samples of the genre, describe its context of use, describe its textual patterns, and analyze what these patterns reveal about the social context. The approach in *Scenes of Writing* is particularly relevant to my own observations of WCGS, as it was from this textbook that Michele drew materials for her final assignment for the course, a genre analysis.

Genre Analysis in WCGS

From the very beginning of the semester, Michele incorporated activities that tuned students into features of academic discourse that surface in many genres. At several points in the course, for example, the students discussed the first-person pronoun "I" and how its use may vary by genre and discipline. In general, elements like these were considered at a discourse level rather than a genre level; that is, discussions focused on their general usage in academic discourse and identified their use in multiple genres throughout the semester. Table 4.1 presents some of these discursive elements discussed and analyzed in terms of their uses in particular genres and their variation across communities of practice.

Table 4.1. WCGS course content with relevance to multiple academic genres.

Relevant Content	Writing Assignment Unit
Informal elements of writing	Writer's Autobiography
Formality and word choice	Writer's Autobiography
Word choice and evaluation	Writer's Autobiography
Disciplinary word choice and adjectives	Writer's Autobiography
Grammar of lists	CV/Résumé
Grammar of figure/table captions	Conference Poster/Slides
Data commentary	Conference Poster/Slides

In addition to these text-level features, students practiced analyzing patterns of organizational structure, as shown previously with the cover letter assignment described in chapter 3. So while Michele had not introduced the term "genre" or "convention," she had gradually exposed the students to the practice of using other texts for building a meta-knowledge of genre- or disciplinary-specific writing throughout the course.

In the final unit of WCGS, Michele made such analysis more explicit, focusing on the more general strategy of genre analysis. This unit was designed to build students' genre analytical skills and to then apply those skills to writing in the genre of their choice. Students first selected a target genre to analyze and write in; their selections ranged from grant proposals, article reviews, conference abstracts, graduate school statement of purpose essays, and a doctoral research proposal.

Class time during this unit was devoted to practicing analysis of sample texts and also to various grammar exercises drawn from Swales and Feak (1994). Genre analysis activities were built around a handout that presented a framework or heuristic, adopted from *Scenes of Writing,* for understanding generic elements of any written text. A general outline of the final unit is presented in Table 4.2.

Table 4.2. Overview of course content for final WCGS assignment.

Day	Content Focus
1	Genre analysis guidelines (Figure 4.1); analysis of sample SOPs
2	Genre analysis guidelines (Figure 4.1); analysis of sample SOPs
3	Conferences with Michele on first draft
4	Grammar exercises: articles
5	Grammar exercises: articles
6	Genre analysis, part 2 (Figure 4.2); analysis of sample conference abstracts
7	Conferences with Michele on second draft

The genre analysis unit was introduced to students immediately after they had completed the third course assignment (a professional poster or set of presentation slides). Michele explained that in the final assignment, students would collect samples of a text type of their choice, and that they would then compose their own text of that type. They began discussing the assignment in detail in the following class session, when Michele explained:

As I mentioned the other day, we're going to start
doing a genre-analysis approach because people are
doing different projects. We've been doing this kind
of, but we're going to go about it more strategically
now. And this is a very general guideline for genre
analysis, how to do it, and then as we go later in the
semester, we'll get more specific. (Classroom transcript, November 1, 2002)

During this unit, Michele provided students with two different sets
of guidelines for genre analysis, shown in Figures 4.1 and 4.2. Both
sets of guidelines were reproductions of presentation handouts that
Michele had received at a composition conference that fall. While they
draw on similar theories of genre, and indeed outline similar questions to guide student analysis, the analytic approaches differ somewhat from one another and also from the more text-based activities
used to teach cover letters. Specifically, the guidelines in Figure 4.1
implement the rhetorical approaches by Devitt, Reiff, and Bawarshi
(described earlier), asking students to first analyze the rhetorical scene,
and then the formal features of the genre, and finally to bring these
elements together by analyzing what the formal patterns reveal about
the scene. The goal of this analysis is for students to explore the relationship between rhetorical form and setting, to understand texts
as socially situated. The guidelines in Figure 4.2, on the other hand,
guide students through a series of questions categorized by Berkenkotter and Huckin's (1995) five characteristics of genre. The goal of this
analysis is for students to explore the tensions between stability and
flux within a genre, by analyzing a range of samples. The slight variation in goals of the two guidelines was not discussed in class; rather,
Michele presented the guidelines as complementary frameworks for
students to use in their own analysis. In fact, the second framework
(Figure 4.2) was distributed to students on the final day of class, after
they had already completed their final assignment.

GUIDELINES FOR ANALYZING GENRES

I. Collect Samples of the Genre
If you are unsure where to find samples, ask a user of that genre for assistance. Try to gather samples from more than one source so that you

get a more accurate picture of the complexity of the genre. The more samples of the genre you collect, the more you will be able to notice patterns within the genre.

2. Study the Situation of the Genre

Seek the answers to questions such as the ones below.

- Setting: Where does the genre appear? Where are texts of this genre typically located? What medium, context? With what other genres does this genre interact?
- Subject: What topics is this genre involved with? What issues, ideas, questions, etc. does the genre address? When people use this genre, what is it that they are interacting about?
- Participants: Who uses the genre?

  Writers: Who writes the texts in this genre? Are multiple writers possible? How do we know who the writers are? What roles do they perform? What characteristics must writers of this genre possess? Under what circumstances to writers write the genre (e.g., in teams, on a computer, in a rush)?

  Readers: Who reads the texts in this genre? Is there more than one type of reader for this genre? What roles do they perform? What characteristics must readers of this genre possess? Under what circumstances do readers read the genre (e.g., at their leisure, on the run, in waiting rooms)?

- Motives: When is the genre used? For what occasions? Why is the genre used? Why do writers write this genre and why do readers read it? What purposes does the genre fulfill for the people who use it?

3. Identify and Describe Patterns in the Genre's Features

What recurrent features do the samples share? For example:

- What **content** is typically included? What excluded? How is the content treated? What sorts of examples are used? What counts as evidence (personal testimony, facts, etc.)?
- What **rhetorical appeals** are used? What appeals to logos, pathos, and ethos appear?
- How are texts in the genres **structured**? What are their parts, and how are they organized?
- In what **format** are texts of this genre presented? What layout or appearance is common? How long is a typical text in this genre?
- What types of **sentences** do texts in the genre typically use? How long are they? Are they simple or complex, passive or active? Are the sentences varied? Do they share a certain style?

- What **diction** is most common? What types of words are most frequent? Is a type of jargon used? Is slang used? How would you describe the writer's voice?

4. Analyze what these Patterns Reveal about the Situation and Scene

What do these rhetorical patterns reveal about the genre, its situation, and the scene in which it is used? Why are these patterns significant? What can you learn about the actions being performed through the genre by observing its language patterns? What arguments can you make about these patterns? As you consider these questions, focus on the following:

- What do participants have to know or believe to understand or appreciate the genre?
- Who is invited into the genre, and who is excluded?
- What roles for writers and readers does it encourage or discourage?
- What values, beliefs, goals, and assumptions are revealed through the genre's patterns?
- How is the subject of the genre treated? What content is considered most important? What content (topics or details) is ignored?
- What actions does the genre help make possible? What actions does the genre make difficult?
- What attitude toward readers is implied in the genre? What attitude toward the world is implied in it?

Figure 4.1. Genre analysis guidelines from *Scenes of Writing: Strategies for Composing with Genres* by Amy Devitt, Mary Jo Reiff, and Anis Bawarshi. © 2004 by Pearson Education. Reprinted by permission.

During Days 1 and 2 of this unit, the students worked with the guidelines presented in Figure 4.1. As a class, they read through the handout, discussing new vocabulary and applying the questions to three graduate school application essays (statements of purpose). After practicing genre analysis as a class, students were to do their own analysis of a genre of their choice, and then compose a text in that genre. Students met with Michele in individual conferences to discuss the first draft of this text; they were not required to write out a genre analysis or to bring copies of sample texts of the target genre. After the conferences, WCGS class sessions consisted of two days of grammar activities, focusing on articles, and then a second round of genre analysis, using the second set of guidelines (Figure 4.2) and a small corpus

Genre knowledge is a form of SITUATED COGNITION. In disciplinary and professional cultures, genre knowledge is the knowledge that professionals need in order to communicate in their disciplinary communication. Genres are flexible and dynamic to respond to users' needs, but also stable enough to capture recurring aspects of situations. This tension, between stability and change, is always present in genre. Genres change when content of the discipline changes.
Berkenkotter, Carol and Thomas N. Huckin. "Rethinking Genre from a Sociocognitive Perspective." *Written Communication* 10-4 (Oct. 1993): 475-509.

DYNAMISM

Genres are dynamic rhetorical forms (speech or text) developed from responses to recurrent situations
Change over time in response to users' needs; constant incremental changes ongoing
New sociocognitive needs change genres (ex: too little time? put abstract at beginning)
Writers in genre are also readers, so on communal *and* individual level, shape genre to needs
Always demonstrate tension, stability vs. change (participants follow the form and resist it)

FORM AND CONTENT

Genre knowledge includes formal conventions, appropriate topics, relevant details
Genres are more sharply and richly defined locally
Traditional genres so broadly defined, only superficial (novel, memo)
Content appropriate to purpose, situation, time
  Epistemology
  Background knowledge
  Surprise value (want to be on "cutting edge")
  Rhetorical timing
Not an all-or-nothing dichotomy, on a continuum of genres
Limit to genre? Not exactly--come out of prior texts and text elements, but some more genre-ish than others
Uses common types shared by participants to make ideas familiar

SITUATEDNESS

Genres are derived from, embedded in, participation in community life
Use to create and position knowledge claims, package communication in ways acceptable to community, work in research networks in field
Apprentices learn genre as socialized in disciplinary community
  Extend as participate in activities of culture (usually picked up, not taught)
  Adopt jargon, imitate behaviors, act according to norms
Genre knowledge is part of the conceptual tool kit
Doesn't translate to different community
New situations and negotiations lead to changes

DUALITY OF STRUCTURE

Genres constitute social structures and reproduce those structures; they are both medium *and* outcome of practices
Human agency AND social structure implicated in each other--not dualisms, individual vs. society, subject vs. object
Sociology usually frames social structure as external and constraining to individuals
  Assume categories and rules are simple and not problematic (actor as puppet)
  See as simple: Sociological categories of status, role, class, religion, external interests, attitudes, beliefs, values
BUT, genre is much more complex: people *choose* genre, enter situation, decide whom they want to speak to in which setting at which time
Social actors are the agents of change, but in a situation not of their making
Resources for conducting affairs are also external and constraining social fact
Social structures come from historical, institutional contexts of people adjusting to time and technology

COMMUNITY OWNERSHIP

Genres signal community's norms, the grounds of knowledge, ideology, and social being
Textual practice reaffirms beliefs and values of disciplinary culture that uses it
Practitioners learn as they go by participation
Community will not listen unless perceived as relevant
Meets the need to talk to others in field

Figure 4.2. Second set of genre analysis guidelines given in WCGS, from Smith (2002).

of sample conference abstracts from an electrical engineering conference. Michele asked students to work in groups explicitly analyzing the samples for particular features or answering a set of the analysis questions. The bulk of class time, however, was spent in teacher-led discussions.

The three days of class discussions that were based on the genre analysis (Days 1, 2, and 6) were not lively. Students found the terminology in the handouts somewhat difficult, and they did not dig very deep in their analysis of social context, goals, or ideologies. While they were able to describe the sample texts and did have some interesting discussions of the genres' procedural elements and disciplinary variations, the class discussions never directly addressed the question of *why* these texts looked as they did and how the forms might be rhetorically situated.

In the discussion of statement of purpose (SOP) essays, the students often asked Michele questions like "Should I include X?" In most cases, her answers came from her own experiences; students often took notes of these responses, leaving me to wonder whether the point of genres as dynamic and social might have been obscured by the students' desire to know, unambiguously, how to write an effective SOP. Participation was also limited in these discussions, with only two students offering significant contribution.

The analysis of conference abstracts was fairly similar. This analysis came on the penultimate day of the semester when Michele brought in the second set of analysis guidelines (Figure 4.2) because some students had requested more work with genre analysis. Michele explained in class that someone had asked for a more specific definition of genre; this second handout provided one, though heavily laden with disciplinary jargon. After reading the definition, Michele emphasized that genres are "more than rules" and stated that genre analysis "can help you identify what's stable" in a particular genre, emphasizing the tension between generic dynamism and stability.

At this juncture in the 15-week semester, however, an analysis of genres—particularly one that seemed more geared toward theorists or discourse analysts than students—seemed to do little to raise student awareness either of the rhetorical and linguistic features of conference abstracts or of the strategies that learners can use to demystify a new genre. Working in groups of two or three, students read through a small corpus of conference abstracts and then discussed answers to one particular set of questions from the handout (e.g., 'Form and Content' or 'Situatedness'). Although Michele gave the students specific analytical tasks and asked them to write their responses on the board, the answers were perfunctory and superficial: conference abstracts require background knowledge in basic algorithms, formal conventions include concise information, apprentices are trained by reading papers and doing experiments, and so on. The class discussion was also limited to the actual texts rather than a broader consideration of the ways in which engineers construct and distribute knowledge (and how those practices influence written text). In observing the task, it seemed to me that students were not extrapolating a strategy for understanding generic writing more broadly; rather, they seemed to be focused primarily on task completion.

While the genre analysis activities were based on the awareness-raising principles advocated by Swales, Johns, Bawarshi, Reiff, and Devitt, students had some difficulty understanding the rationale; I will expand on this important limitation later in this chapter. Of course, students had already analyzed genres throughout the semester without formal analysis guidelines, and in these activities (largely based on the ESP-oriented work of Swales and Feak), they seemed to make connections to their own writing contexts. In doing so, they had become accustomed to looking at texts and identifying structural patterns and then discussing disciplinary variations as a class, as well as possible reasons for such patterns. However, their attitudes and practices in the final genre analysis activity differed markedly from these earlier activities. I will address some of the possible reasons for this difference later in this chapter but would like to note here that Michele herself expressed dissatisfaction when reflecting on this final unit, saying, "I didn't feel like I had some sort of over-arching point to make about it [. . .] and that was, like I said, a problem with *me* not thinking about how it fit in carefully enough with everything else" (December 18, 2002). If she were to teach the course again, Michele said she would still teach genre analysis, but with some modifications:

> I'd front it a lot more. I'd have- I mean, I was trying
> to front it by doing stuff with genre theory in it, but
> I think I needed to *do* genre theory and then tie it
> in specifically into a task—genre, task, genre, task,
> maybe. And I sort of did that, but not as well as I
> wanted. And then to pick out grammatical and lan-
> guage issues that were specifically related to the kinds
> of tasks people are doing. (December 18, 2002)

Clarifying this statement several months later, Michele explained that she felt she should have spent more time practicing methods for analyzing linguistic elements of the genres that the students were writing for the final assignment. She also described her own struggle with filtering her social constructivist approach "through the field of linguistics rather than the field of rhetoric" (electronic communication, September 12, 2003) because of her sense that the course was generally taught at Midwest University through what she called "an applied linguistics approach" rather than a rhetoric and composition approach. This tension, she felt, was strongest in the final unit of the course because it was less "controlled" than the previous units.

I suspect that the tensions that Michele felt in juggling what she perceived to be competing approaches was at the heart of her dissatisfaction with the unit. She seemed to feel compelled to adopt an approach in which she was not entirely invested. I don't mean to suggest that she was resistant to a genre-analytic approach in general, but it was not an approach she felt entirely confident adopting at this point in time. The situation may have been further complicated by her attempt to integrate the orientations of ESP (e.g., in the cover letter unit) and composition studies (in the final genre analysis unit). While such a theoretical and pedagogical integration is entirely feasible—as Ann Johns's (1997) work, for example, nicely illustrates—it may be somewhat challenging.

Uptake: Success and Impasses

One of Michele's goals with this final unit of the course was to allow for individual students to personalize the class, to analyze and write in a genre that was most relevant for them. Because this assignment came at the end of the semester, Michele wanted it to provide flexibility, allowing students to challenge themselves to the degree that they wished. As might be expected, students put varying degrees of time and effort into this final assignment, and they experienced varying degrees of success. Without delving into too much individual detail, I'd like to provide brief snapshots of how John, Yoshi, Chatri, and Paul approached this final assignment, paying particular attention to their application of and reactions to genre analysis as an explicit writing strategy, as well as the extent to which the activity contributed to their understanding of their target genres.

John

John was by far one of the more active members of class discussion during the genre analysis activities. At the time, he was working hard on composing a statement of purpose for his own doctoral program applications, so the discussion of sample SOP essays was immediately relevant to him, and he chose to analyze and write an SOP for this final assignment. He was particularly concerned with how writers can promote themselves in such essays without appearing too arrogant, and the classroom samples provided him with numerous examples of self-promotion.

Throughout the semester, John had focused on building his knowledge of graduate student application materials. As a fairly self-directed learner, he had already gone through his own process of building knowledge of the relevant genres, including the SOP. Prior to and during the genre analysis assignment, John searched university websites for SOP examples and advice, looked at his own SOP from his master's program application, and spoke with various people about their suggestions for writing such essays. Michele had also given John an article about writing SOPs, and he noted that

> . . . basically what that [article] told me *not* to do, was what [the university websites] told me to do. Yeah, [the websites] said, 'Write about your hardships.' And maybe, like, if there was a death of family member or anything. Those are all things to avoid in that [article] because they are so cliché. (November 8, 2002)

John felt he didn't have any such examples in his own life, so his decision to exclude this strategy was fairly easy.

Samples, indeed, were an important influence on John—those encountered both in and outside of WCGS. For instance, John had initially hoped to organize his SOP by topic, but he decided against doing so, saying that "all the sites that say how to write an SOP, they're all in chronological order. I've never seen an SOP not in chronological order" (December 10, 2002). The WCGS classroom discussions of SOPs did not appear to lead to any new epiphanies for John but instead seemed to confirm what he was already learning about the genre outside of class, particularly in terms of formal knowledge. In our discussions of SOPs, John often focused on the reception practices of the genre, emphasizing the importance of keeping the essay to the stated 600-word limit because the evaluators would be reading many essays and would not have the time or patience to wade through a lengthy text.

Despite all of his implicit analysis of the genre, John never systematically went through the WCGS genre analysis guidelines on his own. However, he did gain an understanding of some of the relationships between rhetorical strategies and formal patterns, as he examined samples and solicited advice. The WCGS assignment itself gave John the opportunity to receive feedback from Michele on a very rough draft of his essay; Michele discussed with him ideas for what content to include or exclude, given the short word limit of the text.

Looking at John's task participation from a genre-system perspective (Figure 4.3) highlights some of the interactions that helped in building his knowledge of the SOP genre. Being aware of the variation in opinions of and reactions to SOPs, John wisely tried to examine as many perspectives and examples as possible. In doing so, he drew on both textual and oral interactions, including sample texts, meta-genres, oral advice, and feedback. Because of the immediate relevance of the task beyond the WCGS classroom, John's genre network transcends the classroom, both in the resources that he drew upon and in the final audience(s) of his SOP. This is perhaps the ideal situation for genre-based pedagogy, wherein classroom writing *is* also non-classroom writing and the two worlds blend seamlessly. In fact, when the course had finished, John explained that the primary benefit of WCGS was that he was able to use many of the assignments to complete his graduate school applications (including the résumé, cover letter, and statement of purpose).

Shortly after WCGS had ended, I asked John to reflect on the class as a whole. At this point, he admitted that he "didn't really learn that much *new* information from this class" (December 10, 2002), though he believed it would be useful for students for whom English was a second language. However, when asked if he thought his writing or writing processes had changed at all during the term, John did raise the topic of genre analysis. The process of analyzing genres, it seems, had at least raised his awareness of the ways in which certain texts conform or vary in their use of conventions:

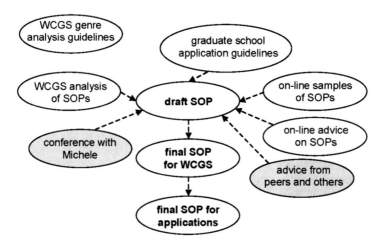

Figure 4.3. Network of genres and interactions involved in John's SOP writing task. Shaded circles represent oral interactions.

I mean, when I write anything, I usually just write it. Like, I don't even look at what's out there, usually, I mean, if I go across it before I write it because I have to know what I have to write, then fine, but if I don't find the exact point, I just write it. But, I guess, um, the whole genre analysis thing made me think twice about just writing it out of nowhere, because, well, I might do more prior article search, I guess. I mean, not prior article as in content, but prior form or I don't know how to explain it. Just to make sure that I conform to the standard. (December 10, 2002)

It is worth noting, as an aside, that John did not always seek to conform to a perceived standard; while he consistently appeared interested in knowing what the prestige variety was, he also expressed interest in expressing a unique identity within that variety. I point this out because one criticism against genre-based approaches is that they encourage students to replicate a normalized prestige variety rather than to question, critique, or even resist generic norms. John's comment above (along with the comments and practices of the other three writers) suggests that the limited discussion of genres in WCGS may have led students to see genre analysis purely as a way of uncovering normalized patterns so that those patterns can then be imitated rather than manipulated or flouted.

Yoshi

Yoshi approached the genre analysis assignment by selecting a genre with which he was relatively unfamiliar: the grant proposal. As an engineer in Japan, he had seen the importance of grant proposals, and he guessed that they would become increasingly central to his own work after returning to Japan. Choosing to write a grant proposal for this assignment would, he felt, help him build his understanding of this genre. This genre was also one option presented to the students by Michele, as she had included sample proposals (written by previous WCGS students) in the WCGS coursepack, along with guidelines for Midwest University's internal summer research grant.

Yoshi was present in each class session of WCGS, and he participated actively, though quietly, in the activities that involved analyzing the sample SOPs and conference abstracts; he also frequently took notes during these discussions. As seen in chapter 3, the strategy of collecting and analyzing sample genres was already a part of Yoshi's approach to writing in unfamiliar genres. Indeed, in the two years that I observed his writing, Yoshi's writing process was nearly always characterized by the strategies of looking to guidelines and samples, identifying conventions—more or less implicitly—and then borrowing textual fragments and/or discursive structures. Yoshi followed this set of strategies in the final WCGS assignment as well, albeit with some modification. Having chosen a somewhat occluded genre—that is, one for which samples are not readily available—he faced some difficulty in locating a corpus of sample texts. In first approaching the task of writing a grant proposal, then, Yoshi went to the Internet to locate advice for grant writers; he also studied the guidelines for the university grant which he would write his proposal for. These guidelines and lists of advice, coupled with his prior workplace experience with this genre, led him to focus rather heavily on the importance of "clarity, precision, and persuasion" (November 8, 2002). Persuasion, he felt, was particularly important but also the most difficult aspect of writing a grant proposal.

As he first began to work on his proposal, I was intrigued by the extent to which Yoshi focused on the contextual and rhetorical features of proposal writing; this attention may well have been shaped by the online advice that he read. He had many questions about the procedural elements of grants, and he understood the importance of understanding the mission of the sponsor and the interests and experience of the proposal reviewers. Still, these dimensions primarily took the form of questions rather than actual knowledge; while Yoshi was aware of the importance of these extra-textual features, he had limited understanding of how they might shape the linguistic features of the genre.

Because he was unable to locate sample grant proposals online, Yoshi used the four student samples from the WCGS coursepack as guides. He did not, however, carry out a formal genre analysis of these samples, and he was not asked to discuss the samples in his conference with Michele. In composing his text, he first summarized ideas for each section of the grant in Japanese and then translated his notes directly (i.e., without any re-organization) into English. His proposal resembled the four student sample proposals to some extent, adopting generally the same moves within each prescribed section of the proposal but differing in his use of certain linguistic features like passive voice or hedging. Although he had many questions for Michele after writing his first draft, she recommended only very minor changes, including making a few sentences more concise, sub-dividing a section of the proposal, and using a bulleted list to describe the plan of research. Praising his draft during their one-on-one conference, Michele gave Yoshi the option of not revising it further. Yoshi did make the minor recommended changes but did not make any more significant revisions.

In our discussions before and after the assignment, Yoshi's genre knowledge appeared fragmented and very partial. Without a great deal of first-hand experience or insider knowledge, this is not surprising. He knew proposals were important for researchers both in the workplace and in academic settings, but he lacked feedback, social discussions, or actual practice that would build his understanding of this complicated genre. In the classroom setting for which he wrote the proposal, he had little opportunity or motivation to draw upon the kinds of resources that would build a more sophisticated knowledge of the genre, one that integrated text form, rhetorical strategies, procedures, and subject-matter. When asked how he might write the text differently if it were to actually be submitted, he explained that he would ask someone in his area for feedback. Specifically, he wanted to know more about the project's feasibility, saying that "I believe I could do this project, but I wanna know another person's advice" (December 4, 2002).

It seemed to me that a great opportunity had indeed been lost here. Yoshi was quite interested in learning more about the grant proposal and wanted the insight of a specialist. Had the assignment built in the requirement of a more formal and systematic genre analysis—perhaps even an ethnographic approach that would require him to talk a grant writer—he would have been pushed to search out such insight, thereby expanding his knowledge of this new genre. With relatively low demands and expectations, however, Yoshi completed the assignment without gaining any significant insider knowledge.

In learning about the grant proposal, Yoshi had access to a relatively limited genre network (Figure 4.4), though he did what he could to expand that network. He sought out meta-genres and drew on provided sample texts to gain an understanding of the generic form, and he built some knowledge of the genre's rhetorical and process dimensions through grant writing advice pages on-line. With some previous experience with grant proposals, he was familiar with the rhetorical function of a proposal, though his experiences were tied to his workplace setting in Japan. Oral interactions, disciplinary participation, and feedback were limited in availability for Yoshi in this task, so his genre network

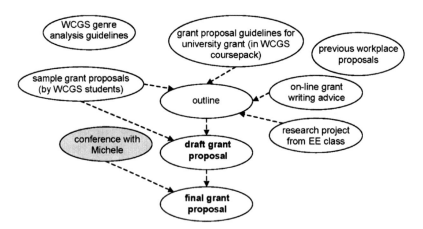

Figure 4.4. Network of genres and interactions involved in Yoshi's grant proposal task. Shaded circles represent oral interactions.

is primarily text-based, as opposed to "real-life" grant proposal tasks that hinge largely around social interactions (Tardy, 2003).

As he reflected on the WCGS course at the end of the semester and again nine months later, Yoshi made no mention of genre analysis—neither the guidelines, the related activities, or the underlying principles. In the time that I observed his writing practices, Yoshi was consistent in applying his tried-and-true strategies of collecting samples and guidelines, and then borrowing selectively, but he never explicitly discussed any attempt to understand rhetorical connections to textual features, at least not in the way that the pedagogical practice of "rhetorical consciousness raising" intends.

Chatri

Like Yoshi, Chatri chose to fulfill the final assignment with a genre that he believed would be important in his future writing practices. In Chatri's case, conference papers were a common genre for graduate students to tackle; not wanting to write a full-length paper, Chatri elected to write a conference proposal. He had had some prior experience with this genre, having written one twice in Thailand (once unsuccessfully as a master's student and once successfully as a researcher)

When he first began thinking about this final course assignment, Chatri faced two difficulties. First, he was unable to find a call for papers (CFP) that asked for a one- to two-page proposal or abstract, as recommended by Michele; all of the CFPs he could locate asked either for the full paper or, in one case, a four-page summary of the paper.

The second difficulty was locating sample conference proposals. Searching the Internet, Chatri was able to find conference papers but no proposals. He did not pursue other routes of locating samples, such as asking his advisor or lab peers. Instead, Chatri drew on his own prior experience, understanding a conference proposal to be "the same format" as a paper, but shorter: "Start with introduction, start with our problem, start with our idea, and tell some short result of our method, that's it" (November 8, 2002). This strategy of developing his genre knowledge through prior experience rather than looking to generic samples, of course, went against the pedagogical goal of the final assignment. Michele had hoped that the genre analysis assignment would help students develop a strategy for demystifying academic genres. For Chatri, however, this goal was unclear at best. "I don't know why we have to do genre analysis," he told me (November 8, 2002). His later feedback was somewhat harsher, as he stated, "something about the genre analysis, I don't like it, and I don't think that it's useful. I don't know its relevance to the writing" (December 2, 2002). Yet it didn't seem to be the principle of consciousness-raising that bothered him; what Chatri disliked seemed to be the rigidity and jargon of the genre analysis guidelines, most particularly the questions that focused on extra-linguistic elements of text, of which he could not see relevance. He explained:

> some question, I cannot give the answers . . . some question is just everyone knows that. It's natural, obvious. [. . .] [For example] "where does the genre appear and what's the medium?" or something. I don't know what's the importance of this. And everyone knows [the answer]. What's the medium? Some answer[s] for this: [it] appear [on] paper. In the paper, in the textbook, in the . . . and that's it. It's not have a significance so much. (November 8, 2002)

What Chatri did find "really useful" from the genre analysis guidelines were questions that focused on the text's structure or patterning.

What is interesting to me about Chatri's experience in this final assignment is (1) his resistance to carrying out explicit genre analysis, and (2) the extent to which this resistance altered the nature of the writing task. Because he was not able to locate sample conference proposals (and perhaps because he did not see the purpose of analyzing such samples), Chatri relied on his own knowledge of the genre in composing his text. He also used content he was already familiar with for his proposal—in fact, this was content that had already been written into a manuscript and submitted to a journal by his postdoctoral supervisor. As he pointed out to me, it would be very unusual in his field to write a conference proposal for a research project *after* having already written it up and submitted it to a journal. Figure 4.5 provides a schemata of the genre system that Chatri engaged in for this task; as I'll illustrate further in chapter 8, the network of genres in this task differed from that of a typical conference proposal task in Chatri's field. Specifically, the WCGS task was initiated by the class assignment (rather than a CFP), and the proposal described research from a previously submitted journal manuscript. The proposal also lacked a disciplinary audience or forum, as it was not written for a particular conference or organization. The only oral interactions in Chatri's WCGS genre network took place with Michele (with the exception of previous disciplinary interactions that led to the journal manuscript).

Perhaps because the writing task had already been shaped by the artificial constraints of the classroom, Chatri acknowledged that his WCGS text differed in specific ways from a proposal that he would submit to a conference. For example, he left out figures and references, both of which he said would be essential to a non-classroom proposal.

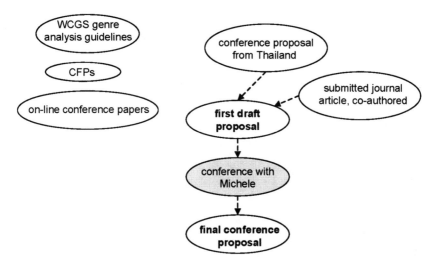

Figure 4.5. Network of genres and interactions involved in Chatri's conference proposal task. Shaded circles represent oral interactions.

In short, Chatri's focus was on completion of the assignment rather than on the process of analyzing and building knowledge of the genre.

Paul

When Michele designed the WCGS course, she purposefully placed the genre analysis assignment at the end of the semester. She knew that students would be very busy with their other graduate courses at this point in time, and she wanted to create a flexible final assignment that would allow them to decide how much time they wanted to invest. Feeling particularly busy at this point of the semester, Paul elected to write an article review for the final assignment, using a review he had already written for a computer science seminar.

In a graduate seminar on peer-to-peer networking, Paul was required to write two article reviews per week. His course instructor had given students some general guidelines on writing these reviews, and Paul was pleased to see his grades increasing over the semester from 4s and 4.5s to the highest grade of 5. As his grades improved, he made repeated use of the genre form that he had found to be successful; however, he expressed limited awareness of how that form related to the audience or context. For the final WCGS assignment, Paul chose to write a review because it was a genre that Michele had mentioned in class and also one that he had both familiarity with *and* a text that he could readily use to complete the assignment. Paul did not see article reviews as a genre that he would need after his final semester of graduate school, but he felt that they used the type of "formal academic writing" that he found somewhat difficult to adopt in his own writing.

When Paul first discussed the final assignment with Michele, she recommended that he look at the sample manuscript reviews provided in the WCGS coursepack. These reviews, however, differed from Paul's, which were written in a computer science classroom, summarizing and critiquing published articles. The coursepack reviews, on the other hand, were blind peer reviews of manuscripts written for a journal editor. Paul explained that he was writing reviews for a graduate course and asked how long the reviews for WCGS should be. Michele recommended two pages but also said that less than two pages would be fine as well. This was the extent of any discussion regarding the genre's form or purpose.

Over the next few weeks, Paul became very busy with his other coursework and missed one WCGS class session and a conference. When turning in the first draft of his article review, he turned in a version identical to one that had already been graded (receiving a "5") for his class. In their conference, Michele suggested minor changes to wording and grammar, and then gave Paul credit for the project without asking for an additional draft. In short, the genre analysis assignment for Paul amounted to virtually no out-of-class work. He re-printed a review that he had already written and handed in for his computer science class, and he discussed the paper with Michele in a short conference. No further changes were made, and the assignment had been fulfilled. Paul never completed an analysis of the genre of reviews, nor did he collect samples written by others. He did participate in the classroom activities related to genre analysis but had difficulty seeing the relevance of these activities to his writing. Taking a genre network view of this task (Figure 4.6), it becomes clear that Paul engaged in a very limited network, with few textual or oral interactions, and no substantive responses or chains of communication.

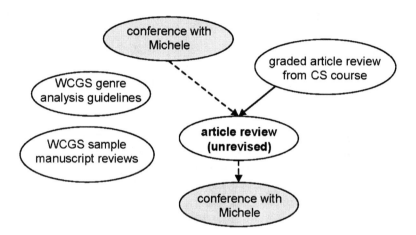

Figure 4.6. Network of genres and interactions involved in Paul's article review task. Shaded circles represent oral interactions, dotted lines indicate relatively visible relationships, and solid lines represent manifest intertextuality.

In reflecting on genre analysis as it was carried out in class, Paul described the analysis guidelines as too long, with many of the points of analysis being too abstract or of little use. He preferred more concrete activities, he explained, such as the exercises looking at article usage or formal versus informal vocabulary. In the week after the course was complete, Paul did describe seeing some value in genre analysis, saying "I think I learned something, but a little bit abstract" (December 12, 2002). Whether or not Paul would later apply the strategy of analyzing a genre—either explicitly or implicitly—will be taken up in chapter 7.

LIMITATIONS TO INSTRUCTION

As the above snapshots suggest, the final assignment of WCGS had limitations. While John and Yoshi did develop some insights into the rhetorical and process dimensions of the genres they wrote in, Chatri and Paul completed the assignment with little to no new knowledge of their chosen genres. Furthermore, none of the writers appeared to develop a more dynamic understanding of the relationship between formal textual features and sociorhetorical context (with the possible exception of John), generally considered to be the goal of genre-based pedagogy. It is worth exploring the possible reasons for these limitations in more depth.

Exigence

As with the job application cover letter task described in chapter 3, exigence played an important role in shaping the approaches that the writers took in engaging in this task. Miller (1984) defines exigence as "a form of social knowledge—a mutual construing of objects, events, interests, and purposes that not only links them but also makes them what they are: an objectified social need" (p. 157). In the case of the WCGS assignment, the writers experienced—and constructed—various exigencies within the task. John fulfilled the assignment by using an authentic high-stakes writing task that he was currently working on outside of the classroom. He was under real time constraints that coincided with the assignment deadlines, and he was in need of feedback and support as he completed the very individualized task of writing an SOP. At the same time, Paul fulfilled the assignment by handing in a paper that he had already written and received a high grade on for another course. John wrote multiple drafts, searched for advice and samples, and solicited and integrated feedback from Michele regarding formal, rhetorical, procedural, and content expectations for the SOP; Paul wrote no drafts, asked no questions about the genre in his individual conference with Michele, and made no revisions to the paper that he had already submitted to his computer science course. This is not to suggest that Paul was a lazy or disengaged student—as other snapshots of Paul's story show throughout this book, he was in many cases a very earnest and engaged student and writer. But each task *for each individual* is constrained by various limitations, possibilities, events, and motives, which together create exigence.

To some extent, this variation among the writers' approaches to the task reflected Michele's goal of creating a flexible final assignment. She had wanted the level of investment in the final assignment to be determined by the individual writers, understanding that they were under considerable pressure in their other courses and that they were receiving no course credit for WCGS. Yet given the choice, most of the students opted for the easier path in completing this assignment, losing the opportunity for a rigorous analysis of a specific genre that might lead to the kind of consciousness-raising that genre-based pedagogues advocate. Students were not required to show any evidence of their genre analysis (they did not turn in or share a corpus of samples or a written summary of an analysis), giving them little incentive to carry out the admittedly time-consuming task. In contrast, the genre-based approaches described at the beginning of this chapter require students to demonstrate their explicit analysis of target genres. The low-pressure approach in WCGS, intended to allow students to experiment with their writing and adapt the class to meet their own needs, in many ways seemed to backfire (see Norris & Tardy, 2006, for a fuller discussion of this conundrum). Without the pressure of a grade or at least high instructor expectations, many of the students found no reason to invest the time and energy necessary for building genre knowledge.

Task

Paul, Chatri, and Yoshi all commented on the usefulness of WCGS activities that focused on language-level or organizational/structural issues of writing, and the majority of these activities took a genre-analytical approach (that is to say, they made some connection between textual form, goals, and community). These writers, however, were unable to identify a connection between those activities that implicitly analyzed the formal features of genre and the more explicit and arduous task referred to in class as "genre analysis."

Student learning appeared to be impeded to some extent by the way in which genre analysis was introduced and framed within the course, and by the jargon and theoretical assumptions that were embedded in the genre analysis handouts. The term "genre analysis" was first introduced to students in the final month of WCGS, but the term "genre" was never discussed theoretically, so students were likely to equate it simply with "text type." Without some discussion of the term, students may not understand why they should analyze contextual and intertextual elements of the texts or what kind of influence these elements might have on formal features. There is, of course, no way to know how students might have responded to the task differently if such a discussion had taken place. Yet, given their questions about the rationale or purpose of the genre analysis activity, I believe that some more explicit explanation of genres as dynamic, social, and intertextual—perhaps through examples that students were already familiar with—could have helped students identify the assignment purpose and the usefulness of linking contextual and formal features in their own analyses, integrating and restructuring their knowledge of form, rhetoric, process, and subject-matter.

An additional limit to the task was the framework that formed the basis of much class discussion. The framework from *Scenes of Writing* (Figure 4.1) would likely be useful for a formal genre analysis project, but was somewhat abstract for a class discussion. This is not a criticism of the framework offered here by Devitt, Reiff, and Bawarshi (2004), which I see as useful for helping students see texts as socially situated, dynamic actions. However, this goal is only likely to be achieved through sustained, systematic analysis in which students develop a strong understanding of the terminology and the goals of the various analytical questions. Devitt et al. present this framework early on in their textbook so that students are introduced to it at the start of a course. It serves as an introduction to the complexities of genre, and it provides a set of guiding questions that students can return to throughout a course as they practice examining various genres of their choosing. Such sustained and systematic analysis is, I believe, essential to developing the type of rhetorical consciousness or genre awareness that genre-based pedagogy works toward.

Sustained analysis of genres—that is, analysis that takes place in cycles over an entire course term—would also allow teachers to break down the quite sophisticated task of multidimensional genre analysis. The frameworks that Michele used in her class cover a great deal of terrain, asking students to examine form, setting, subject, intertextuality, power, ideology, and so on—in other words, all major dimensions of a genre. This is a lot for novice genre users to take in, and may in fact be *too* much in some cases. For learners who already have some familiarity and comfort with particular elements of a genre, it makes sense to examine the genre in a rich, multilayered way. But examining the complexity of a genre that is unfamiliar may be somewhat daunting or even counterproductive. From a pedagogical perspective, scaffolding the learning of genre may be a much more beneficial approach. Learners can first examine a text's formal features, for example; after they have some familiarity with the genre's form, they may return to analyze another dimension, such as the procedures of production, distribution, and reception. What they learn in this later analysis is likely to re-inform and restructure their understanding of generic form. This process of building accumulated knowledge must be long term. While presenting students with a complicated framework for understanding genres can provide a more dynamic view of genre, it is important to remember that holding a holistic view of a particular genre is usually the result of lengthy experience. When learners are contending with linguistic codes, unfamiliar sociocultural assumptions, and possibly conflicting identities, helping them break genres down into "parts," which are later laminated into a whole, may well have value.

The WCGS genre analysis assignment may also have been more successful if the writers had been required to carry out a written genre analysis, collecting and analyzing a small corpus of sample texts and interviewing expert users of the genre. Such an analysis could focus on those elements of the genre that the student finds particularly interesting, problematic, or important. A required component of the analysis could be to link formal textual patterns with social context, obliging learners to address the question of *why* the samples they examine take on particular formal properties; an expert user can provide important insight in this area. In carrying out a more formal genre analysis, students can also benefit from their interactions with other texts and people, both of which become resources for genre learning. Samples of the target genre can provide learners with valuable resources for textual and discursive borrowing, linked genres (including reference guides, antecedent genres, follow-up genres, or supporting genres) illustrate to writers the role that the genre plays in a larger network of texts and activities, and interaction with peers and experts provides first-hand insights while also illustrating to learners the ways in which generic practices may vary for individuals. Michele's intentions for keeping the pressure low for this assignment made intuitive sense, but may have inadvertently led to a missed opportunity for at least the four writers that I observed.

An additional concern related to task is the critical importance of communicating task rationale to the students. As illustrated in the snapshots of the four writers here, students do not necessarily share the understanding that teachers have of task goals or of the theoretical complexity of genre. Without communicating these assumptions very explicitly to students, there is a danger that they will perceive "genre analysis" to be a dressed-up term for learning the standard rules for writing in specific text types. Helping students to unpack the term *genre* and to identify its relevance as a writing strategy is a key to genre-based pedagogy; without doing so, teachers run the risk of unknowingly teaching the kind of prescriptive rules that run counter to a rhetorical view of writing.

Finally, in the stories of the four writers described earlier, I have attempted to show at least a simplified schemata of the genre networks that the writers engaged in as they carried out the genre analysis task. The diagrams illustrate the varying levels of complexity and the distinctions that often exist between classroom-based writing tasks and disciplinary- or practice-based writing tasks. The classroom-centered tasks (all but John's, in this case) were prompted by the task assignment rather than growing out of the work in a more organic way (see chapters 7 and 8, in contrast). These tasks draw on fairly limited textual interactions and even more limited social interactions. In the case of this particular task, the extent of this limitation was left to the devices of the student-writers. The writers could choose independently to dive into a larger genre system, though doing so would require certain social networks (such as mentors or expert peers) that not all writers have access to.

The Genre-Based Classroom

These writers' immediate reactions to the genre analysis task were somewhat negative, and the final assignment was not mentioned by anyone to be the most valuable or useful part of the course. Several months after WCGS had finished, the writers' reactions to it were mixed and reflect the range of needs and experiences that the writers brought to the course. At the end of his MS degree program, six months after completing WCGS, John was able to recall very little from the class as a whole, saying it was now "completely vague" in his mind. In fact his primary lasting impression from the course was that "it was fun" and "didn't put too much pressure on me" (May 3, 2003). For Yoshi, the benefit of enrollment in WCGS at the start of his MS degree program was that it introduced him to U.S. academic writing through practice in multiple genres in English. At the end of the semester, he felt that he was able to write with less difficulty because the course assignments gave him regular writing practice. One year later, Yoshi said he felt more confident in his writing in terms of both speed and level of vocabulary. He credited "practice and experience" for this increased confidence.

Chatri enrolled in WCGS at the end of his PhD coursework and had some question about the relevance of the writing course for his own writing needs as a junior scholar. He described the course as focusing on the writing assignments rather than on *writing,* which he described as issues of language and organization. Chatri's expectations for WCGS (to improve his grammar) clashed with the course goals, and he consequently felt that the course had not benefited him in the ways he had hoped. Although he felt that the individual feedback on his grammar was helpful, he was critical of some of the tasks (such as the résumé and presentation slides) and felt that an alternative approach may have served him better:

> Maybe, for me, I am an international student, I don't have any skills so much about the writing. Because I told you that I took only one writing class in my country, I know that there are some skill to write. Okay, how to organize, and the basic of writing the sentence, how to combine the sentence so that we get the full paragraph or something like that. It's very useful. But I didn't get from this class. I think it's very important. And, after we have the skill, the last half maybe we can use that skill to write the real paper or real application, such as the résumé or cover letter or conference abstract. (December 2, 2002)

Chatri's course goals were likely influenced by his previous educational experience as well as his immediate need for successfully carrying out high-stakes writing tasks.

Select details from WCGS stood out in Paul's mind at the end of the course, and he was optimistic that the content would be of use when he wrote his master's thesis. A year later, he primarily retained from WCGS an awareness of some of the distinctions between more formal and informal styles of writing. While writing his master's thesis, Paul lamented his inability to recall other specific items from the

course and apply them, feeling that he had not received enough practice time:

> Too little practice [in the course], I think. Because
> I was taught several concepts, what I should do, but
> I can hardly apply them. It would be better if I can
> practice those ideas in that class maybe on some as-
> signments to write a technical report. That may be
> more helpful, because I still feel very difficult when I
> write this thesis. (June 6, 2003)

The comments of these students suggest a few lessons about genre
and classroom instructions. First, they illustrate the difficulty of bringing genre to life solely within the confines of a writing classroom—especially a "one size fits all" course such as the WCGS section in which
a range of students were enrolled. As Cheng (2006a) illustrates, however, sophisticated rhetorical knowledge of genres can be developed
through an intermingling of classroom and non-classroom instructional contexts. When the walls between classroom and disciplinary
practice dissolve, students are able to immediately apply and extend
their knowledge to relevant contexts, and to meaningfully explore the
impact of rhetoric, process, and subject-matter on text form. John's experience with the genre analysis task, for example, differs greatly from
the other students, as evident from his processes and the genre system
in which he participated. While certainly the reasons for this difference are related to a host of individual and situational factors, the nature of the task—as an authentic, high-stakes task that had impact on
his life—seems to be crucial. For John, the classroom task was mostly
indistinguishable from the non-classroom task.

A second lesson about genre and the writing classroom concerns
the value of genre analysis as a primary instructional task. Its limitations in WCGS can be explained in part by its placement at the end
of a 15-week semester, the instructor's own discomfort with the assignment, and the low-stakes nature of the task. In contrast, numerous scholars have reported positive student feedback on genre analytic tasks (Bawarshi, 2003; Cheng, 2006a; Johns, 2002a; Johns et al.,
2006; Swales & Lindemann, 2002). It appears that, when carried out
in sustained and systematic ways, genre analysis does have the potential to raise writers' awareness of the dynamic and rhetorical nature of
genre. Nevertheless, consciousness-raising alone is not sufficient for

developing the kind of integrated and multidimensional genre knowl-edge of experts. Students need to see the relevance of the genres they are analyzing and they need to be invested in the analytic task. Blend-ing the classroom and non-classroom contexts—through required in-terviews, observations, or document collection—is, at some point, es-sential for helping students develop such investment and the kind of rhetorical knowledge that gives genres their meaning. In other words, genre analysis cannot stop at the analytic stage if it is to be beneficial for students. Instead, it should include application of analytic skills to the writing students encounter *outside* of class and should aim to engage students in the sociorhetorical contexts of the writing. Carried out in this way, genre analysis may still provide a promising strategy for providing writers with meaningful encounters, practice and experi-ence, and meta-generic knowledge.

5 Accumulated Exposure and the Learning of a Multimodal Genre

> It is now impossible to make sense of texts, even of their linguistic parts alone, without having a clear idea of what these other features might be contributing to the meaning of a text. In fact, it is now no longer possible to understand language and its uses without understanding the effect of all modes of communication that are copresent in any text. (Kress, 2000, p. 337)

As Gunther Kress argues, contemporary texts are multimodal texts, mixing verbal, visual, and even aural/oral modes of communication; the professional and academic genres of graduate school are by no means an exception. In the visual mode, meaning may be created by graphs, photographs, or even layout design or font choice.

Easier access to increasingly powerful technologies has given writers control over aspects of their texts that used to be the province of publishers or graphic designers—such technological changes have obligated writers to contend with new textual choices, including the selection of medium (e.g., paper versus screen) and mode (e.g., verbal versus visual). These choices are not merely cosmetic ones; different modes and media are based on different logics, with paper media dominated by the logic of the word and digital media dominated by the logic of the image (Kress, 2003). For example, in digital texts like websites or presentation slides, images often provide the major source of communication (Allen & Simmons, 2002), prose text is often presented in bulleted lists rather than traditional paragraphs, and information is arranged by screens rather than paragraphs or chapters. Such differing logics have important implications for the learning of multimodal genres, as mixing the logics of verbal text and visual image gives rise to new sets of issues for both readers and writers (Kress, 2003).

As visual and verbal modes interact, one mode is often better suited to carry out certain functions than another; this is what Kress (2003) describes as the "functional specialisation of the modes." Written words, for example, may be more effective in representing event structures, while visual images may be more effective in representing aspects of the world:

> In the new communicational world there are now choices about how what is to be represented should be represented: *in what mode, in what genre, in what ensembles of modes and genres and on what occasions.* These were not decisions open to students (or teachers or textbook-makers) some twenty years earlier. (Kress, 2003, p. 117, emphasis added)

For graduate students, researchers, or even undergraduate academic writers, such decisions have come to play an important role in genre learning.

While rhetoric and composition scholarship has embraced the study of multimodal texts (including how such texts are taught and learned in the classroom), applied linguistics research has remained focused primarily on the linguistic (that is, verbal) elements of text, paying less attention to visual elements. An interest by some ESP scholars in the visuals of scientific texts is an important and relevant exception (e.g., Johns, 1998; Miller, 1998; Rowley-Jolivet, 2001). Visuals often play a central role in scientific discourse, where communication would at times be nearly impossible without the use of displays such as tables, graphs, or figures. As Lemke (1998) notes:

> Visual figures in scientific text, and mathematical expressions also, are generally *not* redundant with verbal main text information. They do not simply 'illustrate' the verbal text, they add important or necessary information; they complement the main text, and in many cases they complete it. (p. 105).

In scientific discourse, Lemke argues, meaning is created through "joint co-deployment" of at least two semiotic modes; such multimodality affords a level of meaning that cannot be obtained through one mode alone.

Multimodal genres also present an interesting case for the study of second language writers because linguistic proficiency applies primarily to the verbal mode. Visual "mastery," on the other hand, depends on the user's familiarity with the visual conventions and standards within a particular disciplinary or social community. One visually-saturated, yet multimodal, genre used frequently by both junior and senior researchers is the conference presentation slideshow. This chapter traces the choices that John, Yoshi, Chatri, and Paul make and the genre knowledge that they draw upon and build as they repeatedly create presentation slides in multiple writing domains, including WCGS, their disciplinary courses, and their professional research.

The Genre of Presentation Slides

Presentations are a common means for knowledge-sharing in conference sessions, seminars, graduate classrooms, or meetings, and their norms and conventions depend to a large extent on the discourse community and forum. Although presentations in some fora are primarily oral, speakers in many contexts make extensive use of presentation "slides"—either as overhead transparencies or LCD projections—to accompany their talk. While papers at the Modern Language Association are generally oral readings of written papers, rarely accompanied by visuals, virtually all of the papers at an IEEE conference rely heavily on presentation slides. Attendance at conferences held by different professional associations provides anecdotal evidence for the generic nature of these slides. Conventions may lean toward use of decorative clip art, LCD-projected displays with animation, or small black font on a white background; during a 15-minute presentation, speakers may use only 5 slides or they may use 30; slides may be used to reinforce or summarize oral commentary, or they may be the sole source for communicating key information through photographs, figures, or video. Conference attendees will also note a large degree of individual variation in how slides are used and formatted, but such variation typically lies within a range of community norms—thus, the definition of a "poor presentation" will vary by community forum.

The most in-depth exploration of conference slides has been carried out by Rowley-Jolivet (Rowley-Jolivet, 2000, 2001, 2002, 2004), who has analyzed slides from 90 papers presented at international conferences in geology, medicine, and physics, focusing specifically on the types of visual images used and the functions that they enacted. Her finding that scientific presentations commonly use visuals to convey fundamental content, rather than to simply add visual interest (Rowley-Jolivet, 2001), is corroborated in Miller's (1998) comparison of visuals used in academic texts and the popular press. At international conference presentations, visuals often play the additional role of facilitating communication among speakers with varying levels of linguistic proficiency in the *lingua franca* (Rowley-Jolivet, 2000, 2002). But despite the heavy functional load afforded to visuals in this genre, they rarely function alone. To varying extents, visuals rely on verbal elements, whether oral or written. Slides may even be purposefully obscure so that verbal commentary is required to give the slides meaning (Gold, 2002).

Within the genre of presentation slides, the role of software technology plays a central role. By far the most common technological tool for the creation of such slides is Microsoft's PowerPoint, a multimedia "slideware" program; indeed, many of PowerPoint's design templates are readily recognizable to business professionals, academics, and students. In an insightful exploration of the "cognitive style of PowerPoint," Edward Tufte (2003) argues that the metaphor that undergirds this presentation style is that of the software's multinational corporation itself: "deeply hierarchical, nested, highly structured, relentlessly sequential, one-short-line-at-a-time . . . fast pace, misdirection, advocacy not analysis, slogan thinking, branding, exaggerated claims, marketplace ethics" (p. 11). Nevertheless, this style has permeated academic and research domains, especially in the sciences. As PowerPoint has come under increasing criticism, however, users have responded by bending the genre, purposefully breaking the bullet-point mold of the software's default forms. Some examples of such genre bending have gained notoriety on the Internet (see, for example, Hardt, 2005; Lessig, 2002).

As writers learn to create presentation slides, then, they make choices about a wide array of generic features. For example, writers must decide how many slides to create, taking into account the length of time allotted them and the density of texts and visuals in each individual slide. They must consider the sequence of the slides and the content of the corresponding oral commentary. Writers must also decide which information is best communicated visually, and then which type of visual might be most effective.

Rowley-Jolivet (2002) provides a useful typology of such visuals, including *scriptural* visuals (that is, visuals that consist of text, as in the case of text-dominated slides), *graphical* visuals (e.g., graphs, diagrams, or maps), *figurative* visuals (e.g., a photograph or X-ray), and *numeric* visuals (e.g., mathematical equations or numeric tables). Rowley-Jolivet draws on Bertin's (1973) crucial distinction between monosemic images, which are unambiguous and encode only one possible meaning, and polysemic images, which are open to more than one interpretation. In her typology of visual types, scriptural and figurative visuals can be considered polysemic, while graphical and numerical visuals are monosemic. While Rowley-Jolivet's work has focused on static images, today's presentation slide writers contend with the added dimension of animation—a modal feature that adds a second layer to the visual typology.

Writers' decisions about visual type are linked to the communicative functions that must be carried out. A systemic-functional approach was designed to understand the multiple functions enacted by single messages and has been applied quite effectively in previous analyses of multimodal genres (e.g., Kress, 2003; Lemke, 1998, 2002; Miller, 1998; Rowley-Jolivet, 2001). Within the systemic-functional framework, Halliday (1994) identifies three functions of meaning-making that any message may play: *ideational, interpersonal,* and *textual.* The ideational function conveys meaning about states of affairs or events in the world, such as an experimental result. The interpersonal function conveys meaning about the attitudes and relations of the writers and readers, such as the authority and credibility or the writers or the finding. Finally, the textual function conveys meaning about the text, guiding the reader through the text's organization. Halliday explains that any utterance can, in theory, enact all three functions. In practice, different modes may be more or less effective at carrying out particular functions (Kress, 2003).

In addition to decisions about content, length, density, rhetorical structure, and visual type and function, writers must consider the design of their presentation slides. While scientific papers and reports may well incorporate and integrate multiple modes, their general format and design is usually dictated by specific requirements of editors or instructors. Slides present writers with an additional range of design choices, including backgrounds, font color and type, and text layout—decisions that are largely irrelevant to more traditional paper-based texts but that carry a large rhetorical impact in visually dominated digital genres. Software programs can greatly aid writers in these decisions through default designs and colors, but writers still have the option of altering templates in nearly infinite ways. In making these design decisions, the astute writer considers how issues of subject-matter, presentation forum, disciplinarity, and writer identity all influence the perceived effectiveness of the visual text.

Procedurally, the presentation slide set is somewhat complicated as well. Although presentations are generally associated with the outcomes of one's work—that is, the sharing of information from a completed or a proposed study—they are not necessarily written as the final *stage* of research. In other words, slides (and their accompanying commentary) may be produced before a formal paper has been written, after a formal paper has been written, or even concurrently with a formal paper. Presentation slides may be given to describe in-progress work, completed work, or future work, and their communicative purpose may be to share research to disciplinary peers and experts, to demonstrate knowledge to an instructor, to persuade an audience to fund a project, or to provoke discussion and feedback. Slides are also linked intertextually to many other research documents, as the visuals often re-appear in corresponding publications or handouts. While slides are most often prepared for an oral presentation, they are often also uploaded to the Internet, on researchers' homepages or Blackboard sites, for wider distribution.

In short, the learning of a multimodal genre like presentation slides presents learners with many decisions that are very unlike more traditional texts. How do writers learn to make effective choices within this complex genre? In the remainder of this chapter, I examine that question by tracing changes in the presentation slides of John, Yoshi, Paul, and Chatri, as they produced slides in WCGS, in their disciplinary courses, and in their graduate research.

PRESENTATION SLIDES IN WCGS AND DISCIPLINARY CONTEXTS

Unlike the cover letter described in chapter 3, presentation slides were a genre with which Yoshi, Chatri, John, and Paul were quite familiar, having already created slides in multiple presentations at work and in graduate seminars. Chatri's experience extended even further to presentations at professional conferences and in his research lab's weekly meetings. While experience in composing and presenting slides was certainly important in building the writers' genre knowledge, the value of simply *viewing* numerous presentation slides cannot be underestimated. All of these writers stressed that they had seen many slides in many different contexts; through such encounters, the writers were exposed to a variety of visual and verbal presentation approaches, providing them with a fairly wide range of stylistic choices upon which to draw in their own work.

Michele's decision to include a conference poster/presentation slide assignment as the third unit of WCGS was two-fold. First, she saw it as a short assignment in which students could review some of the same grammar issues relevant to résumés and CVs (e.g., gapping and parallelism). Second, she wanted to give students an opportunity to practice their speaking skills. Although WCGS was a writing course, many of the students expressed an interest in improving their speaking, and Michele saw the mock poster session as an opportunity to do so. Based on her experience teaching previous WCGS classes, she also anticipated that at least some of the students would be in the process of preparing for an upcoming conference.

Nine class days were spent on the conference poster/presentation slide unit, including five days of classroom activities, two days of individual conferences, and a two-day mock poster session during which time students displayed their slides and posters (see Table 5.1). Although they were exhibited in the classroom, students were given the option of writing for either an expert or lay audience, a point that I will later discuss in more detail. Michele introduced the assignment as a conference poster, with the optional substitute of a PowerPoint presentation. She explained that students may prefer the PowerPoint option if their advisors generally discouraged students from presenting conference posters or if they wanted to gain practice in speaking. All four writers in my study selected the PowerPoint option, primarily because of their experience and familiarity with the presentation slide genre and lack of familiarity with conference posters.

Table 5.1. WCGS schedule for unit on presentation slides and conference posters.

Day	Date	Topic
1	Oct. 9	PowerPoint slides vs. conference posters; sample posters layout; poster layout
2	Oct. 11	Presentation and poster session advice; gapping in captions
3	Oct. 14	Mock conference poster exercise
4 & 5	Oct. 16 Oct. 18	One-to-one conference with PowerPoint/conference poster
6	Oct. 21	Document design for PowerPoint slides; sample questions
7	Oct. 23	Data commentary
8 & 9	Oct. 28 Oct. 30	Mock poster session

The line between the two assignment options was not, however, clear-cut. Michele told students, for example, that "the poster can be made up of separate slides, if you don't want to buy poster board" (Classroom transcript, October 9, 2002). A week later, she mentioned that those students creating slides could either post them to the wall or present them orally:

> . . . with your poster, or your PowerPoint, I'll have you tape them to the wall and we'll walk around and we'll ask each other questions, like "What's your research about?" Take a couple minutes to explain. Or you can try to ask them either a hard or easy question. [. . .] And then some people asked if they could present it just in front of the class, because it's a presentation they're doing for a conference that's upcoming. So some people will be doing that. But that's only if you want to. (Classroom transcript, October 21, 2002)

The lines between the slides and posters may also have been blurred because the two options were never directly compared or contrasted in class (as they were, for example, when differentiating résumés and cover letters). In the individual conferences, Michele told each student that he could present his slides orally, but the students were not directly asked about whether they would present or simply hang their slides for others. John and Chatri had planned to share their slides orally, but because they never stated this intention explicitly, Michele assumed they would post their slides on the wall—which, in the end, they did.

Classroom activities consisted primarily of discussions of conventions and expectations for conference posters (and to a lesser extent, presentation slides). Michele frequently reiterated the extent to which various formal elements of posters and slides were dependent on the given rhetorical situation, including the audience's field and level of expertise and the relative professional status of the speaker. Rather than providing "how to" guidelines for composing slides, Michele encouraged students to draw upon their own disciplinary perspectives.

In one extended activity, the students used a set of data and graphs to create their own mini-posters or slides (see Swales & Feak, 2000, pp. 111–114). During the "presentation" of these posters and slides, students practiced dealing with a range of questions similar to those asked at conferences. Also during the unit, the students reviewed the grammatical feature of gapping, this time applying it to the captions of figures and tables. On the final day of the unit, Michele introduced organizational and lexical elements of data commentaries, an activity that she saw as a transition into the final unit of the class, in which students would choose their own writing assignment (as described in chapter 4).

One major difference between this unit and the résumé/cover letter was the level of individual feedback given to the students. The one-to-one conference took place before students had completed a draft of their slides and therefore focused primarily on discussions of audience and assignment expectations. There was no peer review of drafts either, and no final feedback was given to students. In other words, far less feedback was provided during this unit compared with other units of the course.

In selecting content for this assignment, the writers took one of two approaches: either using material from another course that they were concurrently enrolled in, or adapting presentation slides previously written for another context. John and Chatri used the former approach, while Yoshi and Paul used the latter; both are represented schematically in Figure 5.1.

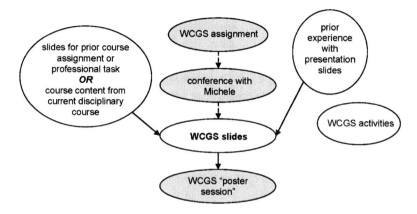

Figure 5.1. Genre network representations of the four writers' WCGS slide assignment tasks. Oral texts and interactions are shaded.

John chose to base his slides on a mock grant proposal that he had written for a graduate seminar the previous year. He trimmed down the content considerably, from approximately 70 slides in the original presentation to 11 slides for WCGS. These slides introduced research related to the improvement of cochlear implants, outlining the research problem and illustrating two algorithms that could be implemented in solving the problem. Chatri's WCGS slides were based on a presentation that he had given to his research group one month previously. His original talk focused on computerized face tracking in American Sign Language (ASL) and the application of a particular model (called the Active Appearance Model, or AAM) in this type of research. While Chatri's research group was not familiar with this specific research, they were all knowledgeable in computer vision research.

Both Yoshi and Paul chose to use content from their current graduate courses in designing their WCGS slides. Yoshi selected content from an assignment in his electromagnetic theory course, described as his "most important class" (November 8, 2002). Paul's motivation for choosing to present content from his current coursework was primarily motivated by time constraints. He explained to me, "I think it will be better if I can use other course's work to be used in this class. So, I do not need to use extra time to do it" (October 15, 2002).

Outside of WCGS, the writers created numerous sets of presentation slides, many of which they shared with me (see Table 5.2). Within their disciplinary courses, these slides were usually presented at the culmination of an individual or collaborative term project, sharing the results of their work with the class. In addition, both Paul and Chatri used slides to present their research to their thesis committees and/or research groups. Within disciplinary contexts, writers received little or no explicit guidelines for preparing or presenting slides.

Table 5.2. Writers' slide sets written in WCGS and in disciplinary contexts.

Writer	Task Purpose and Date	Context
John	To display for a class poster session (Oct. 2002)	WCGS
Paul	To display for a class poster session (Oct. 2002)	WCGS
	To present a concept to a class (April 2003)	Computer science course
	To present master's thesis in oral defense (July 2003)	Thesis defense
Yoshi	To display for a class poster session (Oct. 2002)	WCGS
	To present a published paper to peers (Nov. 2003)	Engineering course
	To present a course project, (Dec. 2003)*	Engineering course
	To present a course design project (April 2004)*	Engineering course
Chatri	To introduce work to research group (Sept. 2002)	Research group seminar
	To display for a class poster session (Oct. 2002)	WCGS
	To present research to potential sponsors (March 2003)	Meeting with sponsors
	To present research to disciplinary experts (April 2004)	International conference
	To present and defend dissertation proposal, (July 2004)	Public defense of preliminary report for dissertation committee and peers

*These slide sets were prepared collaboratively. I have analyzed only the sections of the slides that Yoshi created himself.

GENRE KNOWLEDGE OF PRESENTATION SLIDES

Given my interest in how writers approached the same genre in multiple contexts, presentation slides offered a unique opportunity. Because three of the four writers composed slides in disciplinary contexts after WCGS had been completed, I was able to compare their approaches to these tasks, observe differences in their texts, and discuss their understanding of the genre as they applied it for new rhetorical purposes. In the sections that follow, I share these observations with an eye toward the distinctive nature of presentation slides as a multimodal, yet primarily visual, genre.

John: Individual and Disciplinary Expression

Although he wrote presentation slides in other courses prior to my research, John shared only his WCGS slides with me. Having access to only one set of slides prevents me from tracing changes in John's knowledge of the genre over time and in multiple settings. Still, my discussions with John about his slides revealed many interesting characteristics about the multimodal nature of slides and about issues of identity and disciplinarity. His insights are thus valuable in understanding how learning this genre may differ in important ways from learning more traditional verbal-based genres.

Discussions with John and analysis of his slides both suggest the extent to which writers may see opportunities for expressions of identity within the genre of presentation slides. While such opportunities most definitely exist in all writing, the multimodality and the more personal presentation of presentation slides may highlight this dimension for writers. John's presentation slides show his efforts to align with disciplinary expectations while also exerting his own sense of individual identity within his slides.

Several features of John's slides conform to disciplinary conventions, including the use of disciplinary jargon, the overall rhetorical structure (in this case, Introduction-Method-Results-Discussion, or IMRD), and the numbering of section headings. John noted, for example, that section numbering is quite common among engineers:

> I can usually tell from a PowerPoint presentation or report whether that person is an engineer or not. It's not like 100% accurate, but engineers are usually

more used to having like a numbered system for everything and just going with that. Like, going into a
logical order. I'm not saying that other people aren't
logical, but the [engineering] presentation just, it
could be like a little *too* logical. (November 8, 2002)

In presentation slides, visuals also express disciplinary identities in a
way similar to the use of disciplinary terminology. Visuals are often
field-specific, holding meaning only for those with shared knowledge
of the concepts and visual conventions, as is the case in John's slide
shown in Figure 5.2. In commenting on this slide, John explained
how images can serve as a sort of disciplinary short-hand for writers
and audiences:

. . . explaining the algorithm in words take too much
space, so if you have like a drawing and—especially
for engineers—I mean, this might be hard to understand for somebody who's not in the engineering, but
whoever is engineering and knows single processing,
he could just from this drawing understand what the
algorithm is, so that's why I chose this drawing again.
[. . .] This type of diagram is common for algorithm.
Because it shows- it's like a flow diagram, so it's used
in programming and algorithms, so *basically anybody
who knows discrete algorithms would understand this
diagram.* (November 8, 2002, emphasis added)

Resistance to dominant disciplinary discourses is also evident in
John's slides, where the ideology of traditional scientific objectivity is
subverted in various ways. In all of my discussions with John, I saw
him to be almost fiercely independent, as he questioned standards and
looked for ways to bend and manipulate generic and discursive norms.
As Ivanič (1998) points out,

Writers position themselves by the stance they take
towards privileged conventions. Writers who take a
resistant stance towards privileged conventions are
making a strong statement of an alternative identity,
and are also . . . demonstrating the personal quality
(*ethos*) of non-conformism. (p. 93)

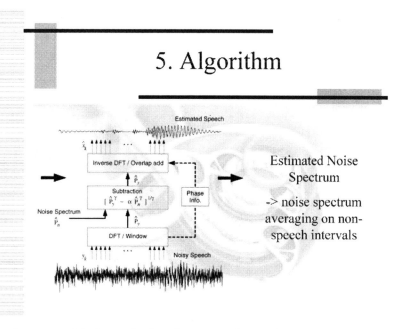

5. Algorithm

Figure 5.2. John's use of a disciplinary-specific visual.

John's slides show an attempt to inject a personal identity into his presentation slides specifically as a way to engage his audience in his research. To do so, John relies on both the verbal and visual modes, taking full advantage of the affordances of multimodality. One such example is his use of a quotation by the philosopher Immanuel Kant, prominently displayed on the third slide of the set: "Not being able to see isolates you from objects; not being able to hear isolates you from people" (Figure 5.3). John hoped that this quotation would help his audience understand the impact of his research by appealing to emotions rather than to scientific evidence. The quote, he said, "gets you thinking about what hearing is" (November 8, 2002). Although fronting a text with a quotation is fairly common in the humanities, it is rare in scientific texts. Therefore, while the content of the quote is jarring, the mere inclusion of a quotation also displaces the reader/viewer in its bending of disciplinary norms. By using a quotation from a philosopher, John further portrays himself as a humanistic and well-rounded individual who reads widely and is concerned with more than scientific data. Indeed, I believe this image does portray John's sense of self, as he described himself to me as someone who is primarily interested in helping others:

> I really enjoy helping people. I mean helping people in a direct way. Like, for example, if I were to earn money and become somebody like Bill Gates and then finance all of these things, I probably wouldn't be that happy because that'd be too indirect for me. But if I developed a robotic leg—which I was very interested in robotic prosthesis when I applied to Midwest University—so that I could change somebody's life, even if I didn't know that person personally, I know that the research I did would directly affect somebody in a good way. (September 4, 2002)

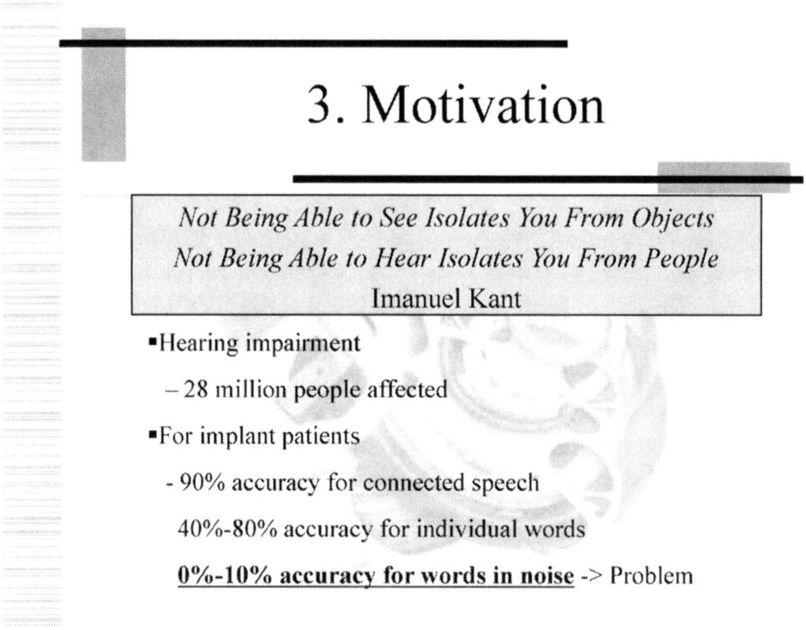

3. Motivation

Not Being Able to See Isolates You From Objects
Not Being Able to Hear Isolates You From People
Imanuel Kant

- Hearing impairment
  - 28 million people affected
- For implant patients
  - 90% accuracy for connected speech
  40%-80% accuracy for individual words
  0%-10% accuracy for words in noise -> Problem

Figure 5.3. Quote in John's WCGS slide set.

For the most part, however, the verbal elements of John's slides do align fairly closely with scientific norms: his presentation is made up of numbered sections with standard headings, like *Experimental Design* and *Future Research,* and numbers and disciplinary jargon permeate his text. Expressions of individuality are primarily found through the visual mode of this slide set. John's final slide, for example, prompts listeners for questions through a self-designed montage of question marks and a cartoon clipart image—a type of visual that Rowley-Jolivet (2004) found to be relatively infrequent in most scientific texts.

John also used color to situate his personal style within disciplinary expectations while simultaneously challenging those expectations. He explained:

> Well, for my personal style, I usually avoid really hard styles. Like, in engineering, they typically have a blue background with like "Midwest University" and have a Midwest mark and something underneath, and go with that. And that's what you see for most every—that's *really* conservative. And most PowerPoint slides are based on that and just diverge a little, but I usually change it a lot to get more visual attention from the people who are looking at the presentation, but I still keep it very like—what do you say? It looks *hard*. I mean, I use more edgy stuff. I think non-engineers or non-scientific people, they usually like more curved stuff. It's the same thing as like cars. Some people like really jagged stuff and some people like really smooth stuff. And I think engineers usually like squares and lines. Like, for example, there are some power points that have like ribbons in the background? And, if you use that in engineering, people would be like, "What?!" But if you use that in other discipline, they'd be like, "interesting background." (November 8, 2002)

The slides in Figures 5.2 and 5.3 illustrate how John maintained some of the "hard" and "edgy" lines that he perceived to be standard in his field, but added a curved depiction of the inner ear to the background and utilized pastel pinks, blues, and browns for a watermarked background image (as opposed to the bright blues and greens more commonly found in scientific presentations).

It is perhaps worth re-stating that John's WCGS were taken directly from a presentation he had given for a bio-engineering course several months earlier. The design of the slides was unchanged, so it is fair to assume that the visual mode was composed primarily with a disciplinary audience in mind. John's creative use of the visual mode and his explicit reference to identity expressions within the genre suggest that his genre knowledge was already rhetorical.

Paul: Audience and Content

Prior to WCGS, Paul had given only two slide-based presentations, both for his computer science courses. One of these slide sets was shortened by a couple of slides and then used to satisfy his WCGS assignment, which consisted of a total of six slides. After WCGS, Paul wrote presentation slides for a computer science class and for his thesis defense. All of Paul's slide sets share a similar rhetorical structure, beginning with an outline, an introduction, and then details regarding method and results, and ending with a conclusion and list of references.

Both Paul's WCGS and thesis defense slides are notable for their simplicity of design, consisting of a white background with black Times New Roman font. Each slide consists of a single, centered heading, and a bullet-point list, sometimes with two levels of hierarchy (see Figure 5.4). After his thesis defense, Paul explained that he had chosen this design because it was typical within his lab:

> In my group, I saw some- I would say *many* presentations in this way. Maybe they only use slides, the transparency, not the projector. And for the transparency, I don't know, because the transparency should have color, they should be able to use more fancy patterns there, but I don't know why they didn't, so I just follow their way. (August 4, 2003)

In contrast to this very simple design, Paul's computer science course presentation was more colorful, having a bright blue background with a geometric wave design. He explained that he had selected this design template because he had borrowed slides from a presentation on-line, modifying the content but retaining the design. Paul liked this more colorful design but astutely connected the effectiveness of its visual design to the audience. He felt that "If the listeners, the audience, are young people, maybe I prefer this one [with colored background]. If the audience are kind of research people like my advisor, maybe I use

Cryptographic algorithms

- Encryption and decryption
  - 3DES: $C = DES_{k3}(DES_{k2}^{-1}(DES_{k1}(M)))$
    - 192-bit key (162 bits in effect)

  - AES (Rijndael): 128, 192, and 256-bit key

- Authentication
  - HMAC-MD5: 128-bit output
  - HMAC-SHA1: 160-bit output

- Simulation using SingleScalar for ARM

Figure 5.4. Sample slide from Paul's thesis defense presentation.

this one [plain white with black font]" (August 4, 2003). Paul's association of the black-on-white design as more traditional echoes Kress
and van Leeuwen's (1996) claim that white and black connote a more
traditional scientific research orientation.

Paul's WCGS slides consist of only six slides, with two of the six
containing diagrams. Paul explained that his use of visuals in this slide
set may have been influenced by the WCGS classroom activities:

> Paul: Because lots of words make the slides looks very
> boring, and I think add[ing] some figures is help-
> ful to make the audience understand the idea of
> the slide. It makes it very easier, I think. Um,
> it's, I think for people, [to] look at a picture is
> easier than [to] read the sentence. Especially for
> the presentation. I think something is covered in
> the English class, you should put some pictures
> in the poster or slides.

Chris: You said it was something you discovered in the
         English class, so before the English class did
         you—
Paul: Before the class, I already knew this, but I would
         say, after this class, I can put this idea into prac-
         tice. [*laughing*] Because before, I only present
         twice, I think, and I use lots of sentence not very-
         not lots of pictures. But after this class, I think
         the pictures is very good for presentation. (No-
         vember 22, 2002)

Paul's later slides continued to make use of visuals, with his thesis defense slides showing a marked increase in this use (see Table 5.3)—primarily because numerous slides in this set included only visual information (no verbal text), with multiple graphs or charts displayed on a
single page in many cases.

Table 5.3. Density of visuals in Paul's slides, October 2002 to July 2003.

Presentation	Total # of slides	Total # of visuals	Average # of visuals / slide
WCGS (Oct. 2002)	6	2	0.33
CS course (April 2003)	24	10	0.42
Thesis defense (July 2003)	35	40	1.14

The later slides also show an increase in variety of visuals used, with
his computer science class slides making use of graphical, figurative,
and numeric images (Table 5.4). His thesis defense slides rely much
more on numeric images (specifically tables and charts) than the other
two presentations; this difference can most easily be explained by the
emphasis in this presentation on sharing results of his research, as opposed to explaining concepts in the other two presentations. Paul's
varying uses of images suggests, then, a facility with visual literacy
and an ability to adapt his visual texts to the ideational and rhetorical
needs of the task. Much of this knowledge seemed to be built through
disciplinary participation. For example, in describing one figurative
visual, Paul explained that:

> This one is like a typical graph in the algorithm. I think maybe I draw it this way because I have already read something about algorithms. I took algorithm course last semester, so I have seen lots of this kind of graphs. (August 4, 2003)

Table 5.4. Frequency of image types' in Paul's slides, normed per 15 Slides.

Presentation	Graphical images*	Figurative images	Numeric images	Total # of images / slide
WCGS (Oct. 2002)	5	0	0	5
CS course (April 2003)	3.12	0.62	2.5	6.25
Thesis defense (July 2003)	1.71	0	15.43	17

*Following Rowley-Jolivet's (2002) typology described earlier in the chapter, graphical visuals refer to graphs, diagrams, or maps; figurative visuals include photograph or X-rays; and numeric visuals include mathematical equations or numeric tables.

But the overall density and frequency of visuals in his later slides is also likely related to the increased substantive load that the slides carry in this case—that is, presenting the results of a six-month long research project. This work is difficult to communicate through words alone, as Paul readily explained.

In addition to in his increased use of visuals, Paul's defense slides are more concise in wording and make better use of parallelism in comparison with his WCGS slides. While his later slides still contain gaps in parallelism or concision, an overall tendency toward clearer expression is evident, as illustrated in Figure 5.5. According to Paul, this improvement was most likely related to the "much better understanding of my subject" (August 4, 2003) in the later slides.

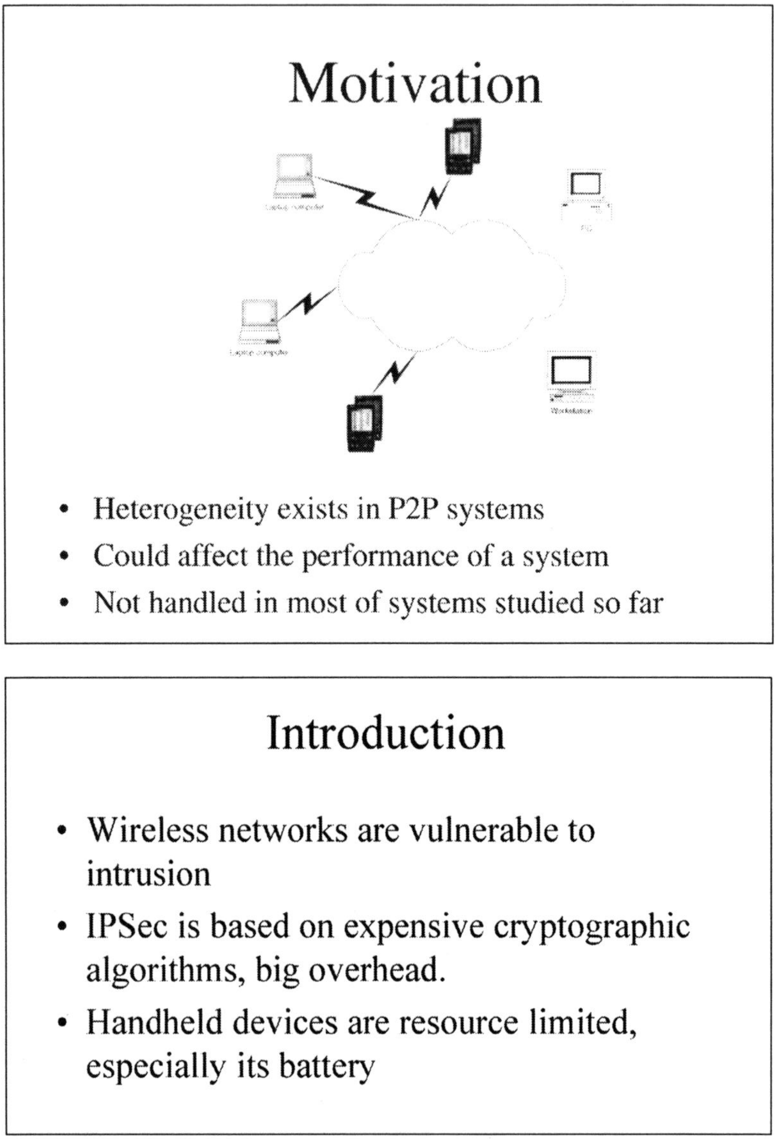

Motivation

- Heterogeneity exists in P2P systems
- Could affect the performance of a system
- Not handled in most of systems studied so far

Introduction

- Wireless networks are vulnerable to intrusion
- IPSec is based on expensive cryptographic algorithms, big overhead.
- Handheld devices are resource limited, especially its battery

Figure 5.5. Comparison of Paul's WCGS slides (top) and thesis defense slides (bottom).

Yoshi: A Tried-and-True Strategy

During the two years of his master's program, Yoshi created four sets of presentation slides: one for WCGS and three for his electrical engineering courses. Two of these slide sets were written and presented collaboratively with peers, and two were written and presented by Yoshi alone (see Table 5.2). There is a remarkable consistency in Yoshi's slides over this two-year period, especially in relation to the visual features of Yoshi's texts. In all four presentations, Yoshi used a standard Microsoft slide template. When writing his WCGS slides, Yoshi searched the Microsoft website for a "scientific presentation theme," and selected the template in Figure 5.6. For all three engineering course presentations, however, Yoshi used another Microsoft design template. This template was intended for presenting project results, Yoshi explained, so he felt "that the style is suit[able] for our project too" (December 15, 2003). The design (Figure 5.7) was in fact identical to the one that Paul had used for his classroom slide set. After using the template for three separate presentations, Yoshi described it as "a very professional look," because of "the font style, or the combination of fonts, and blue background, and gradiation" (May 10, 2004).

Though the general design of Yoshi's presentation slides remains quite similar in each slide set, minor differences are apparent in the later slides; it is impossible, however, to separate these differences from the rhetorical context in which the slides were written. The latter slides were written to share lengthy term projects with a class of disciplinary peers and a disciplinary instructor, a very different setting than the WCGS slides. Nevertheless, the differences are worth exploring particularly as they relate to setting.

Visually, Yoshi's presentation slides continued to conform to the fairly typical design of engineering slides. However, his later presentations share much more content and, because of the nature of the audience, convey that content in more complex ways. His engineering class slides often mix graphical, figurative, and numerical images within one page—a technique that allows him to communicate complex information relatively succinctly, as illustrated in Figure 5.8. The slide in Figure 5.8 further incorporates animation, a technological feature that Yoshi was excited to learn while at Midwest University. Animation, he explained, allowed him to illustrate concepts in more realistic and efficient ways.

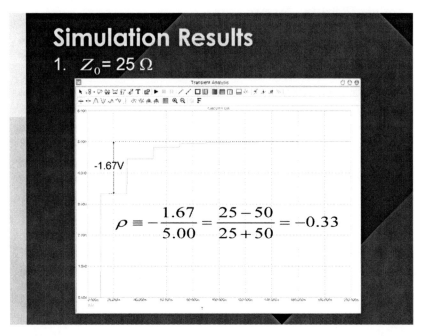

Figure 5.6. Yoshi's design template for the WCGS slides.

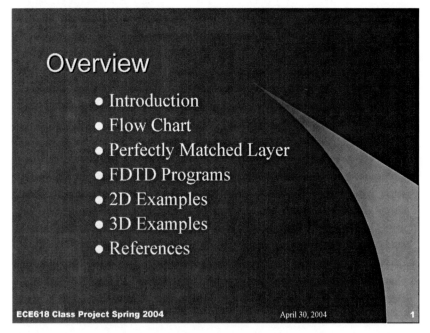

Figure 5.7. Design template used in Yoshi's three slide sets for disciplinary course projects.

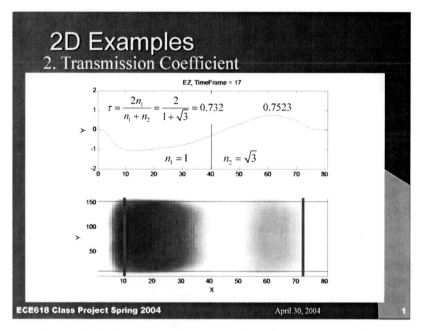

Figure 5.8. Yoshi's mixing of graphical, figurative, and numerical images within a single slide, April 2004.

Because of the heavy load given to visual elements in this genre, writers must learn how to balance the use of verbal text and visual images appropriately. In this area, Yoshi's four sets of slides are relatively consistent. In all cases, the verbal text serves primarily a metadiscoursal function, announcing the structure of the talk through headings and sub-headings. Much of his verbal text also serves an ideational function, though this use is mostly limited to the background, motivation, objectives, and conclusion sections. In contrast, methods are conveyed through a mixture of verbal text and graphical images, while results are conveyed almost entirely through graphical (or, in later slides, figurative) images.

While verbal text does not figure prominently into any of Yoshi's slide sets, there is a slight increase in text density in some sections of his later slides. Specifically, Yoshi's non-WCGS slides make greater use of verbal text in the introductions and discussions of methods. The difference here can be explained by the way in which the slides were shared with others; because the non-WCGS slides were orally presented, Yoshi included more text to serve as memory cues when presenting the slides to his classmates. He explained, "I tried to include this kind of text that I *have* to mention at that slide, so I can explain without these notes" (December 15, 2003).

In sum, Yoshi's slides are marked by a very consistent use of visual design and discursive patterns over the two-year period of his M.S. program. Typical to his discipline, the slides rely heavily on visuals for expressing subject-matter content. His later slides are denser in verbal and visual text and somewhat more jargon-heavy. While the disciplinarity of his audience can explain this difference to a large degree, the heavier content demands are also likely to be influential here. In contrast to the WCGS slides, the engineering course slides relay far greater information, which he had already spent considerable time studying and developing throughout the course. Further, Yoshi worked with multiple peers for two of these later three slide sets, requiring him to take into account the perspectives and suggestions of other group members. Finally, these three engineering course slide sets were in fact verbally presented to a group of disciplinary peers and experts, leading Yoshi to consider his language in the slides more carefully as well as the oral commentary that he would use. Indeed, Yoshi described the WCGS slides as focusing on an experiment for which the "result is quite trivial, so I concentrated on the styles of the presentation" (November 8, 2002). While there are certainly benefits to doing so, Yoshi never suggested that he had in fact learned anything new about the genre from the WCGS task. In contrast, when reflecting on his engineering slide sets, he referred to learning about collaboration, slide design and content selection, presentation skills, and technological elements of animation, apparently building multiple dimensions of his genre knowledge.

Chatri: The Importance of Content Knowledge

Of the four writers, Chatri used slides within the broadest range of contexts during the time I followed his writing, presenting to classmates, his research group, potential research sponsors, an international research community, and dissertation committee members (see Table 5.5). He had a great deal of exposure to presentations within his research group, as informal presentations (using slides) were given on a weekly basis in group meetings, referred to as "seminars." In these contexts, Chatri presented work every two or three months. These seminar presentations appeared to provide an important channel for communication within the research group, allowing them to share their work and provide feedback to one another. Chatri repeatedly referred to the value of this feedback in helping him clarify his ideas as he centered in on a research area for his dissertation. The presentations, including the discussions, were therefore an important part of disciplinary practice and knowledge construction.

Table 5.5. Chatri's slide sets analyzed.

Presentation	Audience	Topic	# of Slides
Presentation 1 (Sept. 2002)	Research group	Computerized face tracking with sign language	33
Presentation 2 (Oct. 2002)	Writing class (WCGS)	Computerized face tracking with sign language	13
Presentation 3 (March 2003)	Potential industry sponsors	Computerized face tracking	11
Presentation 4 (April 2004)	Robotics experts (international)	Active appearance model	25 (+ 5 extra)
Presentation 5 (July 2004)	Dissertation committee and peers	Appearance-based object tracking	50 (+ 31 extra)

In the second year that I followed Chatri's writing, these presentations seemed to become a crucial part of his developing subject-matter knowledge. In preparing Presentation #3, for example, he realized that he did not have a good sense of *why* his research was relevant for the broader field of American Sign Language (ASL) research[5]. He explained that when writing Presentation #1 (on the same topic), he had little sense of the work's significance:

> At that time I don't care. Actually, at that time, I don't know why we need [it]. Okay . . . The time that I had to present this [Presentation #3], it's time to know why, so I had to ask [the linguist who directed the project] *why*, to write this presentation. (April 4, 2003)

Because Presentation #3 was given to potential sponsors from industry, Chatri felt he needed to learn more about the significance of the work, saying that "I need to be clear when I write it [in Presentation #3] because it has some meaning in ASL" (April 4, 2003).

Interestingly, developments in Chatri's disciplinary knowledge of his research also led to changes in his written expression throughout his slides. In this particular case, formal changes such as concision and increased use of disciplinary terminology are evident in Presentation #3, when compared with Presentations #1 and #2. Figure 5.9 shows, for example, changes in Chatri's description of the goal of identifying eye-to-eyebrow distance (the second major bullet point in each slide), with the later slide written in a more concise and precise style. Chatri explained that when he wrote the later slides, he had a much clearer understanding of the subject matter: "At that time [Presentation #1], I still don't- maybe I 50% understand about this, but at this time [Presentation #3], I understand it better, I can use more compact words to explain it" (April 4, 2003).

Within the research group's seminars, presentations were always followed by questions and discussions, and Chatri felt that these discussions played a large role in helping to clarify his research directions and contributions. He credited such discussions with helping him to frame work for his international conference paper as well as a journal manuscript that he had begun to work on in the final months of my research. In addition, the actual preparation of the presentation, including the slides, became a heuristic for Chatri in developing a narrative of his research. He commented that he found it easier to "tell the story" of his research through the presentation genre than through a written paper:

> . . . when I made the PowerPoint, I think the kind of presentation is similar to the writing in another form, right? Because it's not the paragraph, it's just some topic, the organization of the how to tell the story. [. . .] I think it's a better idea to follow the PowerPoint, because when we make the PowerPoint, it seems that we start to tell the story in another format. Instead of we tell the story in writing. And I think to tell the story in PowerPoint is easier, right? We don't have to concern too much about the sentence, the grammar,

My previous work

- In the ASL project, with [Name]
  - Use AAM to develop a very simple *face tracking & pose estimation algorithm*

  - Goal : want to find
    - the distance between *eye* and *eyebrow*
      This distance has some meanings in ASL.

    - the orientation of face

Goal

- Track the face and its features (eye, eyebrow, nose and mouth) from the image sequence of signer

- Measure the eye to eyebrow distance

- One approach
  Using Active Appearance Model

Figure 5.9. Comparison of goal statements in Presentation #1 (top) and #3 (bottom).

just organize the idea. It help me a lot that okay when
I come back to look, and think about when I gave the
presentation what the feedback. Did the listener understand? (January 23, 2004)

In numerous discussions, Chatri expressed this same understanding of presentations being about informing readers in a convincing and
clear way. He learned, over time, that expressing the work's novelty and
contribution was one key. He noted that the difficulty of preparing a
presentation was in refining the topic and deciding "what you're gonna
pick out to present" (January 23, 2004). After a practice-run with Presentation #4 (prior to the formal conference presentation), Chatri received advice from his advisor on making his work more rhetorically
convincing for disciplinary experts by emphasizing its strengths and
discussing negatives only when speaking of how the weaknesses will
be addressed in future work. The advice was new to Chatri, but he followed it, incorporating acknowledgement of his work's limitations in
the conclusion, and following it up with a short discussion of future
work. He adopted the same approach for his preliminary report defense in Presentation #5.

In preparing for Presentation #5, Chatri again showed a strong
awareness of the rhetorical nature of the genre. He was more concerned
about the oral presentation than the written preliminary report, feeling that he had to make a strong argument for the contribution of his
work through his oral presentation and that there was more flexibility
for doing so through the oral genre. His sense of the difficulty in preparing the oral presentation here contrasts with his perception of the
WCGS presentation slide assignment as not difficult at all. He felt the
difficulty of presentations was in selecting content and framing it in
persuasive ways. In contrast, his WCGS assignment required only that
he select and modify slides from Presentation #1.

Like the other writers, Chatri always incorporated visuals that
were highly saturated in disciplinary expertise, drawing on figurative,
graphical, and numeric visuals (see, for example, Figure 5.10). Animation was particularly important in his work, as it allowed him to show
exactly how robot tracking of moving objects worked. Overall, his use
of visuals increased within the 5 slide sets he shared with me. Early
on, Chatri seemed to favor verbal text over visual displays. With the
exception of a handful of slides with animated movies, all of Chatri's

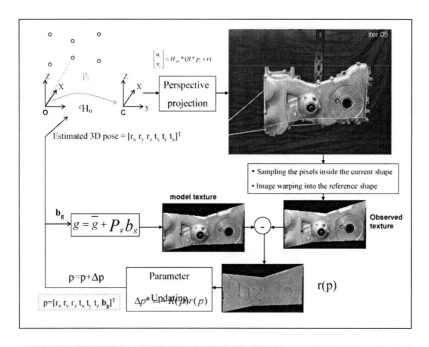

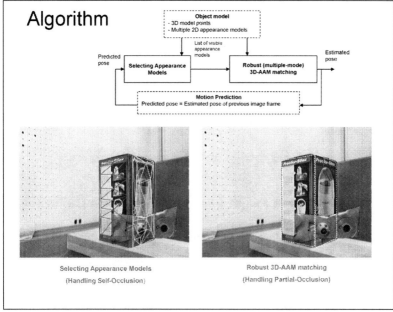

Figure 5.10. Samples of Chatri's use of disciplinary-specific visuals, from Presentation #4 (top) and Presentation #5 (bottom).

slides in Presentations #1 and #2 contain some verbal script—many slides include no visuals. He explained the preference for verbal text this way:

> . . . my idea is, don't put more- Suppose we have the result. Don't put the table in the presentation. Just put some sentence, conclude the result. Because if someone put the table, it's hard to understand the table. Or put the graph. Hard to understand the graph. Just say, okay, what the conclusion of that graph. Okay, the result is *this*. Don't hope that the listener will understand the graph. (October 16, 2002)

His later presentations, however, gravitate toward heavier use of visuals as the sole means of communicating information. Presentation #4 includes eight slides with only visual images (no headings) and Presentation #5 includes four image-only slides. In fact, after presenting Presentation #4 at a conference, he commented on other presenters' slides as being too text-heavy:

> [. . .] many of them is try to use in one slide, they try to put more text, more words. So, when they put more text, more word, I have to read it, and I still didn't finish, they change the slide [*laughing*]. So, I don't- many of them make the slide something like that, but I don't think it's a good idea that there is a lot of text. And if you put a lot of text, people have to read and listen to you also, but he didn't still finish the reading, they change the slide because- So, my idea when I make the slide is try to use the least number of text, of words, in the slide. (May 14, 2004)

He did, however, note that he often used more text than he'd like because it serves as a language aid when presenting orally.

Overall, Chatri's basic design preferences did not change at all in the two years I worked with him. Like Paul, he preferred a simple design, using black Times New Roman type on a white background, with red or blue font used occasionally to accent headings and key words. Chatri explained that his preference for this simple background had been greatly influenced by a presentation that he had seen a prominent researcher give several years earlier in Thailand. He described the talk as "simple" but very effective. Indeed, this visual style resonates with Chatri's own preference for presenting his work in a matter-of-fact, almost understated, manner.

Chatri's slides represent tasks of relatively high investment, from slides presented to sponsors of his lab's funded research to slides prepared for an international conference. These tasks placed Chatri in a position of expertise, even when he did not want or feel prepared to take on that role. His understanding of the genre of presentation slides (or, more aptly, presentations) was very much informed by these settings. For Chatri, presentation slides represented a genre for sharing and extending knowledge, they offered him a heuristic for thinking about his work, and they existed as part of a highly intertextual system of research genres.

Building Genre Knowledge across Contexts

Presentation slides are a unique genre in their frequent use in both classroom contexts and professional practice; it makes good sense to include this kind of writing in a course such as WCGS. Unfortunately, the WCGS task in this case seemed to have little impact on the writers' understanding of the genre. Instead, their knowledge appeared to be built over time through accumulated exposure and use.

In WCGS, the presentation slide task differed greatly from the writers' disciplinary course tasks with the genre. In the writing classroom, the writers did not have to contend with issues of content accuracy or disciplinary convention or expectation. Instead, they focused primarily on audience and explaining their work in lay terms for more their writing classmates. The WCGS task was also relatively low-stakes in that the writers did not need to present their slides orally and no grade was received. Within this context, the writers attended to slide designs and language use.

In contrast, presentation slides presented the writers with more complex tasks in their disciplinary contexts. In those contexts, they contended with not only the verbal and visual modes of the slides, but also the oral mode of presenting. Even more crucially, they struggled with how to make sense of their research and how to share it in ways that were rhetorically effective to their audiences, working out the narrative behind their research. The writers often collaborated in these non-WCGS settings, either in the creation of the slides or in the post-presentation discussions. Such collaborations were a part of knowledge construction, playing in many cases a critical role. Disciplinary tasks were also linked intertextually to a broad range of genres. Figures 5.11 and 5.12, for example, illustrate the many genres that linked to slide sets used by Yoshi and Paul in the engineering classroom and thesis research, respectively. In comparison with the WCGS task (Figure 5.1), these networks are more multimodal and intertextual. In general, the non-WCGS slide sets also presented the writers with more pressure, and the writers approached them with a higher investment in time. Contending with issues of content, audience, process, and form, the writers learned new technologies and narrative frames for sharing their work, and they even developed more concise and specific linguistic expressions for describing their work.

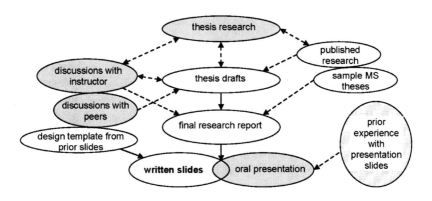

Figure 5.11. The genre network surrounding Yoshi's engineering classroom slides. Oral tasks are shaded; oral-written tasks appear in stripes.

These non-WCGS presentations suggest more interaction between content and rhetoric, in the dual problem space described by Bereiter and Scardamalia (1987). In preparing the slides for WCGS, on the other hand, the writers appeared to be in Geisler's (1994) intermediate stage of acquiring expertise. They were beginning to work with abstractions through tacitly acquired knowledge, but their representations of the rhetorical space are still relatively naïve. Both Chatri and Paul appeared to move closer to Geisler's final stage of expertise acquisition in their later slides. Only in these high-stakes tasks (presenting to potential funders, to conference audiences, and to a thesis commit-

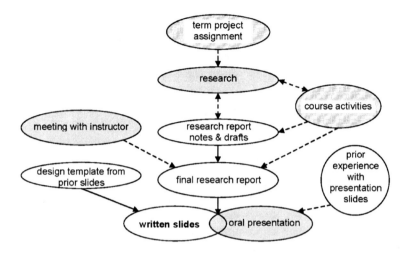

Figure 5.12. The genre network surrounding Paul's thesis defense slides. Oral tasks are shaded; oral-written tasks appear in stripes

tee) do the writers separate the rhetorical and content space, viewing their texts as having claims, credibility, and temporality.

Presentation slides are also an interesting genre to analyze because, unlike the job application cover letters, this was a genre with which all of the writers were already very familiar. All four writers had much exposure to presentation slides and at the time of the WCGS assignment had already developed quite clear preferences for different styles over others; course instruction made little impact on their previously held knowledge. In her study of genre-based reading instruction, Hyon (2001) similarly found that instruction in a particular genre had less impact on her students with more previous experience with that genre. Yet prior experience does not necessarily preclude the influence of instruction (see Beaufort, 1999, for example), so it is important to consider why it did in the present study. One possibility is that the writers did not perceive the genre to be of particular difficulty and already felt relatively confident in their genre performance; perhaps their concerns lie in the oral presentation of the slides more than in the written product. Another possibility lies in the nature of the instruction, which provided very few textual examples for analysis and awareness-raising.

In the case of presentation slides, for these students, accumulated exposure appeared to play a major role in their early development of genre knowledge. Through exposure to numerous slides—as students and researchers—they developed an understanding of convention-al forms and also possible variations on, or even violations of, those forms. All four writers expressed their individual and disciplinary identities through their use of design templates, colors, and visuals. In many cases, their choices were shaped by very particular instances of presentations that they had viewed.

While exposure was important, the use of presentations in knowl-edge making seemed to be most vital in developing the kind of ex-pert-like genre knowledge that integrates formal, process, content, and rhetorical dimensions. Through textual and social interactions, using slides as a means for knowledge construction and distribution, writ-ers can develop more sophisticated awareness of this now ubiquitous genre.

6 Repeated Practice: Lab Reports in the Graduate Classroom

Studies of genre learning in non-classroom contexts are often used to make claims about how genres are learned in general, regardless of context. However, as the previous chapters have illustrated, genre learning may differ in writing classrooms and disciplinary contexts, both in terms of what sort of knowledge is developed and the routes toward development. This chapter explores how two writers—John and Yoshi—built genre knowledge in their engineering and science courses. I consider specifically how their learning in disciplinary classrooms responded to the resources made available to them in that context, and how such learning may differ from writing classrooms in general. The focus on repeated writing tasks illustrates how the practice of re-visiting the same genre influenced these writers' generic expectations and understanding of disciplinary writing more generally. For each writer, the repeated assignment was a lab report, though the textual form and procedural practices of the genre differed somewhat according to the rhetorical context. Interestingly, both John and Yoshi tended not to view these assignments as "writing" at the time, though in retrospect they each noted the value of these repeated tasks on improving their overall writing abilities.

The lab report (LR) is, of course, a common genre for students of science and is indeed one that students begin to learn, in some form, as early as elementary school. In following a group of bilingual fifth-graders learning lab reports, Merino and Hammond (2002) describe the instruction as focusing on

> . . . the need to maintain careful records to understand what happens, to report to others so that other scientists could repeat the experiment and to keep a record for future use. The need to act like a scientist,

>recording faithfully and in detail what transpires in
>the science lessons. (p. 231)

This instructional focus matches the rhetorical goals that Carter,
Ferzli, and Wiebe (2004) assign to the lab report as a genre, as they argue that "the point is not to learn the genre for its own sake, but to apply the genre effectively for the sake of learning in the course" (p. 398).
Crucially, Carter *et al.* point out that students are rarely given explicit
instruction for writing effective lab reports, and they may have little
exposure to genre exemplars; in other words, LRs can be considered an
occluded genre, like much school-based writing. In his historical analysis of science writing, Lerner (2007) provides a convincing a case for
a renewed focus in the science classroom on the relationship between
writing and the scientific process. He demonstrates that science classrooms often incorporate template-like forms for assessing students'
knowledge rather than engaging them in authentic written scientific
argumentation through genres like laboratory reports. It is, after all,
this kind of writing that "support[s] and infuse[s] . . . the communication activities of practicing scientists" (Lerner, 2007, p. 192).

In their studies of student writers, both Carter *et al.* (2004) and
Merino and Hammond (2002) are able to trace the students' genre
knowledge of lab reports by observing the lab itself as well as the subsequent texts that the students produce. Doing so allows them to make
the vital connections between the classroom lab task and the writing
task, truly *situating* the genre. Because I was unable to observe John
and Yoshi's courses or lab participation, my analysis has a somewhat
different focus. While I attempt to bring in some insight into how
the writers learned to practice science through this genre, my primary
focus is on the strategies that they used to compose the reports and
how their understanding of the genre (most particularly the textual
instantiations of the genre) evolved through repeated use.

JOHN: "JUST A LAB REPORT"

At the end of WCGS, John looked ahead to the upcoming, final term
of his two-year master's program. As we discussed the courses he would
be taking in this last semester, he described his uncertainty about an
interdisciplinary bioengineering lab course that he had registered for,
saying that as an electrical engineering major, he had "no idea what
they do in those departments" (December 10, 2002). When we met
again, two weeks into the new semester, he believed that the only writ-

ing he would be doing in this final term included an oral presentation. A few weeks later, however, I asked John if he'd done any writing that month; he pulled out some sheets of paper and answered, "Well, I don't know if this is *writing*, but lab reports" (February 27, 2003).

The bioengineering lab course, it turned out, required students to write LRs nearly every week, composing a total of 13 throughout the semester; John shared and discussed three of these LRs with me (see Table 6.1). The first was called an "Informal lab report" and was written within the first few weeks of the semester; this informal LR consisted of John's answers to specific questions assigned by the instructor. The second LR that John shared was a called a "Formal lab report" (referred to here as "Formal LR1") written immediately after the informal LR. The final report he shared ("Formal LR2") was written one month later, but was not returned to John until the last day of class. These formal LRs followed a boilerplate structure of abstract-introduction-method-results-discussion.

Table 6.1. John's lab reports analyzed.

Text	Title	Date of Experiment
Informal LR	Experiment 3: Explore Phase Measurements, Fourier Series, and Common Monde Rejection Ratio	1/29/03
Formal LR1	Experiment 4: Analysis of Respiration	2/5/03
Formal LR2	Experiment 6: Properties of Excitable Tissue	2/26/03

The LR assignments provided a glimpse into the ways that a writer's knowledge of a genre may develop, or remain relatively stable, within the context of a disciplinary content course. Here, I examine the relatively small changes in John's understanding of this school-based genre over the period of one 15-week course.

Rhetorical Purpose and Composing Process

John began and ended the course with a fairly stable understanding of the goals and communicative purpose of a classroom lab report; this understanding was developed primarily through prior experience with lab-related school genres. Although John had not previously taken a bioengineering lab course, he did have experience with lab-based coursework, and this experience had served to build his repertoire of genres. For instance, he contrasted the LR with a "lab notebook," something that he had been required to keep for a course taken the previous year of his M.S. program. He described the notebook as a meticulous record of his work in the lab, something that served a purpose beyond simply demonstrating one's work to an instructor:

> We had to make a journal of every single thing that we did, just in case we did something wrong, we could [go] back through the journal to find what we did. So that helped me to be pretty strict about writing down everything . . . It was a lab class where we actually had to fabricate semi-conductors. So we were working with dangerous chemicals every day. And if you made one mistake, the devices on the chip wouldn't work, so we have to keep a journal. The course was also concentrating on making us good lab participants. So, a lab journal is important because if I were a scientist in the field and I died, someone could take off where I stopped. If I kept a good journal, they'd know *exactly* what I did. (September 4, 2002)

John felt that one goal of the lab notebook, as a class assignment, was for students to learn how scientists practice science. He believed that the task was part of "making us good lab participants" and did not see the activity as artificial. In fact, John seemed to understand the rhetorical purpose of the lab notebook in much the same way that Merino and Hammond (2002) and Carter *et al.* (2004) describe the rhetorical purpose of classroom lab reports.

Interestingly, John differentiated the LR from a lab notebook, which seemed to hold more authenticity for him. He explained that the "lab notebook is for *me*" and said that "It's more what they do in a real lab" (February 27, 2003). In contrast, John viewed the LRs as a school-based task, saying that "if you're a scientist, researcher, whatever, you don't do an experiment and then write a [lab] report." And it was not just the lab report that John saw as school-based, but also the experiments themselves, which he described as "really interesting, but [. . .] not kind of what you do in a real lab" (February 27, 2003). His understanding of the lab report as serving a learning goal rather than engaging in the practice of science remained unchanged throughout the semester.

During the 15 weeks of the bioengineering lab course, John wrote nine informal LRs and four formal LRs. Although he saw both as school-based tasks, he perceived some distinctions between them. He described the informal LRs as similar to the lab reports he was required to write as an undergraduate in South Korea. He contrasted these with research papers that "would go into *much* more detail" and are "*much* more formal than this sort of thing" (February 27, 2003); in other words, John characterized the informal LRs as more general and less formal than a research paper. The formal LRs were written for "more important experiments" (February 27, 2003). While the structure of the informal LRs was dictated to the students by the instructor's questions, the formal LRs required students to "actually write it like a report." In producing an entire report—rather than responding to a series of questions—students were required to make choices regarding what kinds of content to include and exclude. As John stated:

> For [the informal LR], you know what you're gonna have to talk about in advance because they tell you what questions you should address. For [the formal LR], you have to analyze the data and then find out what you have to talk about. (April 3, 2003)

In this respect, and in its IMRD structure, the formal LR resembled the kind of writing one might do in a research report or article. Nevertheless, John viewed the formal LR—like the informal LR—as primarily a school-based genre rather than something carried out by practicing scientists. He even distinguished the formal LR from the mock grant proposal he had written in a previous graduate class, both in terms of its importance and his own writing process:

> Well, first of all, *this [LR] is for a class, so for a lab report for a class, I don't put that much effort into it as I would for a proposal,* which is the final thing for a class, like a final exam. I think it was a substantial amount of the grade. And, well, other than that, you really have to think a lot before you write the proposal, because you have to know what you're gonna do. But for a

> lab report, you know, you did the lab. *What you have
> to write should be obvious. So, even if this wasn't for a
> class, you know, if I was writing this for somebody, then
> I still think it would be a lot easier to write than a pro-
> posal.* (April 3, 2003, emphasis added)

John saw the real value of the formal LRs as lying in the experimental
work rather than the writing. While he learned a great deal by conducting the experiment, writing the report neither posed a great challenge nor took on any particular importance. He explained that most
students would take 3 to 4 days to write their LRs, but he was able to
write his in the morning on the day it was due. His time investment
in the task was again related to his understanding of genre itself. As
he explained, "maybe the quality suffers, but it doesn't really matter,
because this is just a lab report" (April 3, 2003).

Even at the end of the semester, after writing 13 LRs, John continued to see the genre as divorced from more "real-world" writing. Nevertheless, he thought he might later look back at his bioengineering
LRs as a reference for more important writing tasks. He still viewed
the LRs as relatively low-stakes writing, but suggested that the "learning" element of the task held some value for him. While he gave me
three of his LRs, he made sure to keep a copy of each for himself for
reference in the future, nothing that:

> Because a lot of things [about writing the LR] I knew,
> but if I have a reference, then I just take a look at
> it before I write something really important. I *know*
> I do these sloppy things. I know it even when I'm
> doing it, so [*laughing*] it'll *remind* me not to do it.
> (May 3, 2003)

In other words, John was very aware of his composing processes,
acknowledging that he did not invest a great deal of time into the
LRs. He said that he used some notes to help him write, but wrote
mainly from the ideas in his head. John did concede, however, that his
quick composing process meant that the final texts did not necessarily reflect his writing skills. He described, for example, at times using
vague language rather than citing specific quantifiable results simply
to save time. Linking his composing process to his understanding of
the rhetorical context, John explained, "I don't think it warrants that

much time put into it" (April 3, 2003). The lack of feedback from the instructor—who was slow in returning the LRs to the students, and only returned 6 of the 13—also seemed to de-motivate John from investing more time in the writing process:

> Well, for this [Formal LR2], I was a bit sloppy in the writing itself too, because I wasn't getting any of these back, because I turned in 13 and I only got 6 back, so- if you don't get feedback, you tend to get sloppy, if it's like a every week thing. (May 3, 2003)

Subject-Matter Content

While content-related decisions were relatively straightforward in the informal LRs—in which students responded to a questions provided by the instructor—the formal LRs required John to consider content in more complex ways. The general IMRD structure of these LRs was typical to scientific writing, but students still had to determine what content to include (and not include) in each section of the LR, and how many details to include. John's two formal LRs illustrate an evolving understanding of content appropriate for this genre. For example, John's introduction sections in Formal LR1 and Formal LR2 show a change in content, with the latter LR including more details on the experimental focus and its importance in general (illustrated in Figures 6.1 and 6.2).

Characterizing the mechanics of breathing is important because departure from normal in any of the parameters could be a sign of respiratory illness. In this experiment, we measured the parameters associated with normal pulmonary function tests. Also, in order to understand how restrictive and obstructive respiratory diseases affect breathing, we simulated these conditions and observed how respiration changed. We also observed how we could use a Pneumotachometer to measure the heartbeat. Finally, we related impedance change in the thoracic area to the corresponding volume changes. When we want to measure volume changes in certain situations (such as while a person in playing football), we cannot use a Pneumotachometer. Using electrodes enables us to measure volume changes with more freedom. Also, in telemetry applications, we can obtain basic respiratory parameters such as respiratory rate from the electrodes already used for Electrocardio measures (By using different frequencies for each system: usually low frequencies for the Electrocardiogram, and high frequencies for the Impedance Pneumotachogram. This system is also used to monitor babies in hospitals in case they stop breathing. Basic knowledge of the respiratory dynamics and measurement principles help us diagnose diseases and help create diagnostic devices.	*Topic and its importance* *Summary of experiment* *Explanation of instruments*

Figure 6.1. Rhetorical move analysis of Formal LR1 introduction.

A single stimulus must have adequate duration, ad-equate intensity, and an abrupt onset in order to be effective. Abrupt onset is required because of accomodation in the nervous system. In this experi-ment, we plotted points on the strength-duration curve of excitation of a nerve through the skin and direct excitation of the nerve. We then calculated the Rheobase (The lowest current required for stimulation with an infinitely long duration pulse.) and the Chronaxie (The duration when the current is twice rheobase) of the curves. We then explored the difference in effectiveness of sinusoidal waves compared to rectangular pulses.

Topic

Summary of experiment

Finding these parameters and understanding the dif-ference is very important in engineering medical de-vices because battery life, pain caused by the device, and cost of the device could vary greatly depending on what kind of waveform is used for stimulation. Sinusoidal waves are easier to generate then square waves. Chronaxie is the duration that requires the least energy. It is usually used as the delay in power-critical applications. It is also used when heat generation needs to be minimized. In these cases, 2xRheobase is used as the stimulating intensity. Also, when the curves for different tissue are different, it is possible to engineer the device so that it will stimulate one type of tissue without affecting the other much. (For example, in pacemakers, since the Chronaxie of the heart is larger than the Chronaxie of pain conducting nerves, a long delay would stimu-late the heart with minimal pain. Motor nerves have shorter Chronaxie than sensory nerv es, so short duration pulses would be used to stimulate motor nerves without stimulating the sensory nerves.) If the device is voltage-limited, using the lowest current possible would maximize electrode life, and minimize battery life.

Importance of experiment

Background information

Figure 6.2. Rhetorical move analysis of Formal LR2 introduction.

In Formal LR2, John's introduction included a full paragraph de-tailing the importance of the work and relevant background informa tion, demonstrating his understanding of the basic principles behind the experiment. This paragraph responds directly to the instructor's comments on the introduction of Formal LR1, stating that he "*Would like a little feel for why.*"

$\left(\dfrac{79}{90}\right)$ (passive voice okay)

A. Abstract

Avoid "we" or "I"

"A pneumotachometer was used to characterize..."

~~We used a~~ Pneumotachometer to characterize the mechanics of breathing. The subject's respiratory rate was faster than a normal individual (30 breaths/ minute), and his volume measurements were smaller than average. For example, his vital capacity was only 3.2 L. We also explored how restrictive and obstructive respiratory effects affected breathing. We measured a heartbeat of 63.15 beats/ minute using the Pneumotachometer to create a Pneumocardiogram. Finally, we related transthoracic impedance changes to the corresponding thoracic volume changes. We observed an average impedance/ volume $\Delta Z/\Delta V$ of 3.69 Ohms/L.

$\dfrac{7}{8}$ Should mention ...

Should mention one subject, adult male.

B. Introduction

Since no change was seen with added R and C, should mention, since not expected

Characterizing the mechanics of breathing is important because departure from normal in any of the parameters could be a sign of respiratory illness. In this experiment, we measured the parameters associated with normal pulmonary function tests. Also, in order to understand how restrictive and obstructive respiratory diseases affect breathing, we simulated these conditions and observed how respiration changed. We also observed how we could use a Pneumotachometer to measure the heartbeat. Finally, we related impedance change in the thoracic area to the corresponding volume changes. When we want to measure volume changes in certain situations (such as while a person is playing football), we cannot use a Pneumotachometer. Using electrodes enables us to measure volume changes with more freedom. Also, in telemetry applications, we can obtain basic respiratory parameters such as respiratory rate from the electrodes already used for Electrocardio measurements (By using different frequencies for each system: usually low frequencies for the Electrocardiogram, and high frequencies for the Impedance Pneumotachogram. This system is also used to monitor babies in hospitals in case they stop breathing. Basic knowledge of the respiratory dynamics and measurement principles help us diagnose diseases and help create diagnostic devices.

$\dfrac{5}{5}$ Would like a little feel for why; eg. minute ventilation gives idea of O_2/CO_2 exchange

C. Supplemental Materials and Methods

Figure 6.3. Feedback on the first page of John's Formal LR1.

This change in content, however, is relatively minor. For the most part, John's LRs displayed very similar approaches to quantity and type of content found in each section. Nevertheless, his understanding of content conventions was not always in line with the instructor's expectations. As shown in Figures 6.3 and 6.4, for example, the instructor repeatedly prompted John to include more information in his abstract and introduction sections, such as details about the experiment and explanation of the motivation for this type of experimental work.

[handwritten: 60/90]

A. Abstract

[handwritten: should mention specifically what you were stimulating (sciatic nerve)]

For this experiment, the strength-duration curves for stimulus through the skin of a frog using rectangular and sinusoidal waves were calculated. The strength-duration curves for direct nerve stimulation were also calculated. The Rheobase and Chronaxie calculated using the provided Excel macro are shown in the following table:

[handwritten: An abstract is fully text. No tables or figures. Normally all one paragraph]

	Rheobase (mA)	Chronaxie (ms)	
Rectangular Pulses Through the Skin	0.874	0.329	
Sinusoidal Waves Through the Skin	1.41	0.436	
Direct Nerve Stimulation using Rectangular Pulses	0.134	0.138	

Table 1. The Rheobase and Chronaxie for Various Ways of Stimulating Excitable Tissue

From these results, we can conclude that it ~~is easiest~~ *[handwritten: requires]* (Less current and less duration ~~required~~) to directly stimulate the nerve, and a rectangular pulse can stimulate excitable tissue with less current and duration than a sinusoidal wave.

[handwritten: × Not semantically easier]

Even though it is much harder to create a rectangular pulse than a sinusoidal wave, using a rectangular pulse can save power and extend battery life. Also, when implementing pacemakers or other stimulating devices, stimulating the nerve or muscle directly can extend battery life significantly.

[handwritten: 5/8]

[handwritten: Abstract should only give conclusions that come directly from experiment (we did not look at charge)]

B. Introduction

Figure 6.4. Feedback on the first page of John's Formal LR2.

Indeed, analysis of the instructor's written feedback shows that content-related issues were the primary focus of his comments and

grading. Specific areas of concern in all three LRs included the quality
and quantity of John's analysis and the placement of content within
the LR. Table 6.2 details the focus of the instructor's comments within
each LR.

Table 6.2. Distribution of Instructor's Written Comments (by %).

Focus of Feedback	Informal LR	Formal LR1	Formal LR2
Quality/quantity of analysis (positive)	14%	14%	3%
Quality/quantity of analysis (negative)	47.5	52	52
Misplaced content	0	0	3
Experimental procedure	4.5	0	0
Technical conventions (positive)	4.5	0	0
Technical conventions (negative)	24	17	21
Style	4.5	17	21
Total	100%	100%	100%

As the table shows, the majority of instructor comments focused
on insufficient analysis or detail. In the Informal LR, for example, the
instructor prompted John to include more details, through comments
like, *"But what is phase linear with?"* *"Describe"* and *"Give mathematical
comparison (% difference)."* In Formal LR1, the instructor's comments
prompted John to include more details, giving specific point deduc-
tions for the missing information: For example, *"But what causes it
to appear in the flow? (-2)"* and *"Was relaxed breathing the same shape
as forced? (-3)."* Linking the instructor's written comments with the
points that he deducted from each section of the LRs, it again appears
that content was a primary focus of grading (see Table 6.3).

Table 6.3. Distribution of actual points deducted from final grade.

Focus of Feedback	Informal LR	Formal LR1	Formal LR2
Insufficient content	4.5	10	18
Incorrect content	0.5	0	4
Improper form	0	1	8
Total points deducted	5 (out of 80)	11 (out of 90)	30 (out of 90)

Formal LR2 was the sixth lab report of the semester but the last one to be returned to students with comments. As the instructor handed back the LR on the final day of class, he told the students that he had graded this report particularly harshly; John received 60 out of the 90 total points. Again, the majority of points were deducted for insufficient content, but in this LR a more significant portion of John's final grade was deducted for form. It is not clear, however, if John's increased deduction for content was due to a growing *mis*calculation on his part, or whether it was related to idiosyncratic grading on the part of the course instructor.

Rhetorical Form

The most visible changes in John's LRs are found in the rhetorical form. While the overall structure remained stable throughout the three LRs, John's figure captions and his technical style changed in interesting ways.

Figure Captions. Figures—including graphs, images, and charts—play an important role in communicating content in most LRs, and John's were no exception. All of his LRs included multiple figures and figure captions, with the captions providing one of the more interesting examples of John's developing understanding of generic form. At the start of the course, John believed that these captions should be short and concise; with time, he became less certain about the preferred conventions for this element of LRs. Table 6.4 shows the quantitative change in John's figure captions over time.

Table 6.4. Word length of John's figure captions.

Text	Average # of Words/ Caption	Range of Caption Length (shortest—longest)
Informal LR	7.3	2–12 words
Formal LR1	11.7	4–25 words
Formal LR2	23.5	9–34 words

In the Informal LR—his first report of the three—John's captions were relatively short, the longest reaching 11 words (*"Magnitude Response of Cascaded Bandpass filter that has no Unity Bandwidth"*) and the shortest only 2 (*"Square Wave"*). In his feedback, John's instructor expressed a preference for more detail, writing *"More descriptive labels needed"* next to John's two-word caption. John, however, was uncertain about the TA's preference for extensive detail, saying that:

> . . . usually even when I am pretty satisfied with [the caption], like, "Free Analysis of Square Wave," [the instructor] would want more. [For example,] how many harmonics there are in- which I'd usually write in small print instead of the caption, but he likes using captions. I don't know which one's better. (February 27, 2003)

Conventions for figures and their captions, however, did not appear to be insignificant, with approximately one-fourth of the instructor's written comments in Informal LR focusing on captions or the graphic presentation of data. Only one point was actually deducted from John's final grade for figure caption content/form; still, as he discussed this LR with me, John focused heavily on the extent to which this element had affected his grade.

In Formal LR1, the instructor once again wrote feedback on the figure captions, but this time deducted no points. John's captions in this LR were longer (see Table 6.4) and included more specific details about the data, such as precise experimental conditions or quantitative variables:

> *Output of pneumotach VI when an elastic band is placed around subject's chest to simulate a decrease in compliance.* (Formal LR1)

> *Physiograph output of pneumotachometer and imped-ance change of thorax due to breathing. Note: We have used a 2 point calibration to map volts into ohms.* (For-mal LR1)

Even with these more descriptive captions, the instructor indicated a need for still more details, writing next to the longest caption: *"Should also point out 5Ω calibration from another."*

John had consciously tried to write more detailed captions in For-mal LR1, and he understood the instructor's preference for more detail as a rhetorical issue. The instructor had explained to students that fig-ure captions should be specific enough for readers to look through the data and captions and "know exactly what happened" without read-ing the report itself. (April 3, 2003). Although John understood the purpose of very detailed captions, this style conflicted with his own preference for including the details in the report text (rather than the captions) as a way of engaging the reader:

John: Obviously, in [Formal LR1] I added a lot more captions, but my normal style of writing is- I wouldn't have data on separate pages, I'd have it embedded into it, which I think is a lot easier to read. [. . .] But I normally put it into the paper, and that way the person reading it, you know, like the data and the report itself wouldn't be separate. And- I don't know, since I like doing that, I don't put *that* much emphasis on the cap-tion. [. . .] I need a little more detail on this informal [LR], but for the formal [LR], I think I put a little *too* much detail, but he obviously likes it even more detail than this. I like writing it in the paper, so that somebody would have to read it.

Chris: I see. So, you would normally have more of it in the text?

John: Mhm. Well, I'd have a lot of it on this too, but just
       too much data on this would confuse people. Like,
       if somebody looks at the data, they shouldn't be
       able to know the whole picture, but they should
       be able to know what this data means, and, you
       know, not like every single detailed detail than
       this. I like writing it in the paper, so that some-
       body would have to read it. (April 3, 2003)

John further explained that including so many details in the caption
seemed unnecessary because "the person looking at this should know
how to get these values for themselves." John knew that this view conflicted with his instructor's, and he expressed confusion about which
approach was preferred in general.

Figure captions remained an issue in Formal LR2, even though
John's captions had become even longer and more specific. One figure
caption in this report, for example, read:

> *The Strength-Duration Curve for Rectangular Pulses*
> *(The current axis is plotted on a logarithmic scale, and*
> *the pulse duration is plotted on a linear scale.)* (Formal
> LR2)

The TA wrote underneath this caption: *"Be more specific in the description: stimulating a frog's sciatic nerve transcutaneously (or with a biopo-
lar surface electrode)."* Pointing to this comment, John again expressed
some confusion—and even skepticism—about the feedback:

I thought I was pretty specific in this [caption], but
[my instructor] still wanted it more specific, so I don't
know. I mean, I understand what he's trying to say,
but sort of if it gets too long, then it gets a little slop-
py, I think. Because everything is explained in the
contents . . . A lot of it is probably because he was
reading too fast. (May 3, 2003)

John's reference here to reading speed is somewhat intriguing. On
the one hand, he implies that the instructor's quick reading would
not be a typical way of reading the genre; on the other hand, John
described his own reading practices of research articles as very fast,
quickly scanning the abstract, figures, and captions:

> I go through and look at the data, [?] graphs or pic-
> tures, whatever, and then from that data, I should
> know what, basically what they are trying to do. Of
> course, they won't give me the whole idea, but still.
> So, the captions are pretty important I guess. (April
> 3, 2003)

If John reads research articles quickly, looking at figure captions before reading the text, it may be somewhat surprising that he would
write the captions in his LR so that they depended on the prose text.
One possible explanation is that John understood research articles and
LRs to be fairly distinct genres. Because of their different rhetorical
purposes—the research article written to convey information to disciplinary peers, and the LR written to illustrate one's knowledge of
specific subject-matter content to an instructor—John likely assumed
different reading practices. In other words, John may have believed
that his instructor would read the LR quite carefully because he was
evaluating and grading it. Such an explanation suggests that John differentiated research- and learning-based genres; unfortunately, it also
suggests that John's understanding of the LR genre conflicted in some
ways with that of his instructor.

These tensions between John's understanding of the genre and
his instructor's expectations point to some of the blurry boundaries
of genres and the multiple communicative purposes that they are intended to serve *for different genre participants*. While John continued
to see the LR as a knowledge-telling task and approached it as such,
his instructor seemed to view the goals more broadly, expecting the
students to write as scientists might within a larger academic discourse
community.

Style. The instructor's feedback related to technical writing style addressed three primary areas: use of personal pronouns and passive
voice, use of parentheses, and capitalization. The latter two were addressed primarily as mechanical issues, but comments regarding the
use of personal pronouns and passive voice were embedded in larger
rhetorical issues. Because John perceived the informal LR to differ
with regards to formality and style, I focus here on just the two formal
LRs.

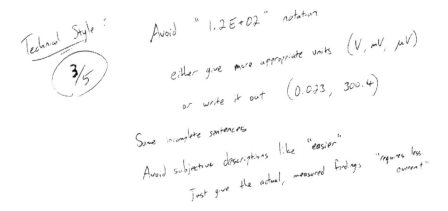

Figure 6.5. Feedback on the last page of John's Formal LR2.

In Formal LR1, the instructor re-wrote the opening sentence of John's abstract into a passive construction and then wrote in the margin *"Avoid 'we' or 'I' (passive voice okay)."* This comment was repeated at the end of the LR. John expressed confusion about this suggestion, because he had used "we" in his previous LRs (both formal and informal) and had received no negative feedback. The use of "we" in LRs was preferential to John because he felt an overuse of passive voice could become very "tiresome," requiring long constructions and more words. Active constructions, he believed, often conveyed the ideas more clearly. While John knew that it was conventional to avoid the use of "I" in much academic writing, he was unsure as to why the pronoun "we" would be frowned upon in this particular genre: "I don't use 'I' but I thought it was fine to use 'we' in a *lab report*. I mean, it's not even a paper" (April 3, 2003).

As John and I discussed Formal LR1, he tended to fixate more on the structural or stylistic weaknesses of his LRs than on level of detail or content. He referred to the single point that had been deducted for technical style, and explained "I think it's just like an exercise for writing later in academic career" (April 3, 2003). In fact, only one-fifth of the TA's written feedback focused on form, while one-third of it focused on insufficient content.

In Formal LR2, the instructor focused more heavily on form than he had in the previous LRs. Here, points were deducted for John's "technical style," including notational errors, grammatical errors, and an overuse of *"subjective descriptions like 'easier'"* (see Figure 6.5). John agreed with the suggestions and explained that he had been unaware of many of these conventions.

Interestingly, one convention that the instructor did not comment on in Formal LR2 was John's continued use of "we" pronouns. Despite the suggestion in Formal LR1 to avoid the first person plural pronoun, Formal LR2 contains numerous instances of "we" in the both the abstract and introduction sections; its presence, however, is diminished in the results and discussion sections, where John uses more passive voice than he had in the previous LRs.

Summary of Knowledge Development

From the beginning of the semester through to the end, John viewed the bioengineering lab reports as a learning-based genre in which the primary purpose was to demonstrate his lab knowledge and ability to present this knowledge effectively. He consistently differentiated this genre from more "real world" writing tasks of scientists, such as a lab notebook or mock proposal, and his unaltered, rapid composing process suggests that the LR task did not gain any increased importance for him over time. John's knowledge of the LRs did, however, develop in other ways. He demonstrated an increased understanding of his immediate audience (the course instructor) and shaped his text in various ways to meet the expectations of that audience. The inclusion of a research motivation in his introduction section, his longer and more detailed figure captions, and his increasing use of the passive voice all illustrate changes in John's understanding of audience expectations.

Yoshi: Lab Reports as "a Building Block"

During his second year at Midwest University, Yoshi took two courses that required students to write regular reports on lab work. In the first of these courses, taken in the fall term of 2003, students needed to complete computer simulation labs and summarize their procedures, results, and analysis in a short hand-written report. In the second course, taken during Yoshi's final semester, students carried out more formal lab experiments in small groups; the groups composed written responses to required questions and then handed in a typed report for each lab. Although the forms of these reports in these two courses differed, I discuss them together here in order to illustrate how Yoshi's understanding of technical writing style changed through the practice of writing these reports.

Lab Assignments, Fall 2003

During the third semester of his master's program, Yoshi enrolled in two engineering courses and a course in oral communication taught by an English-language specialist within the Electrical Engineering department. One course, on the topic of very large scale integration (known in engineering parlance as "VLSI") circuit design, required students to carry out four laboratory computer simulations and to then write up their results as "lab assignments." Although these LRs were less formal in structure and format than John's and did not take place in a physical laboratory space, the reports shared the same purpose of asking students to demonstrate their ability to carry out and analyze "laboratory" work.

Yoshi wrote four LRs between the end of September and the end of October 2003, and he shared them with me in November after all four had been graded and returned. Like John, Yoshi did not initially consider these assignments to be examples of writing. Unlike John, however, Yoshi never received feedback on his writing in these LRs; his instructor simply wrote a point total on the top of each assignment (Yoshi received full credit for each LR). It was perhaps this lack of feedback on the writing that led Yoshi to conclude that the LR was graded primarily on the result of the lab simulation. With 20 students in the course each handing in an individual report, Yoshi even doubted that the instructor was able to read the LRs carefully.

My discussions with Yoshi about these four LRs were much less extensive than those with John and they provided less insight into his understanding of the genre's rhetorical purpose or form. However, an analysis of Yoshi's texts illustrate slight changes to his writing over the one-month period that they were written, while his discussions of these texts suggest that Yoshi saw them as important practice in his writing development. While his first lab assignment consisted primarily of data and very scant explanations, his final LR contained more detailed explanation of both procedures and analysis. A comparison of the first pages of LR1 and LR4 shows a representative illustration of the changes here (see Figure 6.6).

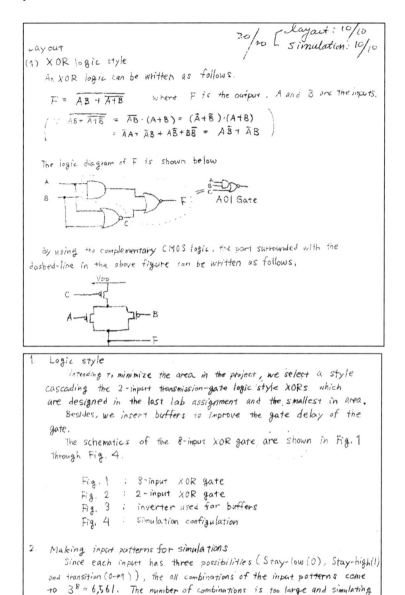

Figure 6.6. First page of LR1 (top) and LR4 (bottom) for Yoshi's VLSI course, Fall 2003.

As LRs are written to report on data, they require writers to display data in ways that are easily accessible to readers; therefore, tables and figures are a typical feature of the genre. Writers must find ways to refer to figures and tables throughout the LR, and this rhetorical act is typically carried out through metadiscourse, such as *"As Table 1 illustrates . . ."* Yoshi's LRs are in fact heavy on data display (through tables, figures, and formulas) and lighter on prose text, in comparison with John's. In fact, much of Yoshi's prose is simply meta-discursive, referring readers to relevant data. Particularly common are *endophoric markers,* or expressions that refer to other parts of a writer's text (Hyland, 2000). Table 6.5 shows the meta-discursive lexical phrases used in each LR. In LR1, for example, four lexical phrases (listed in the table) account for nine instances of metadiscourse in the report. In LR3, two nearly identical phrases account for all 14 instances of metadiscourse found in the text.

Table 6.5. Metadiscourse in Yoshi's LRs, Fall 2003.

	Endophoric Markers	**Logical Connectives**
LR1	In the above figure, is/are shown below as follows is the following	Besides, Thus,
LR2	are shown in as follows	In contrast, In this/such a case, Thus,
LR3	is/are shown in are shown below	Before..., Similarly as...,
LR4	in the above figure is/are shown in is described below is also attached to are summarized in	As far as X [is] concerned, Besides, From the simulation result, Since..., Then,

In learning to write in a style appropriate to this genre, Yoshi adopted essentially the same strategy he had used (successfully) in WCGS— he looked at other texts that he perceived as similar in style. In the case of homework and LRs, he described much of the writing as "kind of a textbook explanation style" (October 1, 2003). So, Yoshi looked to textbooks as resources for his own writing. He explained to me that he found a few useful phrases and then used those repeatedly. His limited range of such expressions, however, was a concern for him:

> . . . sometimes that sounds stupid or something, because I am, for example, [writing] *"this form can be written as following"* etc., the same type of explanation repeatedly. So, I want to improve my explanation style. [. . .] Recently, I try to read carefully about how to explain in textbook, and I think if I could memorize the phrases or something, it would be good. (October 1, 2003)

This conscious practice of broadening his range of endophoric expressions through the sampling of other texts seemed to have some impact on Yoshi's writing. His fourth and final LR for this course included a slightly wider range of such expressions, as the nine instances of endophoric markers were carried out through five different phrases.

Yoshi's use of textbooks as a linguistic resource becomes apparent not only through his growing repertoire of endophoric markers but also through an increase in his range of logical connectives (e.g., thus, since). Once again, the slight change in Yoshi's writing was by no means unconscious. Rather, Yoshi made a deliberate effort to use more of these meta-discursive phrases after being given a list of logical connectives and sequence markers in his oral English communication course, taken in the engineering department. Although that course focused on using these kinds of lexical phrases in oral presentations, Yoshi hoped to begin integrating some of them into his writing. Tracing his use of logical connectives throughout the four LRs for his VLSI course, it seems that he was able to draw on a somewhat expanded repertoire in his final LR (see Table 6.5); no sequence markers were used in the LRs.

A final area of stylistic change can be found in Yoshi's use of the first personal plural pronoun *we*. Although the pronoun is absent from the first three LRs, it is conspicuously present in LR4, which contains eight instances of *we*. In all of these instances, *we* is used either to describe the lab procedures (e.g., *"we insert"* and *"we reduce"*) or analysis (e.g., *"we find"* or *"we can satisfy"*). The extensive use of *we* in this last LR illustrates Yoshi's typical learning process. As he attempted to expand his linguistic repertoire and to approximate the language that he was reading, he tended to try out new forms. When he received positive feedback or, more often, no negative feedback, on those forms, he would often re-use them and gradually take ownership over them. He described this process to me months later, saying that:

> . . . honestly, now I felt I borrow someone [else's] writing . . . Although my variety is getting larger and larger, [. . .] but I coming to my mind another person's writing. I find, "Oh, this is a good expression for-" and I memorize the expression, and later I remember that. (January 22, 2004)

Yoshi went on to explain that he had followed the same process in Japanese from as far back as junior high. He felt, however, that "practice and experience will solve that problem" (January 22, 2004).

In fact, Yoshi already viewed these four LRs as valuable for providing him with practice in writing quickly in a fairly limited about of time. He estimated spending about four hours composing each report, and explained that the writing became easier with each LR "because I repeatedly write similar documents, so I got accustomed to writ[ing] these things . . . Writing these documents [has] become a building block for me" (November 5, 2003).

Formal Lab Reports, Spring 2004

In the fourth and final semester of Yoshi's two-year master's program, he enrolled in another engineering course that included a laboratory component. In this course, which focused on high frequency wireless systems, students worked in small groups to carry out lab work and prepare a written report. The students in each group divided up the sections according to their strengths in different areas and then compiled the parts into a complete version to hand in. Students participated in three labs and wrote a total of seven LRs (see Figure 6.7). Yoshi was assigned to work in a group with three other students, including a native English speaker from the U.S., a native Chinese speaker from China, and another Chinese speaker from Taiwan; a second native English speaker was added to the group for the last three reports.

Lab Report 1 (LR1), February 6, 2004
Lab Report 2 (LR2), February 13, 2004
Lab Report 3 (LR3), March 5, 2004
Lab Report 4 (LR4), March 26, 2004
Lab Report 5 (LR5), April 9, 2004
Lab Report 6 (LR6), April 23, 2004
Lab Report 7 (LR7), May 6, 2004

Figure 6.7. LRs written by Yoshi in Spring 2004.

Process and Rhetorical Goals

At the start of the semester, Yoshi told me that he had never written formal LRs in English, though he had written them as an undergraduate student in Japan. He contrasted this course's lab work from the LRs on computer simulations in the previous semester, describing this current work as "real experiments," something he said he had not done in quite awhile. He did, however, hypothesize that the contents of these reports would be "similar as [the reports] I wrote last semester" (January 22, 2004). As he wrote the reports throughout this semester, Yoshi noted that the writing helped develop his understanding of the concepts from the lab:

> Through the writing, I can understand the questions deeply. Sometimes, when I writing the results, I notice my analysis was incorrect or something. And then I re-think about that. (February 26, 2004)

In other words, these LRs seemed to serve for Yoshi the rhetorical goal that Carter *et al.* (2004) outline: they were applied in order to learn the material of the course.

In contrast to the previous semester, the instructor of this course provided students with numerous materials describing how to prepare for, carry out, and report on the lab. These materials included lecture notes, background reading, and instructions for what to include in the report, such as specific plots and calculations. In addition, he provided students with a set of questions for each report; these questions formed the "sections" of each report, much like John's "informal LRs" described in the first half of this chapter. An excerpt from Yoshi's first LR for this course is found in Figure 6.8.

Self-calibration of your raw data

Look in the online manual of the network analyzer (www.agilent.com) and perform your own calibration on the data of the extended short. Compare the calibrated results from step 5 to your own calibration procedure, specifically the calibrated short to the uncalibrated short.

5.) Show these two reflection plots as the magnitude and phase in the frequency domain and discuss differences in your routine.

Making use of the one-port error model [I], we carried out a self-calibration on the data of the extended short. According to the model, the actual reflection coefficient (S_{IIA}) is given by the following form
[equation]
where
        [variables]
From these uncalibrated measurements (a perfect load, short and open), the following relations between SIIM and the above errors are obtained
        [equations]
[. . .]
The frequency response of the calibrated short and self-calibrated short based on eq. (I) is shown in Fig. 5. From the figure, the calibrated short (red) shows that the amplitude of the reflection coefficient is not exactly one and that the phrase of the reflection coefficient is shifting as frequency increases. Whereas the self-calibrated short (blue exhibits an ideal shorted circuit response.
We think these results are reasonable from the following two reasons. First, the reference plane of the short standard is electrically offset from the calibration plane of the test port. And the offset can be regarded as a small length of transmission line. Thus after the calibration, it does not appear to be a "perfect" short and shows a certain amount of phase shift.

Figure 6.8. Excerpt from Yoshi's first LR, spring 2004.

Yoshi described the instructor's grading as "very strict" (April 1, 2004), focused on the accuracy of the group's analysis. Points were deducted if the report did not fully address the questions posed by the instructor, but points were never taken off for writing style, at least in Yoshi's case. He believed that "the instructor graded very quickly" (April 1, 2004). Yoshi did not share with me his graded reports, so I have no record of his group's scores on these LRs. At the end of the semester, though, he explained, "I think [the instructor] didn't care much about the writing" (May 10, 2004) since he never provided any feedback on it.

After writing LR1 and LR2, Yoshi described his composing process for these reports as fairly time consuming. He estimated spending approximately one day writing each report, noting that producing the equations and formulas on the computer took a great deal of time. As the semester went on, he believed that he was able to write more quickly, but that this speed was offset by the increasing content expectations for each report.

Rhetorical Form

Because the instructor did not explicitly address in class his expectations for the writing in terms of format or structure, Yoshi relied on "basic format or styles [that] I've learnt from now" to prepare his reports. The lack of feedback on the report writing, however, led Yoshi to the understanding that his group's approach to the writing was acceptable. As he said, "At this moment, professor doesn't say about our report, so I guess it is OK" (April 26, 2004). In the first LR of the semester (LR1), Yoshi's writing shows many similarities to the writing in his final LR from the prior semester. Once again, his text includes a number of endophoric markers, logical connectives, and the pronoun *we*, many of which are used in the excerpt in Figure 6.8.

As he wrote his reports, Yoshi considered his lab group to be his primary audience. He read everyone's work and quickly began to notice stylistic differences among the writers. He was especially interested in some of the discursive conventions adopted by the native English speaker in the group:

> We have one native English speaker in our group[6].
> Here is his part and I noticed almost all sentences are passive tenses. And last semester my project partner also wrote like that, so now I [am] thinking I better change my style like this for these kinds of reports.
> (February 26, 2004)

He noted that the pre-lab handouts given by the instructor were stylistically similar to textbooks, making frequent use of "we." This more active and interpersonal style was what Yoshi had consciously tried to mimic in the previous semester as well as the first two LRs in the current course. In fact, Yoshi remembered reading a technical writing textbook in Japanese that described English technical writing as using more active voice constructions than Japanese; after reading that, Yoshi "kind of avoid[ed] writing passive tense in technical writing" (February 26, 2004). Now, however, he began to question whether an active and interpersonal style like this was appropriate for report writing. He noted, "I know this style sometimes work[s] well, so it is difficult to decide which style is better. But I think I definitely use active tense" (February 26, 2004).

In writing the fourth LR that spring, Yoshi made a conscious attempt to avoid the active tense; his writing in this LR shows no instances of *we,* replacing them with either inanimate subjects or passive structures, as in the example below:

> *From the figure, it is obvious that the loaded Q varies linearly with S21. A fitted line can be obtained by using Matlab as follows.* (LR4)

At the end of the semester, Yoshi again commented on his deliberate effort to modify his style, saying that "I think for the first time I got accustomed to textbook style writing, then later as I read another group members' documents, so I changed my mind to try to use passive tense in this kind of lab report" (May 10, 2004). His understanding of voice was, however, more complex than it had been in the previous semester when he specifically asked me whether active or passive voice was better to use. Now, he had a sense that voice (and style more generally) was dependent on issues like context and genre. In the future, he said, "I think I need to balance the both passive and active tense, but [for] this kind of report issue, I think I will use passive tense more" (May 10, 2004).

Yoshi's reports continued to include the metadiscourse found in his writing the previous semester, though with still more variation. New phrases, like "the following figure shows" or "in the next page," appeared and were integrated with ease into Yoshi's writing. Commenting on his use of such phrases, Yoshi explained that "at first I saw these sentence[s] in a textbook, and now I think this is kind of *my* pattern to write" (April 26, 2004). Yoshi had also begun to use sequence markers (e.g., *first, finally*) regularly, and used a more diverse range of logical connectives. He attributed this increased lexical diversity to his exposure to scientific discourse through the extensive reading he was doing. Likewise, when I commented on his use of more "academic" words like *obtain*, Yoshi laughed, describing this kind of language as "knowledge from my reading and my textbooks—very, not oral expression" (April 1, 2004). By the seventh, and final, LR of this semester, Yoshi's writing incorporated metadiscourse and passive voice in ways that differ from his first LR of the fourth semester and from his first LR of the previous semester, as illustrated in sentences like these:

> *By adding the DC bias network designed with Bias_ Network.dsn and three decoupling capacitors, which were used to decouple the RF amplifier and the DC bias network, to the FinishedAmp.dsn, the following final amplifier schematic were obtained.* (LR7, spring 2004)

> *Since the automatic layout generator did not work well for the example schematic for some reason, several modifications such as inserting transmission lines, flipping components, and elongating transmission lines were needed to make the automatic layout generator work properly.* (LR7, spring 2004)

Summary of Genre Knowledge Development

An exploration of the formal changes in Yoshi's LR writing shows an increasingly formal discourse style and an expanded repertoire of written expression. At the end of the semester, reflecting on all of his writing experiences during his two-year graduate program, Yoshi believed that the two courses in which he wrote the lab reports were the most useful for improving his writing. In this final "high frequency wireless systems" course, he noted the value of having to write a great deal on a weekly basis. In the previous "VLSI" course, he found the final term project (not discussed here) to be most helpful, because it required him to learn to write in what he described as "a more formal style" (May 10, 2004).

WCGS and Disciplinary Contexts:
Connections and Contradictions

Although lab report writing was not a focus of WCGS, some of the discursive features relevant to LRs were discussed in class at various junctures. For example, Michele presented several "informal elements" of writing, including the use of first person singular pronouns, contractions, sentence-initial "*But . . .*" or "*And . . . ,*" direct questions, imperatives, and two-word verbs. These elements were presented and revisited throughout the semester as tools students could use to control the style and tone of their writing—and they would later have *potential* relevance to the LRs that John and Yoshi wrote in subsequent semesters.

In class activities, Michele often asked students to evaluate texts—both their own and published samples—in terms of formality and to explain what elements made the writing more (or less) formal. Formality was a complex issue for John; throughout my study, he described it as both a strength and weakness of his writing. At the end of his graduate program, five months after having completed WCGS, John still felt uncertain about how to vary his level of formality for different written genres. In terms of the linguistic elements of informality discussed in WCGS, John's writing changed very little over time. In a mock grant proposal, an engineering course project, and his lab reports, John made no use of most of these informal elements, with the exception of only a few instances of contractions or two-word verbs. He did, however, frequently use the first-person plural pronoun (we/ our) in much of his previous writing. John explained that he saw the use of "we" (as opposed to "I") as a way to build credibility, saying that "even if it was one person, just using "I" would probably- most people wouldn't think it's not as credible because, 'so you're doing this by yourself?' [. . .] I think it's just a credibility language" (April 3, 2003).

Formality was also an area with which Yoshi was concerned, as he struggled to reconcile the language he saw in textbooks and class handouts, advice he had seen about English-language technical writing, and the writing of his peers. In the end, he seemed to be most swayed by his classmates' frequent use of passive constructions, which appear more pervasively in his final lab report. In discussing with me his uncertainty about the use of first person pronouns and passive constructions, he never referred to the related discussions in WCGS. Instead, he tied the issue to the immediate contexts in which he was reading and writing—student report writing, textbooks, and handouts.

A second element of academic discourse discussed in WCGS that had potential application to John's LRs was figure captions. One WCGS class session focused on captions, specifically encouraging students to use gapping to create short and concise captions by eliminating articles, prepositions, or other unnecessary words. Because this class session was part of the conference poster/slide unit, it was implicitly tied to the poster and slide genres in terms of medium and rhetorical context. At the same time, no distinction was drawn in class between captions used in posters or slides and those used in other written genres like research reports.

This WCGS class content did not seem to influence John's subsequent use of captions in his LRs. As described earlier, John preferred using relatively short figure captions, much like those in WCGS. This preference is evident in his mock proposal written prior to WCGS, his course project written during WCGS, and his informal LR written shortly after WCGS. But, as illustrated above, John's LR captions changed both quantitatively and qualitatively over time in response to his TA's feedback. Although the feedback conflicted with both the WCGS instruction *and* John's own personal preferences, the TA's expectations "won out," as John wrote increasingly descriptive, lengthier captions. It appears that John treated his immediate audience (the course TA) as more imperative than prior instruction or his own preferences.

Tracing John's and Yoshi's knowledge development of the LR genre is difficult without having access to all of the input that they may have received in their courses or through discussions with their peers; the connections made here can represent only a very partial view of their changing genre knowledge. Nevertheless, neither John's nor Yoshi's discussions of their LRs reveal any visible links to WCGS course instruction, suggesting that they did not draw conscious connections— at least during our discussions—between course activities on formality, data commentary, or figure captions when applying these features in their LRs. Indeed, in John's case, the changes made in the form of his captions conflicted with WCGS instruction.

The strategy of analyzing genres, as taught in WCGS, also had potential carry-over into the writers' disciplinary contexts. Yoshi did explicitly look to textual samples as a way of learning more about the formal dimensions of the technical writing, but he did not appear to analyze these features in relationship to rhetorical, process, or subject-matter, as was the goal of the WCGS genre analysis. In other words, Yoshi analyzed the textual elements of the writing and borrowed particular expressions just as he had been doing since junior high. In writing his LRs, John did not attempt to analyze the genre in an effort to learn more about the formal or rhetorical dimensions. Instead, the most apparent source of John's knowledge was feedback from his immediate audience.

In both cases, the writers turned primarily to the immediate rhetorical context in their learning process, building knowledge of the most local instance of the genre. Given the presence of an identifiable, local audience and the exigence of receiving a course grade, the writers' turn to the local seems strategically wise.

Building Knowledge through Repeated Practice

Yoshi's and John's experiences with lab report writing illustrate the central importance of context in shaping the possibilities and strategies for genre learning. In each case, the writers had the opportunity to re-visit the same genre repeatedly within a relatively short period of time. Through this repetition, they built their rhetorical, process, and content knowledge of "doing lab work"—a practice central to scientific research. I have focused my attention here on the formal traces of that genre knowledge, and in this area repetition also proved a valuable resource for the writers.

For John, repeated practice allowed him to respond to the feedback received from his instructor, which appears to be a primary influence on his changing formal knowledge of the LRs. In response to this feedback, John began composing more detailed figure captions, he modified the content of his introduction sections, and he increased his use of passive voice. In addition to this textual evidence, John's comments in interviews provide further support that feedback influenced his understanding of the genre and for academic discourse more broadly:

> [The feedback] made me more aware of my [?style?]
> even though I was unaware of it when I was writing
> it. And other than that, like the new insights, like I

> didn't know . . . you know, like what to capitalize
> and the exact format, like, for grant proposals. Like
> that's a completely new form of writing that I just did
> here. Even for lab reports, there's- you know, from
> the comments, there are some things I *didn't* know.
> I don't remember them right now, but they might be
> worth, like- as I am writing the new report, I always
> catch myself doing something- "oh yea!" So that's
> probably affecting my writing. (May 3, 2003)

In Yoshi's case, carrying out the same task repeatedly allowed him multiple opportunities for looking to other texts and mining them for formal expressions and written style. As he worked collaboratively with his peers, he gained insight related to the process of laboratory work and he gained access to their writing. Over time, he became familiar with his peers' writing, noted differences among group members' approaches, and contrasted these with other texts in which he was immersed. Yoshi never received feedback explicitly focused on his writing form, but he interpreted this *lack* of feedback as a generally positive (or at least neutral) sign indicating that he had at least met basic expectations.

Tracing the formal changes in the writers' knowledge and the influences on those changes further emphasizes the extent to which their knowledge is situated in the local. Rather than returning to the more general strategies discussed in WCGS, however, both writers' knowledge development was shaped primarily within the local disciplinary domain. In this way, their practices align with Carter's (1990) model of expertise in which experts gradually move toward the use of highly contextualized strategies.

John's knowledge development, for example, was tied to the bioengineering classroom environment insofar as he responded to local goals and a local audience. One explanation for his contextual dependence is that many strategies that John had used previously relied on the availability of other texts, such as samples of the genre or instructional guidelines. In the case of the LRs, John did not have access to such textual resources. He could not look at sample LRs, as he had when writing his cover letter, nor did he have the accumulated experience as a reader of the genre that he had with presentation slides. While John had written LRs before in different settings, he lacked extensive exposure to LR texts written by experts or even peers. Furthermore, John did not actively seek out information about lab reports as a genre. Instead of looking to outside resources for advice, as he had for the other writing tasks, John relied solely on the feedback of his course instructor. His decision suggests that John distinguished between genres intended for wide audiences (such as CVs) and those tied to a very local context (such as a LR). Finally, John's view of the LR as relatively low-stakes seemed to influence his decision to spend less time learning to write in this genre. He believed that the main purpose of the LR was to learn the subject-matter content and that it was a genre of limited use outside of the classroom.

Yoshi's classroom contexts differed from John's in that he was not given any feedback and his writing was at times collaborative. In the absence of feedback or mentoring, Yoshi turned to other texts—and, indeed, the classroom context offered him multiple textual interactions. Not limiting himself to the lab report, Yoshi looked at a range of genres, attempting to improve his more general sense of technical discourse. Yoshi's local situation also offered social and textual interactions with peers, so that he was able to learn more about how other student writers approached the same task.

Finally, the repeated practice that these tasks offered may have benefited the writers' more general writing improvement. For Yoshi, the repetition and extensive writing practice—something that is not always common in science and engineering classrooms—helped him build fluency with and confidence in his English writing skills. John similarly felt that his writing had changed during the eight months he met with me, and he attributed at least some of that to the feedback on his LRs, saying that the feedback had led to "not a *huge* change in how I organize my writing or how I go about writing, but like the small details that I didn't actually realize. It changed" (May 3, 2003).

7 The Culmination of Graduate Research: Learning to Write a Master's Thesis

Paul spoke about his master's thesis when I first met him in late August of 2002. He knew that he would be writing a thesis by the end of that academic year, but he had not yet decided whether or not he would continue for a doctoral degree in Computer Sciences; by December, he had decided against doing so. With his lack of interest in academic research and his preference for working on concrete applications, Paul saw little point in completing a PhD. He was also no longer interested in his advisor's research area but did not want move to a new research group. Instead, he said, "I just want to finish my master's degree" (December 12, 2002).

As he began the project, Paul realized that it would be impossible to complete his entire thesis in only one semester, so he planned on conducting the research during the spring semester of 2003 and the writing during that summer, graduating by August. This chapter traces Paul's path through the master's thesis writing task, focusing particularly on his emerging knowledge of the genre and the important role that his advisor's feedback played in the process of knowledge building.

THE THESIS GENRE

A master's thesis can pose many challenges for students as it is usually their first piece of extended academic writing and may also be their first attempt at presenting their own work to a scholarly audience consisting of more than a single course instructor. With few exceptions, students lack previous experience in writing a master's thesis, or similar genres, and must learn the expectations, procedures, and conventions of the task while carrying it out. To further compound the difficulty, disciplinary fields, geographical locations, and institutional departments may display variation in their expectations. There is indeed a wide range of thesis types and discourse structures, and these variations are not always reflected in published advice on thesis and dissertation writing (Paltridge, 2002). Additionally, the majority of research on actual thesis texts or writing practices has focused on doctoral students; in contrast, very little research has examined students' master's thesis writing. The few studies that exist have affirmed the disciplinary situatedness of the genre (Samraj, 2006) and the importance of a productive advisor/advisee relationship (Krase, 2007).

Sociocultural research of thesis writing, at both the master's and doctoral level, is fairly unanimous in describing the central role that a mentor (particularly a graduate advisor) can play in supporting advisees. Dong's (1998) survey of 137 L1 and L2 graduate thesis writers, for example, found that the L2 writers tended to work in more isolation than the L1 counterparts and tended to rely more heavily on their advisors for advice and support. The same writers described the most helpful comments from their advisors as focusing on forms of expression, organization and coherence, presentation of subject matter, and style and format. Unfortunately, Dong also found that these writers generally expressed a desire for more support overall. In addition to support from advisors, novice thesis writers may turn to other textual and social resources, and may also draw upon their knowledge of other genres with which they have become familiar through their work as Research Assistants (RAs) or through independent course projects.

PAUL'S PREVIOUS EXPERIENCES

Paul had not completed any extended writing in English prior to his master's thesis. In fact, he had done very little writing at all until he began his master's program. As an undergraduate student in China, however, he had written a 48-page bachelor's thesis in Chinese with an English-language abstract. He had also helped another student write and translate her bachelor's thesis, though he explained that it was quite short, at only six pages.

During the time in his master's program, Paul's writing consisted primarily of course homework assignments. These assignments, many of which he shared with me, varied in purpose and structure, and included 7- to 10-page descriptions of algorithms, 1-page reviews of published articles, program source codes, and short answers to problem sets. Paul had also written one longer paper as an independent course project and a section of a conference paper submitted by colleagues in his research group.

Outside of school, Paul had written many reports in his internship position at a local computer company. Weekly reports summarized work completed on a regular basis, while longer design documentation reports summarized finished design projects, following a prescribed template for writing. Paul noted that this workplace writing differed from that completed in his graduate courses, primarily in terms of its overall focus or goal:

> I think the difference is between the research and the implementation. In the implementation, everything is on hand, and there's very little to think. But in the research, the most important part is to think, to find a way to solve the problem. In implementation, I mean the programming, there's just how to implement it, not the way. I mean, there's no uncertainty, I think. So, I think the difference is because the difference between research and implementation. (January 23, 2003)

From his own perspective, the workplace writing felt more "natural," requiring him only to write down what he had done to create a program. Academic writing, he believed, required more explanation and more focus on writing style:

> For example, I think in [a course project] paper, there's lots of statistics formula and theory, and not everybody have that background. So, I have to give a background, what's the paper, of a problem, and at least I think that's necessary for the people who are not familiar with statistics. And I will explain my idea step-by-step from the easiest thing to difficult. But for [workplace] documentation, I think that it's not necessary. I just write down what I did. I think it's obvious. Because I want to achieve this, so I do this. It's very obvious. There's no difficult algorithm,

no difficult theory. I think when I write some paper,
I think they also make things easier to understand.
But the documentation is just follow the format,
what you should say, what's not necessary. For paper,
there's- although there's also some format, but I think
how to organize the content is very free. The goal
is to make yourself understood [. . .] in the paper.
(January 23, 2003)

Prior to writing his master's thesis, then, Paul had experience with
a variety of writing tasks, engaging in school-based genres, workplace
genres, and a few research-based genres. The extent to which these
experiences corresponded or conflicted with the master's thesis task
would become more apparent throughout Paul's final year as a graduate student.

Finding a Focus

During the period of August through December of 2002, Paul had
not yet begun to work on his thesis, but he did participate in a variety
of other writing tasks in his English writing class (WCGS) and his
disciplinary content courses; some of these tasks would later come to
bear on his thesis-writing experience. By December, Paul had begun
to think ahead to his final semester in his master's program, and he
knew that the main task in front of him was the writing of his master's
thesis. His knowledge of the thesis at this stage was understandably
rather limited. He had "heard from somebody" that a thesis would be
30 to 40 pages in length, and he expressed some uncertainty about its
resemblance to other genres with which he was familiar:

> I think both part are new—the volume is high and I
> should have a lot of research work. It's like a report,
> but I think it's maybe similar to a paper, but not so
> formal. Actually, I have no idea! [laughing] (Decem-
> ber 12, 2002)

Paul expected that his advisor, Dr. Xu[7], would provide guidance in
the writing and researching process. As Paul stated, "I think he will
not help you to *write*" (December 12, 2002), but would instead provide feedback on the written drafts. Paul's understanding of the thesis-

writing process at this time was based on his experiences watching his advisor work with the doctoral students in the research group.

During the final semester of coursework in his master's program, Paul began thinking more concretely about his thesis. In late January, Dr. Xu helped shape Paul's thesis topic, suggesting an area that would be more practical than the work he would have done had he continued for a PhD. For the next few months, Paul conducted experiments in this area, gathering data and results so that he could begin writing. In this researching/pre-writing stage, Paul still had limited knowledge even of what a master's thesis looked like. He had read only a few theses and had some vague expectations of page length:

> Paul: But when I was in China, I read some theses written by Chinese student. I think that maybe there is some difference.
> Chris: The ones that you looked at in China, were they written in Chinese?
> Paul: Yeah. Only with a English abstract.
> Chris: You said that there might be some differences.
> Paul: I think that the difference is in China, I think the master's thesis is not so high quality. In U.S., I think most of the master's thesis is very high quality. Some of them can be published as paper. Oh yeah, I read a thesis before, written by Columbia University guy, and the volume is very big. I hope I can write a huge volume thesis, but my advisor told me 20 to 30 page. (April 2, 2003)

Although he said that this would be longest document he had written in English, he had the understanding that much of it would consist of the words of *other* writers:

> I think someone told me most of the contents should be the phrase of other papers. Only part of- maybe very small part of are written by myself. (April 2, 2003)

Transforming Knowledge

In mid-April, Paul began planning and organizing his thesis; the actual writing, and some of the remaining research, was conducted during the three-month period from May through the beginning of August. He wrote four drafts during this time period, receiving extensive feedback from his advisor on two of these (see Table 7.1).

Table 7.1. Paul's thesis drafts.

Draft	Time Period Written	Length in Pages	Written Feedback Received?
Draft 1	early May	24	No
Draft 2	early June	49	Yes
Draft 3	late June	54	Yes
Draft 4	late July	62	No

This period finds visible leaps in Paul's understanding of the genre and in academic discourse more generally. The most interesting aspect of Paul's development was the extent to which the various knowledge dimensions—formal, rhetorical, procedural, and subject-matter—became increasingly integrated over time. Below, I outline Paul's knowledge of specific generic and discursive elements, illustrating their increased interdependence during this writing-intensive period.

From Formality to Elegance

For Paul, one of the most salient features of the thesis genre was its style of language, and indeed this was an element with which he expressed a great lack of confidence. After completing his first draft, Paul described language style in much the way he had during WCGS—that is, primarily an issue of formality. In fact, Paul attributed some of his understanding of formality, and of style more generally, to his experience in WCGS, saying that it was the most useful content of the course:

> I think most useful thing [in WCGS] is how to make your sentences more formal. That's the most useful, appropriate word. And I . . . I think I used- to avoid duplicate sentence format. Like if I use "we can see,"

> I will not use "we can see" in the next sentence. (May 13, 2003)

Nevertheless, the issue of formality still posed difficulty for Paul, and he repeatedly returned to it when describing his writing:

> I think I encountered some problems to express my idea in English. I think in my thesis, everything should be formal, but what I first wrote down, always look like very informal. I have trouble with that. (May 13, 2003)

> Because I read lots of papers, they were written very formal. And I feel their way is very comfortable, but I do not feel the same way with my writing style. I don't know why. [*laughing*] Maybe it's . . . I don't know. Maybe it's just a feeling. (May 13, 2003)

Paul was able to identify specific sentences in his first draft that he felt were "not very good," but which he did not know how to revise. He also faced questions about certain features of formal writing, such as the use of "we" versus "I," a feature discussed in WCGS (see chapter 5):

> I don't know how if I- for my thesis, I use "we" as a pronoun. Because I think I did the work. If I write "I," it looks strange. Instead of that, I wrote "we" but I don't know. [. . .] Usually [publications] use "we" because there are several authors. But I think the only author for my thesis is me. Maybe I should write "I." (May 13, 2003)

Indeed, Paul's confusion is echoed in his infrequent and inconsistent pronoun usage in his first draft, where he manages to avoid using almost any first-person pronouns outside of the sections describing research procedures. In this draft, there are four instances of "our," four instances of "we," and one instance of "I." With the exception of one case, Paul used first-person pronouns only when describing research methods (e.g., "*The handheld device used in our experiments is a Compaq iPAQ . . .*" or " *. . . we measure the voltage on a small resistance . . .*").

Two drafts and six weeks later, Paul still expressed dissatisfaction with his writing, but he no longer articulated this dissatisfaction in terms of formality. Instead, he focused on features like redundant sentence structures and a general sense of style that he was unable to pinpoint:

> I keep thinking my writing style is very bad. I don't know why. Maybe it's not so bad, but I think that the sentence I write is ugly, it's just a repeated pattern from the previous one. I'm trying to write sentence more . . . I write sentence in some different style. I do not want to repeat the same style. But I cannot- what I can write down looks like what I usually write in email. Maybe looks a little bit formal, but the sentence is still not very good. That's my feeling. (June 26, 2003)

> I think there are two levels in writing in English. The first one is make others understand what you are saying. I am confident about this one. Second one is the others think your writing is good . . . how to say it . . . it's elegant. Elegant. I'm not confident about this one. You can see that I have no difficulty writing emails, but I have difficulty writing this formal technical report. (June 26, 2003)

By this point in time, Dr. Xu had written rather extensive feedback on the second and third drafts of Paul's thesis. While comments on the second draft focused on technical content and rhetorical structure, feedback on the third draft was primarily language related (see Table 7.2).

Table 7.2. Distribution of Dr. Xu's written feedback in drafts 2 and 3.

Area of Focus	Draft 2	Draft 3
Content	30%	17%
Organization	12	1
Audience	3	0
Purpose	3	0

Area of Focus	Draft 2	Draft 3
Language	0	65
Deleting phrases, sentences, or paragraphs	6	16
Format	27	1
Figure Design	18	0

Much of this feedback in fact served to restructure Paul's original writing. Specifically, Dr. Xu's revisions often changed the subject or agent within a clause or they altered the logical connection among clausal or phrasal elements (see Table 7.3).

Table 7.3. Sample revisions to language that restructured Paul's original expressions.

Revision Type	Paul's Original Text	Dr. Xu's Revisions
Logical connection	variable length of messages	messages of variable length
	. . . takes the 64-bit key and from it creates a set of sixteen 48-bit key blocks.	. . . creates a set of sixteen 48-bit key blocks based on the 64-bit key.
	Although using SHA-1 is more expensive than using MD5, the difference is quite small.	Using SHA-1 is more expensive than using MD5, but the difference is quite small.
Change of subject or agent	It can be concluded that . . .	We conclude that . . .
	The desktop server is a Dell Dimension 4100 which has a 1GHz P-III processor.	It communicates through a wireless LAN with a Dell Dimension 4100 desktop computer which has a 1GHz P-III processor.
	In this experiment, in order to justify that without compression, different types of data result in the same energy consumption, the compression of IPSec is disabled . . .	To verify this experimentally, we disable the compression . . .

As is evident in the examples, these revisions were often quite minor, but by restructuring Paul's phrases or sentences, the changes de-emphasized some elements in favor of others. In many of these cases, Dr. Xu changed passive constructions to active voice, adding "we" as the agent. Dr. Xu's apparent preference for active constructions and use of "we" provided Paul with guidance in formal conventions, an area in which he had been uncertain.

An additional focus of Dr. Xu's revisions to Paul's language was sentence boundaries. A substantial number of Dr. Xu's changes broke longer sentences into one or more shorter sentences, as in Figure 7.1. While it would not be surprising for Dr. Xu to shorten sentences that were originally lengthy, the changes were often made to sentences that were already quite short. Dr. Xu's preference for separating clauses into multiple sentences, therefore, may be a strategy for emphasizing certain technical content.

Paul's Original Text	Dr. Xu's Revisions
Before going into specific experiments on energy cost of IPSec, it is helpful to get some idea how significant the overhead of IPSec is under some given workload.	It is useful to present certain facts about its computation cost. This will help explain the focus of our energy-cost study in this thesis.
Each of these is used in turn at each of the 16 rounds of the cipher function which alters the plain text in accordance with the specifications of an S-Box.	Each of these blocks is used in one of the 16 rounds of the cipher function. Each round alters the plain text in accordance to the specifications of an S-Box.
Although 3DES is considered secure for now, it is quite slow.	3DES is considered secure at the present. However, it is quite slow.
Only three lines of assembly code is needed to send a signal, so the overhead of invoking the interrupt handler is quite small.	Only three lines of assembly code is needed to send a signal. Therefore, the overhead of invoking the interrupt handler is quite small.

Figure 7.1. Revisions made to Paul's sentence boundaries in Draft 3.

At the beginning of August 2003, with his final thesis draft in hand, Paul again reflected on his advisor's feedback on his third draft, describing Dr. Xu's revisions as "the proper way to describe the idea" (August 4, 2003). It seems as though Dr. Xu's focus on phrasing served to extend Paul's understanding of stylistic form beyond the issue of formality; unfortunately, Paul was unable to see exactly where his weaknesses were, having only a vague sense that his language style was inadequate.

What is notable is Paul's changing view of what language style entails. During this time period, he moves from viewing language use purely in terms of formality to a more complex notion of disciplinary style. While the latter view is much fuzzier in Paul's mind, it is at the same time more sophisticated and touches upon the notion of disciplinary discourse.

From Formal Organization to Rhetorical Structure

Organization posed difficulties for Paul from the very early stages of thesis writing, and he described it as the most difficult part of the writing task. One of the most striking changes in Paul's genre knowledge was his move from a primarily formal view of organization to a fully rhetorical view of generic structure. When he began work on the first draft of his thesis in April, Paul said that he spent a great deal of time reading papers and "thinking how to organize my results, how to organize my thesis, how many parts, how many sections there are" (May 13, 2003). He explained that this was the biggest challenge he had had up to that point, and that it would also be a challenge if he were to write in Chinese.

The organization that Paul decided on for his first draft was based on his goal of providing readers with sufficient background knowledge of the key concepts germane to his research. When asked how he had determined the overall structure of this draft, Paul explained:

> I think my objective is to make my thesis complete. Every concept in my experiment should be explained well in some introduction section. In my topic, I need to- this concepts include networking, some security, and [?]. Also, IPSec itself is very important. What is IPSec? So, for each of them I need to explain first what the concept is and what's the state of the art of that concept. After that, when I show the result about concept, it will not be strange to the reader. So, I think maybe to make my thesis readable, understandable, I decide the organization in my thesis. (May 13, 2003)

Looking at the organization of another master's thesis provided Paul with some ideas for organizing his own thesis. He explained to me that he was able to adopt largely the same organization as the sample he had looked at.

Paul spoke with me in some detail about the introduction in his first draft. The purpose of this section, he felt, was to provide a "high-level overview" of his topic. Drawing upon knowledge accrued through reading academic papers, Paul had built a sense of the purpose and appropriate length of this section:

> I think for the first part, it should be- they should not be too detailed information. And, it should not be more than one page. I read some papers, and I think they all have a very brief introduction, an overall view about the paper, about the topic. I think if some person didn't have time to go through my thesis, he can look at the abstract and introduction and get the idea. (May 13, 2003)

This comparison suggests that Paul noted a resemblance between the thesis genre and academic papers. With limited experience with thesis writing, he applied his knowledge of another genre that he perceived to be similar, though overgeneralizing some of the formal features to a different rhetorical situation.

After reading his first draft, Dr. Xu told Paul that the draft was "extremely terse." Paul interpreted this comment to mean that he needed to go into more detail. He believed that "mainly the volume is too short, but the contents of this thesis is pretty good" (May 13, 2003). In revising this first draft, Paul decided to expand the content but keep the organization largely the same. In fact, the second draft resembles the first draft in terms of overall organization. Much of the writing is identical, with the addition of information regarding two new experiments. When Dr. Xu read the second draft, he wrote extensive feedback, much of it focusing on organization.

Key suggestions from Dr. Xu appear on the first page of Paul's second draft (see Figure 7.2), where he advised re-organizing the thesis by integrating some of the background details into the experimental results rather than outlining them all in the beginning. He stressed the importance of showing the work's significance: "*It is boring to read IPSec details (which are other people's work) before understanding why one*

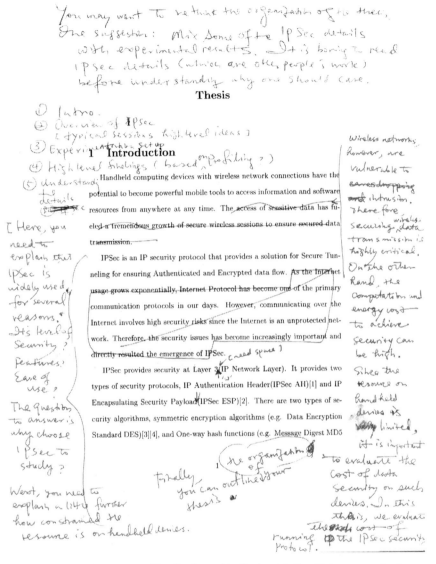

Figure 7.2. First page of Paul's thesis (draft 2), with Dr. Xu's written feedback.

should care." Elsewhere on the same page, Dr. Xu re-emphasized this point, writing, "*The question to answer is why choose IPSec to study?*"

Dr. Xu's comments prompted Paul to thoroughly revise his introduction, which increased from 291 words to 581 words. A comparison of these passages in the two drafts (see Appendices K and L) shows that Paul made the following revisions to the organization and content: (a) added a direct statement of the need for this research; (b) added the purpose of the research; (c) revised background details to provide a more general overview; (d) omitted details about IPSec security protocols and algorithms; (e) added metadiscourse to clarify the advantages and disadvantages; (f) added details about the use of IPSec on handheld devices; and (g) added a roadmap of the entire thesis.

When describing his organizational revisions, the changes in Paul's understanding of the rhetorical goals are evident. Whereas he previously had focused on building his readers' background knowledge, by late June he believed that readers would be interested in the *logic* of his thesis:

> The results will be important, but because what I was doing here was not new, it's just technical report, technical evaluation for some kind of new technique, I think what [readers] should care about is the logic of my thesis. If the way I explain it makes sense. Because the results should be correct. I just do it in a different environment, but the results should be correct. So the way I organize my results should make sense to them. *I should convince them my experiment is important for understanding this new technique.* (June 26, 2003, emphasis added)

Paul explained that understanding this goal of persuasion was what led him to add two more experiments after the first draft:

> For the first [draft], I think I just report some experimental results. It's not clear why I should go this way, why should people care about what I was doing. So I was trying to improve this by re-organizing it and adding two experiments. And I think now it follows the natural way to explain things. I first emphasized the importance of my research, why people should care about it. And then I give a high level of idea, what kind of problem people may encounter. And then I follow it step-by-step. First, this component, then the next. [. . .] This [third draft], I feel it should

be better, much better, than this [first draft]. In order to re-organize, I have to add more experiments, so that's one effort, but two gains! [*laughing*] (June 26, 2003)

In Paul's much-revised third draft, only three of Dr. Xu's comments focused on organization, all of these referring only to one- or two-sentence passages that Dr. Xu recommended moving to other (unspecified) locations in the thesis. Paul was able to respond to each of Dr. Xu's rather open-ended suggestions.

By August, with his thesis completed, Paul spoke about organization much differently than he had three months earlier. He now viewed organization as inextricably connected to both content and the rhetorical goals of the genre. In addition, he was able to extend this understanding to other similar genres:

> One thing I learned from this is when I wrote something quite long, I *must* make it *clear* that what I try to express is interesting to readers. I cannot just put lots of experimental results in my writing without explaining what's the importance of this result and why we should care about this experiment. (August 4, 2003)

> The volume is not so important. Even [if] I wrote only 10 pages, I would rather to say more about the background and the importance of my work than the numbers. Or maybe I can- I think it's okay to put every results in the appendix, because that part is not the most important thing. Yeah. I think- *I thought my advisor said it's important to let readers know what's the technical impact of your work.* For the first draft, it's really very hard to see why I did so many experiments. Or for this one- yeah, I think for this one, at least readers should have a feeling that my work is, somehow it's really not so significant, but it's better than nothing [*laughing*]. (August 4, 2003, emphasis added)

If I were to write something in the future, I will first introduce the background clearer before I go ahead to other parts. It is like a process of convincing people, and the whole thing should be very- like a story. It's a complete story. It has some other part needed, and the reader should not feel foreign when he is reading my writing. I think, for example, in my first draft, which is 10 pages long, I just state the fact and the result I got without giving solid evidence why it's important. *And so I was likely to be questioned by readers why we should care about your work.* If I got a defense based on my first draft, I'm going to be in big trouble! (August 4, 2003, emphasis added)

At several points in our final interview, Paul returned to this notion of convincing readers of the importance of his work. He conceded that he had "seldom consider[ed] this an issue before," but that he thought that he would think about this in the future when writing "similar things to convince people, like a proposal" (August 4, 2003).

One strategy used to convince readers of a work's significance, and also to help guide them through a document as lengthy as a thesis, is metadiscourse. Particularly in Draft 3, many of Dr. Xu's written revisions added or deleted metadiscourse, particularly in the form of frame markers that illustrate sequencing (e.g., *first, next*) and announce goals (e.g., *we focus on . . . , for this thesis . . .*). While Paul had added some metadiscoursal devices to his third draft on his own, including an outline of the thesis chapters, Dr. Xu's subsequent feedback included 19 comments related to metadiscourse. Four of these revisions actually deleted sequencing markers that Paul had written—*first, second, then,* and *finally*—suggesting that Dr. Xu perceived an overuse of these forms (see Figure 7.3). In addition, Dr. Xu added 11 instances of metadiscourse used to announce the goals of the text or to directly state the significance of the work (see Figure 7.4).

In our discussions, Paul never explicitly referred to these overt markers of sequencing or goals, but he did implicitly describe the need to clarify the logic of the thesis for readers. Even when working on his final draft, Paul explained that the issue of organization still posed difficulty for him because of the sheer volume of text with which he had to contend:

> The overhead comes from the fact that IP stack must be either changed or extended. [First,] authenticate and encrypt/decrypt packet are expensive operations that increase the delay. [Second,] adding headers on IP packets for authentication and encryption increases the size of IP packets, which in turn may lower the effective bandwidth.

Figure 7.3. Sample from Paul's text in which Dr. Xu deleted two sequence markers.

> Therefore *it is important to evaluate* the resource, especially . . .
>
> *For this thesis, we focus* on the Transport mode only . . .
>
> The facts *reported in this section* are collected using . . .
>
> Hence, these numbers strongly suggest that *we must focus our attention on* . . .

Figure 7.4. Examples of metadiscourse announcing goals (in italics) incorporated into Paul's third draft by Dr. Xu.

> As the volume gets larger and larger, it's more and more difficult to keep it straightforward, keep the organization clear. I think that- what I read my thesis, I always read- when I read later parts, I always forgot what I said in previous parts. So, it's very hard for me, even [though] it's written by me. (June 26, 2003)

The metadiscourse written by Dr. Xu provided one tool for navigating the lengthy text—for both Paul and his readers. At the same time, this tool did not seem to be overtly recognized by Paul. Because he incorporated nearly all of Dr Xu's written comments when revising his thesis, and because this was the last writing that I saw of Paul's, there is no way to know whether or not Paul would implement this particular writing strategy in future tasks.

Building Subject-Matter Expertise
and a Researcher Identity

As Paul worked through the various stages of writing his master's thesis, he moved gradually toward expertise in his subject matter. This
move is relatively easy to trace in his interviews from January through
August of 2003. During this seven-month period, Paul gradually depended less and less on his advisor as he made independent decisions
in his research and became more confident in his own knowledge of
his topic.

Dr. Xu was in fact responsible for pointing Paul in the direction of
a thesis topic in late December of 2002, recommending a topic that
would be manageable in the given time period. Paul explained that
Dr. Xu recommended he work on something "concrete" because such
work would be easy to present in a thesis and would also be useful
research. Although Paul had some experience with the instruments
and methods he would use in this research, the topic area was new.
After a month of working in this new area, Paul was frustrated with
his progress. Nevertheless, Dr. Xu encouraged him to continue his
work, suggesting to Paul that "there's something valuable" (February
26, 2003).

By early April, Paul was still concerned about the value of his research, saying that, "I'm afraid my thesis will not be very deep as an
experimental thesis," but he was again reassured by his advisor that
"it's okay for a master's thesis" (April 2, 2003). At this time, Paul began
reading up on the topic and planning the written part of his thesis task.
During this planning stage, Paul realized that his topic area—Internet
protocol security—was too broad and he would need to focus it much
more. He decided that he would concentrate on energy consumption
and cryptography algorithms. But after narrowing the topic and preparing a first draft, Dr. Xu's comment (that the thesis was "terse") led
Paul to believe that he needed more detail. At this point, he made a
key decision on his own:

> I think the first draft I only handle some cryptogra-
> phy algorithms. I do not mention how to reduce the
> energy cost on transmission. I think that's the reason
> I decided to add two more big experiments. [. . .]
> *What I feel good is I can find out what's the deficiency,*
> *what's the flaw in my thesis.* What should I improve.

> Yeah. Otherwise, I cannot make this one twice lon-
> ger than the previous one. [. . .] Because all of this
> experiment I newly added, it's all I think should be
> done. It's not from my advisor's comment. (June 26,
> 2003, emphasis added)

Paul clearly had a feeling of success at this decision to add these two
experiments. He later described the decision as a "hunch" that in the
end helped him understand his work more clearly:

> [my understanding of the research] has improved be-
> cause *after I wrote down this introduction, I began to
> realize the real important things inside here, not the su-
> perficial experimental results.* I think it's very strange
> why I should start this experiment at the first place
> without knowing the importance. I think that's be-
> cause- maybe because I wanted to do more work, so
> that way I can put more materials in my thesis. But
> I was very lucky that my work was not wasted. They
> are all helpful for my research. So I think my hunch
> is good. Yeah, I feel what may be important, so I go
> ahead with that. (August 4, 2003, emphasis added)

Just days before depositing his final thesis, Paul explained that he now
had a "much better understanding of my subject" (August 4, 2003).

At the same time that Paul was becoming a more independent
researcher, he seemed to wrestle with his own researcher identity.
Throughout the thesis-writing process, Paul referred to himself as a
novice, and described the extent to which he relied on the work of
others:

> I read some papers including some good comments
> on the current data from IPSec and the handheld de-
> vices, so I borrowed their ideas, maybe paraphrased
> them to write down in my thesis. But I think I can-
> not think anything better idea about this. They are
> experts. I am a beginner. (May 13, 2003)

At the same time, Paul realized that he likely had more knowledge
of his research than the members of his thesis committee, who had
been selected by his advisor. Though always aware of his status as a

relative newcomer, Paul felt quite confident with his subject-matter knowledge by the time of his oral defense:

> My defense is the easiest part of the whole process [*laughing*]. Because I think after I did so much work on my thesis, I have- I would say the . . . adequate knowledge about my research. It's difficult for others who are questioning me about some technical details-of course, they can question me about some high-level things, like the importance of my work, but after this draft, I was prepared for that kind of question. So, really, I didn't encounter very difficult questions during my defense. (August 4, 2003)

INFLUENCES ON GENRE KNOWLEDGE DEVELOPMENT

During the 11 months in which I worked with Paul, I watched his knowledge of the thesis genre grow from just a vague sense of length to a fully rhetorical understanding of presenting research effectively to his readers. Paul's first draft and his interviews from January through May illustrate his nascent—yet evolving—knowledge of the thesis structure and subject, as he learned to focus his topic, expand his research, and recount all necessary background knowledge to guide his readers clearly through his work. Later drafts and interviews show an increasingly sophisticated understanding of the genre, as Paul began to grapple with issues such as illustrating the significance of his research, convincing readers of this significance, and articulating his work in an elegant and expert manner. That is to say, Paul was moving *toward* the kind of genre knowledge that is characteristic of expert genre users.

Paul's knowledge development was gradual, but visible. In response to this high-stakes task, he marshaled his resources and adopted multiple strategies to approach the task to the best of his ability. Mentoring from Dr. Xu led Paul to his topic area and provided reassurances that his research would be both valuable and appropriate for a master's thesis. Much of his initial understanding of form, as well as subject-matter content, was influenced by his exposure to other research genres. Paul was explicitly aware of structures common to these research genres, and he drew upon this awareness as he organized and wrote his initial draft:

Paul: . . . because I have to read lots of papers, maybe
I caught some feelings from those papers. Some
of those papers are written very good. I think,
maybe I can borrow some ideas there. Even some
sentence [*laughing*].
Chris: How did you decide, like, if you borrow sentences—
Paul: I just feel the way *they* wrote is much better than I
could, so instead of paraphrase those sentences,
I just borrow them here. Of course I include the
reference. (August 4, 2003)

On the desk, I put several papers related to my topic.
On the screen, I put several papers there. So, I look at
this and this, and I put them together, select the best
of them . . . [*laughing*] (May 13, 2003)

I read the other student's thesis. I think- because he
has *two* topics, so his organization is different from
mine. He first divides the thesis into two parts, one
for each topic. Still, with each topic, I think the organization is very similar to mine. But he also has a
overall conclusion. (May 13, 2003)

For Paul, these other texts served an important resource.

When writing his first draft, Paul focused on linguistic rather than
rhetorical elements. He described his writing process as slow and concentrated on language:

I pay attention to every word I use. For a report like
this [course project], I didn't. I think maybe informal
is okay for this kind of report, but it's not okay for my
thesis. I want it to be perfect. (May 13, 2003)

As he wrote both the first and second drafts, Paul seemed to be at
least somewhat influenced by his experiences in WCGS. He thought
about language use in terms of formality and sentence variation, two
topics from the course that had stuck in his head. At the same time, he
expressed frustration at not being able to apply other ideas that he had
learned: "I think I should use the idea I learned from that class, but
what's the specific idea, I cannot remember now" (May 13, 2003).

In later drafts, Paul's feedback from his advisor took on primary importance, influencing Paul's understanding of the genre. Situating himself as a novice and his advisor as an expert, Paul repeatedly referred to his advisor's knowledge and experience. Although Paul made many independent choices—in both his research and the writing of his research—he nearly always followed the advice of Dr. Xu when it was available. The social status and symbolic capital of a master's student relative to his advisor surely explain the importance of Dr. Xu's feedback to some extent. Dr. Xu had both more academic and linguistic capital than Paul—a fact that Paul frequently referred to—making it unsurprising that Paul would defer to his advisor. But other factors may also explain why Paul almost never countered Dr. Xu's advice when revising. Paul's lack of interest in academic research and preference for "concrete" work with practical applications were in conflict with the type of academic writing required in his master's thesis:

> Paul: I personally do not want— I don't like [the] research area.
> Chris: It's not your interest?
> Paul: No. I prefer industry style. To build something, not *purely* theoretical. There should be- it's better to involve more realistic things. [. . .] This [thesis] is kind of theoretical, although there is no *real* theory there. But the conclusion is still hard to be employed by real product . . . So, I'd rather to build something more realistic. Develop some benefit from this product. This one [the thesis], this is just research work. Only research people benefit from it. But it's— I admit that it's a required process. Maybe in the future it can be employed. Maybe me or other people can take advantage of this. (August 4, 2003)

It is possible that if Paul had intended to become an academic researcher, or at the very least to continue on for a doctoral degree, he would have questioned more of Dr. Xu's advice and suggestions, rather than integrating them rather mechanically. Certainly, time pressures were also a factor, as Paul himself noted on numerous occasions. As his final deadline approached, Paul felt that he had no choice but to simply incorporate his advisor's suggestions, even when he did not understand how they differed from his own writing:

> I doubt about some changes. I think the original way
> I wrote was fine, but maybe I'm not sure if the modi-
> fication is better than my way. But I just followed the
> instruction. (August 4, 2003)

In addition to the influences of his advisor's feedback and the extensive reading he did for his research, Paul saw "practice" to be important in improving his writing in his thesis. That is, he felt the very act of writing—and writing a lot—was instrumental in developing his skills. In our final interview, Paul said he felt much more confident in writing than he had at the start of my study, and he credited his thesis:

> I feel more confident. Yeah. Yeah, this [thesis] is the
> source of my confidence. I can finish this, so why not
> others? [. . .] Without this one, I can hardly tell if my
> writing ability fulfill the requirement of my further
> development- in my future career, maybe I probably I
> need to do this kind of task. (August 4, 2003)

It is important to emphasize that Paul felt that much of what he learned through writing his thesis could be extended to writing in other genres and discourses. While the master's thesis served as a culmination of Paul's academic education, he also saw it as a pathway into future writing tasks.

Paul's knowledge development, while unique and situated within a very local context, also shares similarities with other advanced multilingual—and monolingual—writers. Like other writers, Paul both wanted and used the feedback of his advisor (Dong, 1998; Leki, 2006b). In the absence of feedback or other mentoring interactions— or perhaps to augment these—written texts became important sources of information. Turning to samples of the target genre or related genres can help writers build a general frame or schema for the genre they are approximating (Beaufort, 1999; Gentil, 2005). And, crucially, immersion into the world of disciplinary practice provides writers with these social and textual interactions, as well as the important subject-matter knowledge that are all central to carrying out the genre. So, while Paul's story is in many ways unique to him, it echoes the central influences on genre knowledge found in multiple case studies of disciplinary and professional writers.

8 Writing for/in a Discipline: First Forays into the Larger Research World

As Paul's story shows, some tasks seem to exert more force than others, pushing writers into new domains where they must write for new readers for new purposes. Some writers, like Paul, will invest more in the task, drawing on more resources and implementing more strategies to build a richer view of the genre at hand. This "richer view" is characterized by an integration of formal knowledge, rhetorical knowledge, process knowledge, and subject-matter knowledge. Paul's story illustrates how mentoring and feedback play an important role in integrating genre knowledge dimensions.

In this chapter, I consider two additional resources for building genre knowledge: participation in increasingly complex genre networks and adoption of shifting roles and agencies within those networks. These resources are not available to all writers—in my research, only Chatri, the sole doctoral student, worked at a level of disciplinary participation that allowed him access to such resources. Nevertheless, these are important resources that are likely to characterize the learning of other writers in similar settings, such as workplace writers or other new researchers.

Chatri's roles within his disciplinary community differed in many ways from Paul's. Having already earned a master's degree and having worked full-time in a research lab in his home country, Chatri had been an active researcher for several years by the time I met him. After completing his graduate coursework, his principal focus was to search for a research problem that would be valuable enough to take him from "student" to "candidate" status. He frequently spoke of the importance of finding a good problem to study and of presenting and publishing work as a graduate student. He knew that the path to graduation was metaphorically paved with research genres and that the research paper was of primary importance.

In our meetings, Chatri repeatedly focused on the conference paper as the most valued type of research paper in his area. He explained that, while journal articles had a more rigorous review process, conference papers tended to be more cutting edge as they could be presented and published in proceedings relatively quickly. In fact, Chatri claimed to approach any research paper as if it were a conference paper in terms of overall structure; it was, in a sense, the foundational research genre for him. I was able to trace Chatri's changing knowledge of research genres, including conference papers and the other "satellite" genres, through the texts that he wrote and interacted with over a four-year period (see Table 8.1).

Table 8.1. Chatri's Conference-Related Research Writing.

Paper	Task Description	Rhetorical Context	Time Period Written
Paper #1	Conference paper	Submitted to a conference	February-March 2000
Paper #2	Conference paper	Submitted to a conference in Thailand, based on the submitted proposal above	June-August 2000
WCGS Proposal	Conference proposal	Written for WCGS	November-December 2002
Paper #3	Internal research paper	Written at request of supervisor to organize and synthesize research to date	June-August 2003
Paper #4	Conference paper	Submitted to an international conference in robotics	October-November 2003
Paper #5	Conference paper	Submitted to an international conference in robot vision	March-April 2004

I begin this chapter by illustrating changes in Chatri's knowledge of the conference/research paper genre through his texts and our oral interviews. After showing his growing sense of rhetorical awareness and the ways in which this awareness informed his written text, I explore the ways in which genre networks and changing roles and agencies pushed Chatri beyond nascent knowledge into an intermediary level of expertise.

Tracing Textual-Rhetorical Changes

Far from being "blank slates," writers enter any generic encounter with attitudes, preferences, and personal senses of who they are and how they want to portray themselves in writing. But for those learning new genres, writing is not simply a matter of expressing these tastes and identities but also learning *how* to do so effectively. In Chatri's process of learning the *how*, he turned to rhetorical strategies like claiming significance and credibility along with an evolving sense of self as a member of a disciplinary community.

Novelty and Contribution in Claims of Significance

As Chatri faced greater exigencies for writing—knowing that he had to present or publish work in order to graduate—he focused increasingly on his work's value and significance. He began to see over time that expert writers adopted various discursive tools for showing their work's significance, and he spoke frequently of the importance of "novelty" and "contribution," rhetorical elements that underlie claims of significance in the fields of engineering (Hyland, 2000). To build significance claims, researchers must not only show how their work is situated within existing knowledge frameworks, but also that the work extends that knowledge in a new and valuable way, contributing to the advancement of the discipline (Kaufer & Geisler, 1989). Tracing Chatri's significance claims over time reveals his increasingly sophisticated grasp of the notion of novelty and how it may be expressed in writing.

Chatri's early papers from Thailand lack explicit reference to the novelty or contribution of his work. Taking an indirect approach, Chatri's first paper expresses novelty by focusing on the paucity of prior work, thereby situating his own work as new:

> *For the previous work about Thai sentence extraction,* **we found only one publication** *[Longchupole 1995] presents the method of splitting Thai sentences from paragraph.* (Paper #1, Spring 2000)

This statement is the closest that Chatri gets to an explicit reference to the novelty of his work in Paper #1. Readers must infer the newness of his work from the lack of previous research on the topic. Paper #2, also written in Thailand, draws a somewhat clearer connection between the prior work and his work. Here, Chatri shows the limits of prior research and then situates his own work within those limitations, identifying a niche and immediately occupying it:

> *After having reviewed the approaches which have been successfully applied for English or other languages text-to-speech synthesis (TTS),* **we found that they can not be applied directly for the Thai language. In this work, we focus our research on handling the unique characteristics of Thai** *for improving the naturalness of our Thai TTS system.* (Paper #2, Summer 2000)

While this claim in Paper #2 is more explicit than that in the previous paper, it still lacks any evidence of the work's significance. In other words, readers are told that the work is new, but they are still left without any direct statement or proof of its importance.

As he reflected on Paper #2 in an interview, Chatri noted that its key weakness lay in the research itself. Even at the time of writing this paper, Chatri admitted that he felt the research was weak:

> This work has no key research. [. . .] In English there is some well done research in this. It's all done. But we just try to apply that technique to our language. So there is nothing interesting except it's our language. So, when I read it, it seem that this paper have no key point, key idea in the research. So, I don't know how to change this writing, except change the research work. [*laughing*] (December 16, 2003)

When I pressed him to consider how he might revise this paper now, Chatri explained that the text needed to show the motivation for the research, describing specifically why the work was important.

Nearly two years after Paper #2 had been written, Chatri found himself in the U.S. writing a conference proposal for WCGS (the proposal described in chapter 4). Although a proposal differs from a full-length conference paper, it still requires that writers emphasize a work's significance to readers. At this stage in his writing development, however, Chatri continued to struggle with this rhetorical task; his strategy for expressing novelty in this task was simply to compare his approach to that used in previous studies:

> *The clustering in the eigenspace is carried out by using the Koontz-Fukunaga non parametric clustering algorithm **instead of** the K-means clustering algorithm used in [1–3].* (WCGS Proposal, November 2002)

The significance claim here is relatively subtle, relying on the reader to evaluate the extent to which this alternative approach is in fact new. In addition, there is again no real explanation of the motivation for the research, a point that Chatri noted when re-reading the proposal one year after it had been written.

Chatri's WCGS proposal suggests a nascent rhetorical understanding of the conference submission task. At this time, he was still uncertain as to how conference proposals and papers were evaluated by reviewers. After some hesitation, he identified four criteria that he thought might be used to evaluate the work: "originality," "contribution," "results," and clarity of the writing (December 2, 2002). However, he was unable to describe these criteria in any depth, explaining that he had had very little experience with this genre.

Several months later, in the summer of 2003, when he had completed his graduate coursework, Chatri's supervisor (a postdoctoral student in his research group, whom I'll call "Roberto") suggested that he write up the research he had been working on for the past several months. The purpose of this internal research paper (Paper #3), in Chatri's words was to "organize the ideas[s]" (August 29, 2003) that he had been working on, including the large amount of literature that he had read. Although the text was at least twice as long as a typical conference paper in his field, Chatri wrote the paper in the form of a conference paper, as he understood it at that time. His writing in his paper displays more explicit attempts to address the evaluation criteria that he perceived to be important—most particularly, the notion of novelty:

> *By virtue of the above advantages, we would like **to de-**
> ***velop** the 3D rigid object pose estimation algorithms
> that use the AAM-based object localization as a core
> component.* (Paper #3, Summer 2003)

Here, Chatri links his work directly to the advantages of the AAM approach—an approach that he has reviewed in the previous paragraph (using the introductory clause "*By virtue of the above advantages . . .*"). In doing so, he provides motivation for his work and situates it as an extension of prior research in the field. In the latter half of the sentence, he stresses his goal of *development* of a new algorithm, using a verb whose very meaning implies novelty. Following this sentence, the paper details Chatri's proposed approach and then completes the paragraph with a summary that directly states his work's contribution:

> *Particularly **our contribution in this work is to (i)**
> **propose the feasible approaches** to use AAM in esti-
> mating the 3D rigid object pose, (ii) report the experi-
> mental results obtained from the workspace that simu-
> lates from the real and practical application.* (Paper #3,
> Summer 2003)

The decision to write the contribution statement in such direct language was influenced by Chatri's reading of another paper (written by a member of his research group) that included a similar expression. He found the explicit references to contribution useful as a reader and thought they might help persuade reviewers of the work's importance:

> [Some papers] will say what is the- for example, "The
> contribution of this paper is . . ." and they will say
> something that no one ever proposed before, some-
> thing like that. So that, okay, when the reviewer see
> [it, he or she thinks], "Ah! I understand what you
> mean!"[. . .] I think normally we have to put some-
> thing like that. [. . .] I think the good paper should
> state clearly what is the contribution, what is the nov-

elty. I think the first thing is the novelty in this area.
That's very hard for me. (September 12, 2003)

Chatri in fact emphasized the importance of novelty several times after having written this paper. He discussed at length the intertwined
relationship of novelty and contribution, and he explained that as he
now wrote, he repeatedly considered how to illustrate these concepts
to his readers:

> I think that to write a paper in this area, I think one
> thing we should have is the novelty. If we have nov-
> elty, [it's] very easily to present the data for that. For
> example, in the first paragraph [?], "*The contribution
> of this paper is . . ..*" "Contribution" it means the nov-
> elty that is provide in this paper. It's not difficult,
> right? But in this paper, it seems that the novelty of
> this paper is 5% because I just- I didn't propose the
> new technique, just bring those technique [and] put
> it in my work, so that the motivation is not too much.
> I try to- I think when I write conference paper, I'm
> thinking about that- how to present so that even [if]
> my paper is bad make it just not good. I will think
> about this. Right now, I'm thinking about this. I'm
> not sure that I will get accept or not. I have to find
> a way to present what is the contribution, for exam-
> ple. I mean, the novelty. Not think about the novelty
> too much, but maybe the contribution. In contribu-
> tion, there is something novelty. Something like that.
> (September 12, 2003)

This was in fact the first point at which Chatri had begun using the
term *novelty*, and it had already become a key consideration for him.
At the same time, it remained somewhat elusive, and Chatri expressed
difficulty defining it. After much thought, Chatri was able to pinpoint
an important parameter of novelty, which is to illustrate the novelty
of one's work by using the backdrop of current literature (Kaufer &
Geisler, 1989):

> . . . novelty is something is- just someone don't do
> something like this before. [. . .] But no one may
> think about that, but never published. But you had

> to work hard in the literature survey to, okay, make
> sure that may think about that, but never published.
> You show that no one do something like that. [. . .
>] Suppose there is some formula, some mathematical
> formula we have to devise, and in the division, we
> just change two or three [?]. And maybe we get an-
> other result that may be better or equivalent. I think
> that we can call that, it's novelty. *Because novelty is
> based on another work.* (September 12, 2003, empha-
> sis added)

Chatri further elaborated that a definition of novelty depends on the reader—specifically, he explained that a reader who is unfamiliar with the research problem may be more likely to find the work novel. Paper #3 then instantiates Chatri's growing awareness of this notion and how it informs formal features of the genre.

The development of Chatri's claims of significance between Paper #3 and Paper #4 is striking. In contrast to Paper #3, which was written for an unspecified audience, Paper #4 was submitted to an interna- tional conference. In this paper, Chatri includes a very explicit state- ment of the gap in prior work:

> *However* **none has tried to apply the AAM tech-
> nique for the robot vision area especially for** *track-
> ing rigid object pose in 6 DOF which the accuracy is the
> major requirement.* (Paper #4, Fall 2003)

When I asked Chatri why he had written such a direct statement of the research gap, he pointed to the importance of convincing the reviewer that his paper had something to contribute to the field:

> This is the key point of my paper. Because I know
> that my work is just extension of the idea AAM, and,
> as I told you, when we wrote the paper, we have to
> find some contribution, right? [. . .] But maybe the
> idea is, okay, no one tried to use [AAM] in the robot
> vision area. Then maybe the reviewer, "Oh!" I want
> the reviewer to agree with me that this paper should
> be got accept because if somebody in robot vision
> area never know this, why don't we inject this paper
> to those guys?! (December 16, 2003)

The sentence above also serves as an important link between the literature survey and Chatri's own work—a discursive strategy that he had not employed in his earlier writing. After this explicit statement of the gap in research, Chatri immediately situates his own work within this niche, as follows:

> *Therefore, in this work, we would like to **propose a feasible way to applied the AAM technique** to tackle the problem of object pose tracking in 6 DOF and verify to see if their accuracy is good enough for using in the vision-based industrial robot control system. In particular, **our contribution in this paper is to** propose two different pose tracking algorithms based on Active Appearance Model (AAM) and then report the results which are performed in the workspace that simulates from the real/practical situation (the assembly line).*
> (Paper #4, Fall 2003)

Using the connective *"therefore"* further serves to position his work as a logical outcome of the research gap, persuading readers of the work's motivation and contribution.

Despite Chatri's best effort to showcase his contribution in the excerpts shown here, Roberto later deleted the explicit statement (" . . . *our contribution is . . .*") when revising the paper with Chatri. Although Chatri was unsure exactly why this change was made, he suspected that including the contribution statement up front might prevent the reviewer from reading the whole paper and was thus a risky strategy. The expression did not appear in Chatri's second international conference submission, Paper #5. Instead, in this paper, Chatri stresses novelty lexically (through *"new"*) and through direct comparisons with previous research. These strategies are especially prominent in the introduction:

> *In this paper, **we propose a new method** that combines a sparse 3D model with multiple appearance models to accurately estimate the 6 DOF pose of objects. **Unlike the range maps in [3], our 3D model is very simple** and can be created using a few mouse clicks on a pair of stereo images. However, despite the simplicity of this 3D model, **our method provides means to** deal with both*

> *partial and self occlusion with high accuracy—typically*
> *a few millimetres in translation and less than one degree*
> *in rotation. Besides, **unlike the work in [17]**, which*
> *handles both self and partial occlusion using a robust*
> *estimation, **our method allows** self and partial occlu-*
> *sion to be treated **more robustly** by doing it separately.*
> (Paper #5, Spring 2004)

But Chatri's understanding of contribution and novelty in this paper were also heavily wrapped up in a more complicated sense of audience. Because the conference was organized by a leader in the field of computer vision, the person who had established the model on which Chatri's own word was based, Chatri considered this individual as his primary audience. Chatri saw the work in Paper #5 as an extension of that in Paper #4—but he was not sure that the reviewers would see it as a real extension of the original model. He commented:

> I know that if I submit this to British Machine Vi-
> sion, I think . . . the guy who invent the concept of
> AAM will read this paper, and he will say, "Oh! Do
> you think that it's [an] extension? I think it's a slight
> extension! [*laughing*] Okay, reject it!" (March 16,
> 2004)

A look at Chatri's significance claims over time (bolded below) reveals increasingly more explicit attempts to illustrate novelty and contribution. As the subtlety of his early writing gives way to more overt statements of his work's significance, Chatri appears to hold a keener sense of the accepted strategies for convincing readers that his work has value—even when he himself lacks confidence in this value:

> *For the previous work about Thai sentence extraction,*
> ***we found only one publication** [Longchupole 1995]*
> *presents the method of splitting Thai sentences from*
> *paragraph.* (Paper #1, spring 2000)

> *After having reviewed the approaches which have been*
> *successfully applied for English or other languages text-*
> *to-speech synthesis (TTS), **we found that they can***
> ***not be applied directly for the Thai language. In***
> ***this work, we focus our research on handling the***

unique characteristics of Thai for improving the naturalness of our Thai TTS system. (Paper #2, summer 2000)

The clustering in the eigenspace is carried out by using the Koontz-Fukunaga non parametric clustering algorithm instead of the K-means clustering algorithm used in [1–3]. (WCGS Proposal, November 2002)

By virtue of the above advantages, we would like to develop the 3D rigid object pose estimation algorithms that use the AAM-based object localization as a core component. (Paper #3, summer 2003)

Particularly our contribution in this work is to (i) propose the feasible approaches to use AAM in estimating the 3D rigid object pose, (ii) report the experimental results obtained from the workspace that simulates from the real and practical application. (Paper #3, summer 2003)

However none has tried to apply the AAM technique for the robot vision area especially for tracking rigid object pose in 6 DOF which the accuracy is the major requirement. (Paper #4, fall 2003)

Therefore, in this work, we would like to propose a feasible way to applied the AAM technique to tackle the problem of object pose tracking in 6 DOF and verify to see if their accuracy is good enough for using in the vision-based industrial robot control system. In particular, our contribution in this paper is to propose two different pose tracking algorithms based on Active Appearance Model (AAM) and then report the results which are performed in the workspace that simulates from the real/practical situation (the assembly line). (Paper #4, fall 2003)

In this paper, we propose a new method that combines a sparse 3D model with multiple appearance models to accurately estimate the 6 DOF pose of objects. Unlike the range maps in [3], our 3D model is very simple and can be created using a few mouse clicks on a pair of stereo images. However, despite the simplicity of this 3D model, **our method provides means to** deal with both partial and self occlusion with high accuracy—typically a few millimetres in translation and less than one degree in rotation. Besides, **unlike the work in [17],** which handles both self and partial occlusion using a robust estimation, **our method allows** self and partial occlusion to be treated **more robustly** by doing it separately. (Paper #5, spring 2004)

Chatri's struggle with this element of writing was clearly bound up with many other features of context and identity. To illustrate his perspective at the end of my research—just a month before he completed his oral defense of his preliminary exam—I quote Chatri here at length:

Chatri: I think my advisor is very good, and he will teach me a lot in writing, in presenting the idea, in how to present the idea. But I think he will not teach me how to invent the idea. *That's* the problem. Because he always say that, you know what, how to present the idea is important. But I want to tell him, but I'm scared, "Why don't you tell me how to invent the idea?" [*laughing*] That's, in my idea, I think it's also *important* for the PhD, also, how to invent the idea. But I cannot learn that skill from my advisor. Or my advisor don't tell me. That's why.

Chris: So you still have that idea that, "my work is not that good"?

Chatri: Always. Until maybe I have some- Oh, this I found out, something like that. If you saw the movie *Beautiful Mind?* Something like John Nash finds that idea during in the pub, right? And then he can finish within, I think, his thesis only less than 50 pages. And he can finish in one year after he had that idea.

Chris: Yeah. So, is that the kind of feedback that you-
I mean how do you know when your work is
good?

Chatri: I don't know. I still don't have that idea. I try to
find, but you know what? To have a really great
idea is a complicated process. There is no methodology to come up with that, right? It's creative. Sometimes it comes up accidentally. I don't
know.
[. . .]
It seems that, okay, I know, let's say three years
ago, I didn't know many things in this field. But
after I read more and more and especially when
I write down the literature survey [Paper #3], the
picture about the relevant work that's related to
my current work is more clear. I mean clearer
right now. So it seems that, if you think about
that, it's still- I have more confidence about my
work. But to graduate, I have to give more contribution about that idea.

Chris: Contribution to the field?

Chatri: Yes, to the community, to the computer vision
community, something like that. I still trying.
[*laughing*] (June 25, 2004)

Wrestling with Identities: Self-Identity and the Selling of Research

In promoting their research, expert writers portray themselves as credible researchers who are knowledgeable in their subject area, framing
their work to highlight its value, importance, and novelty. Chatri's
early difficulties in displaying the novelty of his work illustrate the
extent to which such claims are closely wrapped up in the writer's personal sense of identity. Even when researchers *know* the rhetorical tools
used to promote their work, they may feel tension between what they
perceive to be "effective rhetoric" and what they feel more accurately
represents their own sense of self. Community newcomers, like graduate students, often have particular difficulty with this, as they may
face more self-doubts about their own credibility or legitimacy as full-
fledged members of the research community.

The issue of credibility first came up in our discussions when Chatri asked me to clarify the term *ethos* after it had been used in the WCGS classroom during the genre analysis unit. At this time in November 2002, Chatri seemed to hold a fairly narrow understanding of what it means to build credibility as a writer, seeing it merely as explicit statements of one's ability to conduct research:

> Actually, I didn't like this kind of writing so much, because, okay, so you show you are good. But, I don't like that kind of people to tell that. Okay, I'm good, I'm good. I think everyone will decide that this guy's good or not by his work or his experience, and that's it. You don't have to show that, okay, think I'm good enough to- Just show, okay, what is your publication, your qualification? Everything will be imply from that. (November 8, 2002)

In fact, researcher credibility may be promoted through various strategies, including illustrating the researcher's disciplinary knowledge base, stressing the positive elements of the work, and pointing to limits in prior work.

Displaying Disciplinary Knowledge. Writers display their disciplinary knowledge through strategies like referencing key works, explicitly appealing to shared knowledge, and hinting at the vastness of their own knowledge (Dong, 1996; Giltrow & Valiquette, 1994; Hyland, 2000). Over time, Chatri learned to use these strategies to claim an insider status that often belied his own sense of self as "just a PhD student."

Textual citations are used for multiple purposes, the most pragmatic of which is to acknowledge and reference the work of others. But citations also serve to illustrate the writer's familiarity with well known or pioneering works, to align the writer with particular orientations, or even to promote the writer's own previous work, as in the case of self-citation. Chatri's use of citations in his introduction sections increased over time, as illustrated in Figure 8.1.

During my study, Chatri illustrated an understanding of these various functions of citations. When discussing his conference proposal for WCGS in December 2002 (not included in Figure 8.1), he explained that including some references was important for showing the reviewer that he was familiar with the standard literature work and to

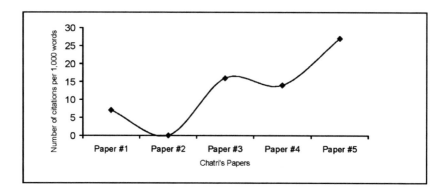

Figure 8.1. Number of citations in Chatri's paper introductions, per 1,000 words.

refer the reviewer to the specific articles that he had used. Because the proposal was only 751 words in length, Chatri included minimal references, selecting those that he felt were key references in the research area.

Several months later, when writing Paper #3, Chatri spoke in more depth about his citation choices and his process for deciding which references to include in and exclude from his literature survey. He admitted that he had not read some of the papers cited, but had included them because they were cited in so many other articles. When asked why he had cited those primary sources instead of the secondary sources, which he *had* read, Chatri demonstrated an understanding of how some citations carry more academic capital than others:

> For example, you have to refer [to] someone that [is] very famous, so that, okay, you are . . . you- otherwise, I can't refer to some work that unknown people wrote. [. . .] We have to refer some paper that published in a good journal, in a good conference, right? So that, "Okay, you're work is valid." I can refer to, for example, the paper or the conference in the local, maybe in my country, in Thai. But no one knows, right? Who know? You have to refer to something so that, okay, your work, "Hmm . . . sound good." (September 12, 2003)

As Chatri's purpose and audiences for his texts became more varied and more high-stakes, he wrestled with citational practices in different ways. By the time he wrote Paper #5, in the spring of 2004, his decisions about which work to cite and where to cite it were more complicated, and he even began using citations strategically. In this paper, for example, he made an effort to foreground his citations to similar work so that he could immediately show how his own work was unique.

Stance. Writers' ethos is built not only through displays of disciplinary knowledge, but also through the stances that they take through their writing. One way in which writers engage in their work is through the use of hedges and boosters—lexical tools for qualifying or increasing the writer's commitment to his or her knowledge claims. Hyland's work has contributed much to an understanding of how these strategies work rhetorically. According to Hyland (2000):

> In academic discourse their importance lies in their contribution to an appropriate rhetorical and interactive tenor, conveying both epistemic and affective meanings—that is, they not only carry the writer's degree of confidence in the truth of a proposition, but also an attitude to the audience . . . Writers need to invest a convincing degree of assurance in their propositions, yet must avoid overstating their case and risk inviting the rejection of their arguments. (p. 87)

A writer's use of hedges and boosters then serves multiple purposes of persuasion and ethos. Text-based research has shown patterns of use to be influenced by disciplinary epistemology, they are also influenced by individual writers. Second language writers, for example, may use hedges in ways that differ from standardized norms created by native English speakers (Hyland, 1995). Examining postgraduate students of engineering, Koutsantoni (2006) found that student writers tended to use more hedges and to distance themselves from their claims, and she suggests that these rhetorical choices were related to the students' awareness of the power differentials within the research community. For any writer, many factors are likely to influence the stance(s) that he or she takes in a text—cultural capital, linguistic capital, subject-matter knowledge, and relationship to the intended audience are just a few examples. The stances that Chatri took in his research writing provide a window into his struggles with his sense of self-identity, the discursive identity that he strove to portray, and his attempts at rhetorical persuasion.

In his early conference papers written in Thailand, Chatri avoids boosting claims almost entirely. Generally, his strategy was to cite quantitative or qualitative measurements of his results without drawing any direct comparisons between his work and previous work.

> *The average accuracy of space classification, break-space detection and false-break rate tested on the ORCHID corpus are 85.26%, 79.82% and 8.75% respectively. Furthermore, **we found that** the error rate of POS tagging in the sentence that achieved by the product in our algorithm comparing with the tagger that works on token-by-token **is reduced by average 11.3%**.* (Paper #1, Spring 2000)

> *After implementing the system with the above approach and evaluating the synthetic speech, **we found that the quality was acceptable**. However, the improvement of the naturalness of the speech is suggested.* (Paper #2, Summer 2000)

Two years after he had written these papers, Chatri and I discussed the issue of persuasion in research writing. At this time—still early in his doctoral study—Chatri knew that he needed to persuade readers of his work's contribution, but he was unsure *how* to do so. The only strategy that he could name was to "conceal our weaknesses" (November 8, 2002).

After nearly one year had passed, Chatri had developed a better sense of how to highlight his work's strengths. In Paper #3 (the internal research paper), he makes direct claims that his work has something to offer *over* previous work. For example, he writes:

> *Also, from the above results which show that **both methods can perform at least equivalent to** the typical feature/model based approach, this can confirm us to **hopefully** proceed in making more progress with the appearance-based approach.* (Paper #3, Summer 2003)

Despite his direct comparison to prior work, Chatri's text still contains hedges like "at least" and "hopefully," serving to qualify his claims and suggesting a lack of confidence in his work. Chatri was aware of the hedging and described it as problematic, saying "I think these sentence show . . . that I'm not the kind of researcher that [is] convince[d] [of] my work. Because I know that the work is not perfect . . . Finally, I think, believe me, we have to change this. I know. Otherwise, even my boss, he will not write this" (September 12, 2003).

Chatri admitted at that this time that he was still uncomfortable taking a stance that was at odds with his own sense of self, saying, "it seems that we have to boast about your work, but my character is not something like that" (August 29, 2003). This tension illustrates an interesting stage in the development of genre knowledge: although Chatri has some awareness of what he should do rhetorically (and formally), he is still unable to "buy in" and so continues to resist the generic norm.

Chatri's fourth paper represents the first real "high-stakes" writing among these texts—his first submission to an international conference. His writing in this paper shows less hedging and even a few boosters. For example:

> *From the above results, **we found that the accuracies of our both methods are somewhat similar even the second method may be slightly better. Clearly our methods outperform** the geometrical feature-based method especially if we consider the maximum error. Furthermore, **we found that the stability of estimated pose our both methods is better than** the one of feature-based method.* (Paper #4, November 2003)

Because of the task's importance, Chatri revised the final version of this paper with Roberto. During this collaboration, many of the hedges were deleted and more boosters were added. Although Chatri was not entirely comfortable with some of these changes, he deferred to Roberto, whom he described as a more experienced researcher and writer.

Despite his discomfort with many of Roberto's discursive strategies, Chatri implemented many of these strategies on his own when writing Paper #5, his second international conference submission. In this paper, Chatri's claims contain almost no hedges and spell out very explicitly the contribution of his work in relation to previous work. In a paragraph quite similar to his abstract from the same paper (shown earlier on pages 262–263), Chatri writes:

> **Unlike the range maps in [3], our 3D model is very simple** and can be created using a few mouse clicks on a pair of stereo images. **However, despite the simplicity of this 3D model, our method provides means to deal with both partial and self occlusion with high accuracy—typically** a few millimetres in translation and less than one degree in rotation. Besides, **unlike the work in [17],** which handles both self and partial occlusion using a robust estimation, **our method allows self and partial occlusion to be treated more robustly** by doing it separately. (Paper #5, Spring 2004)

Chatri's commitment to his work appears quite strong in this passage and in the abstract, but these appearances should not be read to mean that Chatri himself had grown more confident as a researcher. In fact, the use of boosters belies Chatri's concern that this passage and the abstract exaggerated the contribution of his work. The final statement in the abstract had been revised by Roberto, and in the interests of time, Chatri had failed to push for a further revision before submitting the paper. In the end, Chatri's concern was indeed warranted as one of the reviewers of Paper #5 pointed out the potential inaccuracy of the claim. The reviewer writes:

> The claim that no other AAM paper has used "ground truth" to demonstrate the accuracy of tracking needs to be substantiated. I believe this to be a false claim (but don't have any other AAM papers at hand to provide references against this). (Review, Spring 2004)

When reading his review, Chatri agreed with the comment. He admitted that it was inaccurate as written and that the statement should have been qualified in certain ways. When I asked him how he might revise it if he were to continue working on the paper, he responded:

> Maybe eliminate it because . . . because the way that we- in the abstract, it seems that if you write down this. I mean this sentence. It seems that we commit us

that this is the one contribution, or maybe one thing that you have to notice about this . . . But, as a reader or as a reviewer, as a researcher, I don't think this is a one thing that we should notice about this point. So we can say move this sentence into the experiment when we talk about that. Because this is about the experiment, we can talk and then give more detail about it. Okay, like this work that uses ground-truth in this way, we use the ground-truth in this way. We think that it's more reasonable, blah, blah, blah. Something like that. So, right now, if I have in my mind is I will remove this [original sentence in the abstract]. Just not totally remove, just move into another section. (July 15, 2004)

By this time, Chatri had developed several strategies for selling his work. While two years earlier, his only strategy for persuasion was to conceal any weaknesses, he now had a greater understanding of how to use tools like hedging and boosting to show confidence in his work and to foreground the work's contribution in accurate and meaningful ways. Certainly, he had not yet mastered these strategies, and he was still far from confident in his ability to persuade. Yet, he had begun to enact a discursive identity that was somewhat more in line with the preferred generic norms, and in doing so, he had hoped to build a new ethos and to illustrate his authorial credibility.

BUILDING GENRE KNOWLEDGE

As Chatri struggled with his research and the pressures of writing up that research in order to complete his doctoral degree, he gradually developed the skills necessary to sell his work to a larger community— that is, he began to view all dimensions of the research paper genre in a rhetorical way. His increasing moves toward emphasizing the novelty of his work and building his credibility as a researcher represent the tools that he used to do so. The changing textual features of his research writing were thus informed by his growing knowledge of the rhetorical scenes of the research world, a world that he was growing increasingly involved in and increasingly comfortable with. Was it simply this involvement that led to Chatri's growing rhetorical insights?

How can we understand this legitimate peripheral participation or cognitive apprenticeship in more fine-grained ways? In Chatri's case, at least three resources appear to have contributed to his increased rhetorical awareness and richer genre knowledge: increased participation in the networks of research genres, a fluid movement among and across genres within this network, and the adoption of multiple roles and positions of agency within the network.

Russell (1997) has linked genre networks (or systems) to the activity systems that learners participate in—such as, classrooms, workplaces, or disciplinary research—arguing that involvement in a genre system provides students with access to discursive and material tools that can in turn expand their involvement in the larger activity systems of the discipline. Ethnographic research illustrates how increasing participation in a social group coincides with increasing engagement in one or more genre systems (Beaufort, 1999; Prior, 1998). Through this process, newcomers gradually become more expert-like as they gain familiarity with how things get done within the group.

As learners participate in interlinked genres, they must contend with multiple exigencies, audiences, and goals. They take on shifting roles and alternative positions of agency. This kind of expanded participation in genre systems, it seems to me, can also help learners develop a more sophisticated understanding of the system's "core genres" (such as research articles), including an understanding of how to manipulate those genres for their own purposes.

Immersion in a Genre-Networked World

Participation in a particular community is obviously crucial for understanding that community's values. Bazerman (2002) has described such participation quite simply: " . . . if you hang around a place long enough, you will become the kind of person who hangs around that kind of place" (p. 14). Genre networks provide a very powerful heuristic for understanding this "hanging out."

Mapping Chatri's participation in different tasks reveals important changes in the nature of the tasks. By means of comparison, it is especially interesting to first chart Chatri's participation in the WCGS classroom task surrounding his proposal ("WCGS Proposal"), taking place between Papers #2 and #3. The genre chain here is simple and unidirectional, as illustrated in Figure 8.2.

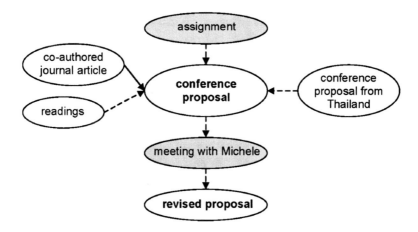

Figure 8.2. Genre chain in Chatri's WCGS conference proposal task, November-December 2002. Oral interactions are shaded.

The chain is first instigated by the WCGS course assignment. In this case, the assignment was given orally in class and then discussed with each student individually in a conference. Chatri chose to write a conference proposal because it was a genre that he had at least some familiarity with, as he had written two conference papers and one conference proposal while working in Thailand. After selecting a genre (the conference proposal), Chatri considered the subject matter that he would use, eventually deciding to write a proposal based on research that he had done under the supervision of his previous postdoc supervisor. The supervisor had submitted the research to a journal, so it already existed in article form. To review the work, Chatri re-read the article manuscript and a small number of published papers on the topic; these texts served as support genres in the chain, informing the "core genre" of the conference proposal. Because he was unfamiliar with writing conference proposals (as the genre is relatively rare in his field, where writers are more likely to submit full conference papers), Chatri wrote a scaled-down version of a conference paper. After having written a first draft, Chatri met with Michele in a conference, in which he received additional feedback primarily related to grammar and usage. Finally, Chatri submitted the final draft. He did not receive any formal written feedback on this final draft, and the task ended here.

The underlying exigence for this genre chain was a course assignment, the task involved social interactions only with Michele, and the network involved a total of two written genres—journal articles (published and unpublished) and the conference proposal itself. The task was also artificial, as Chatri noted, in that he wrote the conference proposal *after* the work had already been submitted to a journal. Because of this unique circumstance, and because this research was no longer Chatri's current focus, his conference proposal written for this task was never used again—Chatri simply put it in his folder and forgot about it. This was, in other words, a very contained and short-lived genre chain.

In contrast, Paper #4 offers expanded social interaction with both the local and global communities that Chatri functioned within and obliged Chatri to interact with multiple genres within the system of research writing (see Figure 8.3). In this case, the genre chain was initiated by a call for papers (CFP) for an international conference in Chatri's field, held this year in the U.S. After deciding that he was ready to present his work to the larger research community, Chatri began the difficult work of preparing a paper for submission.

In this genre network, Chatri interacted with many genres. Some of these genres served to navigate him through the genre set (i.e., the call for papers and supporting conference information, the acceptance letter, and the paper reviews), while others helped him produce the core genre of the paper itself (i.e., the research paper he had written for himself a few months earlier, a presentation he had given to his research group, and published papers he had read). In addition, social interactions were critical both in guiding him through the process and informing his work on the core genre. Early on in the process, his advisor gave him important feedback that led him to reconsider some issues in his work, and Roberto collaborated with him on revising the paper at the later stages. This collaboration significantly influenced Chatri's genre knowledge as well as his written text, as described earlier. The entire task, from beginning through the presenting of the work, took place over a period of seven months, though the bulk of the writing was completed in two months during the fall of 2003.

The genre chain surrounding Paper #4 starts to resemble more of a genre system (as described in chapter 1), bringing in more genres from other sets and being shaped in unpredictable ways by Chatri's social interactions. In addition, the system involves multiple levels of

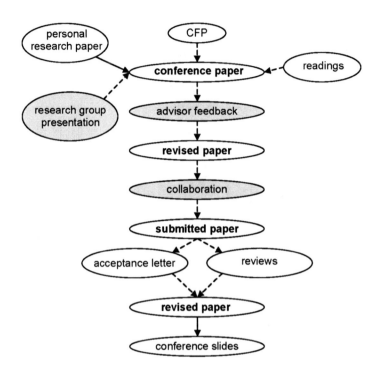

Figure 8.3. Genre network in Chatri's international conference proposal task, October-November 2003. Oral interactions are shaded.

discourse communities (Chatri's research lab, the conference reviewers, and finally the conference attendees), taking Chatri out of the local setting in which he was fairly comfortable and into the larger community responsible for judging what counts as new (and valuable) knowledge. At the later stages of this genre chain, Chatri starts to engage in more "occluded genres," which are less public but which also provide newcomers with more sophisticated knowledge of the group's organization and gatekeeping devices. So, as Chatri participates in this longer genre chain, he gradually develops increased insight into the research community—insight that feeds back into his knowledge of the conference paper.

Chatri's second international conference submission, Paper #5, offers an even more expanded interaction with people and texts (Figure 8.4). By the time Chatri was engaged in this task, his views of writing were fully rhetorical in that he had begun to consider the impact that his research topic and written form would have on his intended audience (both individual readers and the larger target community) from the very start—not just later in the process as he had in the past—and he constantly considered the "means of persuasion" available to him at various nodes of the set.

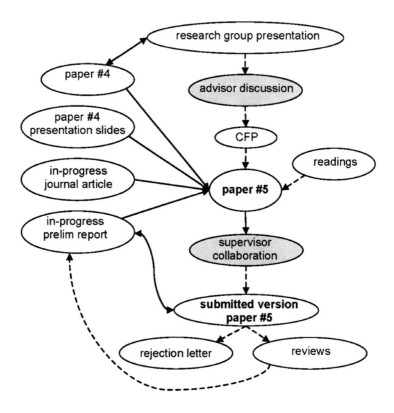

Figure 8.4. Genre network in Chatri's international conference proposal task, March-April 2004.

Multiple exigencies underlie this genre network: (1) Chatri felt increased pressure to present his work, as it was expected for graduate students working with his advisor, (2) he was particularly motivated to present at this conference because it was very specifically related to his research area and the conference organizer was the leading pioneer in his work, and (3) he had learned, searching on-line, that a researcher at another U.S. university was currently working to solve the same research problem as him. This final exigence influenced his writing from the very beginning, as he considered how to show the strengths of his work in comparison to this other researcher's work. Throughout the task of writing Paper #5, Chatri was strongly motivated to succeed, though his timeframe for working on this task was much more limited than it had been in Paper #4, as he had only about four weeks to write the entire paper.

In addition to the multiple goals and exigencies here, Chatri had to contend with an even larger range of peripheral and support genres. Presentations to his research group informed his paper greatly, as did Paper #4 and the presentation slides for Paper #4. At the urging of his supervisor, Chatri was also concurrently preparing a journal article, and he had begun working on his preliminary report (a kind of "pre-dissertation text" that included multiple chapters and a lengthy literature review). These three genres—Paper #5, the journal article, and the prelim report—began to inform one another, shaping Chatri's ideas and his texts. Chatri described the process as cyclical, with the various interactions and genres influencing each other and prompting new tasks. Chatri also stressed that as he became more engaged in his research and his research community he found himself thinking of and working on multiple genre tasks at once. He admitted to thinking ahead to his dissertation as he worked on various papers and his prelim report. In other words, by Paper #5, he had become immersed in a generic research world.

The Slipperiness of Generic Boundaries

When I first met Chatri, he shared with me the writing he had done in his engineering courses and for WCGS, as well as slides he had written for his research group seminars. After almost one year, he had finished his graduate coursework and his writing had moved completely out of the classroom—reviews, internal research papers, conference papers, presentation slides, and preliminary dissertation chapters were the new genres in Chatri's discursive world. But the change between the early days of classroom genres and the later days of research genres was not simply one of exigence or community. The classroom tasks— whether in WCGS or engineering—tended to be relatively isolated or contained. Chatri would typically receive an assignment, work his way through the genre chain, and complete the task. These tasks had clear starting and ending points, and they had little immediate relationship to other concurrent tasks in which Chatri was engaged in his lab.

As Chatri participated increasingly in the networks of research genres, however, the boundaries between tasks and genres became much more blurred. In the spring of 2004, he presented Paper #4 to his research group in preparation for the upcoming conference. After the presentation, Chatri received feedback from both his peers and his advisor, and this feedback influenced his work in other genres. He recounted, for example, his advisor's comments about the discursive structure of his presentation:

> . . . my advisor mentioned that, he said that this kind of presentation is a kind of old-style fashion- old style of presentation. He mentioned that, "You never talk about the negative point of your work. Because in the conference paper everyone just show what your good point, but every work have the negative point, but you didn't say it in the presentation." And actually he want me to add something to show the result that your work is negative. I mean, show the negative point of your work, and show in the presentation and maybe just mention that in the future work that we gonna solve that problem. Because he told me, don't try to make [?] for the listener, 'oh, this work is good!' Actually, every work has some negative points, but you have to show that also to make your work be more realistic, and many one may [copy your work?]. (April 16, 2004)

Chatri took his advisor's advice and revised his presentation slides to include a section of weaknesses and future work. Furthermore, he included a similar section in the conclusion to Paper #5:

> ***The proposed method presents one drawback*** *in terms of the speed of the object in the scene. This problem can be partially solved using a simple motion prediction model, but in the future a better prediction model should be employed.* (Paper #5, Spring 2004)

But the relationship among the tasks went beyond applying advice from one task to another; Chatri built knowledge of one genre while working in another genre. The most profound example of this was his experience working on a journal paper manuscript in January of 2004. While the paper would focus on the same research that he had been working on for several months, Chatri began thinking of the framing of his work in new ways after presenting the research orally to his research group. He described to me how this experience made him rethink how he might organize his work in a journal manuscript:

Chatri: . . . I have to give a seminar [presentation] every two months, and in that time [two months ago] I didn't write the paper that I am writing right now. I have to report some idea and make a PowerPoint. And, at *this* time, I try to think by myself what the organization should be, even [though] I forgot that last time I make some PowerPoint. And I think about the organization, just think about the organization, and I realized that, okay, at that time remember that I made the Power-Point. It's similar. Maybe I can recognize it by- maybe I will forget it. "Oh, I made something before!" But when I made the PowerPoint, I think the kind of presentation is similar to the writing in another form, right? Because it's not the paragraph, it's just some topic, the organization of the that's how to tell the story.

Chris: So that's for the *current* paper that you're working on? That the PowerPoint—

Chatri: Yes and that time, okay, I think it's a better idea to follow the PowerPoint, because when we make the PowerPoint, it seems that we start to tell the story in another format. Instead of we tell the story in writing. And I think to tell the story in PowerPoint is easier, right? We don't have to concern too much about the sentence, the grammar, just organize the idea. It help me a lot that okay when I come back to look, and think about when I gave the presentation what the feedback. Did

the listener understand? [. . .]I don't know if
this approach is- If you make a PowerPoint first,
and try to present the idea, and then, okay, come
back to write. Is it helpful or not? I'm not sure.
(January 23, 2004)

As he worked on so many tasks concurrently—presentation slides,
conference papers, a journal article, and his preliminary exam for his
dissertation—the tasks themselves became blurred, as did the genres,
as they seemed to seep into one another. Chatri's description of the
various tasks he was working on in the spring of 2004 gives some insight into the slipperiness of it all and the somewhat chaotic nature of
the relationship among these genres and tasks:

I think first I made a- because before I write down
this sentence, this paragraph, this section, I give a
talk in the seminar, some detail about this, but in
different way. Maybe let's say, if you see the pictures
[in the presentation slides], it change a lot from the
first presentation that I have. Let's say "our method"
[?], this different from the last- I start to present this
from the last semester, and okay, it changed when I
talked [to my research group] and then it changed a
little bit even [though] in detail, you can think that
it's the same thing. Right? The way to give the title
of this document [is] different, and then . . . in the
beginning of this semester, I told you that my supervisor want me to write a journal. And he want me
to, okay, bring that [Paper #4] and extend something
from that paper. I used the Microsoft Word file from
that paper and add something in another section, and
that thing is similar to the section 3 [in Paper #5].
And then, I think this semester I have another presentation about this, and when I make the presentation, I re-organize it again [using] the words that [are]
easier to understand. And then, I write the prelim report. I bring the writing that I want to make for the
journal and then read it and re-organize it into the
preliminary report. Modify something based on the
last presentation, I think, okay, modify it. And so the

current- the latest version should be something in the
preliminary report, right? So, and then when I write
[Paper #5], okay, I bring the preliminary report with
me, and then modify it, and then change something
and then . . . okay . . . modified *many* versions, and
then right now we changed the topic, okay, I bring it
here to this section. Here you will see in this section,
and you will see how the picture is changed, but this
idea—at least this topic, this title is changed. (April
16, 2004)

Working with Chatri at this point, I began seeing a focus on genre
as limiting; what Chatri was learning was not individual genres so
much as the networks of genres and the disciplinary discourses of his
field. Or, more aptly, Chatri was learning what Gee (2005) defines as
Discourses with an upper-case "D"—"ways of combining and integrating language, actions, interactions, ways of thinking, believing,
valuing, and using various symbols, tools, and objects to enact a particular sort of socially recognizable identity" (p. 21).

The change between learning in this context of disciplinary practice and learning in the classroom was striking. Primarily, it is an issue
of access. As he became immersed in a generic research world, Chatri
had access to more people, more genres, and more choices. He began
working with a larger genre repertoire, and these genres were interlinked in ways that helped him build a more sophisticated knowledge
of individual genres *and* of the Discourses of academic research, of his
research lab, and of the computer vision field.

Shifting Roles and New Positions of Agency

Over time, Chatri increasingly encountered research genres from multiple roles and positions of agency. He was a developing research writer
and also an active *consumer* of research, reading articles on a daily
basis as he searched for useful algorithms and methods to adapt to his
own research. Reading also gave him insight into the ways in which
other authors presented their work to the community in effective and
persuasive ways—he repeatedly referred to the influences of his reading on his research, his writing, and his disciplinary participation. But
reading research was not the activity that most influenced his knowl-

edge of research genres; instead, it was his participation in the task of reviewing a manuscript for a journal in his field.

In the spring of 2003—just before writing Paper #3—Chatri was asked to review a manuscript by his advisor, a journal editor. Having never reviewed a manuscript before, Chatri struggled greatly with the task, and one of his more-senior peers helped him write the final review. He read the manuscript multiple times, and found himself looking at it from a new perspective from what he was accustomed, now trying to judge the validity of the claims and the strength of the contribution rather than simply reading for content. Even a year later, Chatri referenced the review experience in explaining his understanding of research writing and the publication/acceptance process. Several months after the review, he explained that:

> . . . after I did that review, it changed my writing or my working, at least my working. Because I know that when I work, or when I think about the research problem, something about writing, when I think about my research problem, I have to think about if I finish, suppose if I done this idea, and if I have to write, what's gonna be in the paper? I have to imagine and think about if it's possible that cannot be in the paper, and that paper will gonna get accept. I have to think something about that. If it's good enough, if it's reasonable, if it's a bad idea, if there is some weakness that I can hide. [*laughing*] I have to think about writing also. I think it made me change the way to think about the idea and the way to present that idea in the paper. At least in my idea, my goal is to publish the paper, to publish that idea, right? Not to sell that idea to a company, or to get it into patent. Because my goal is to get this idea to publish in a conference or in a journal. So I think it changed my way to think about the research problem and to write a paper. (December 16, 2003)

Multiple conversations and analyses of Chatri's writing suggest that his understanding of the research writing process became much more sophisticated with time, and that taking on this role of reviewer was critical in building knowledge. As he wrote future papers, he thought specifically of how to persuade the *reviewers*—not the conference audience. He found phrases from other papers (including the one that he had reviewed) that he believed were particularly effective at selling the research, and he integrated these phrases into his own writing. He built a stronger understanding of the procedural elements of the genre, and this understanding was fundamentally rhetorical. As he read articles, he found himself viewing the authors as people with motives—writing for tenure or promotion, writing to be the first to publish on a new method. He focused much more on what he called the "tricks" of writing and even went so far as to say that—though he disagreed with this—he felt that often the persuasiveness of the writing was more important than the research itself.

Taking on new roles gave Chatri new positions of agency, allowing him to "think like a reviewer" and to take on a position of power within the genre system—whether or not he felt it was a position that he deserved. In doing so, he entered the genre system at a different node, gaining a new glimpse at the entire process of research genres (see Figure 8.5). The effect that this act had on Chatri was unmistakable—he referred to the task repeatedly, even a year later. The task impacted not only Chatri's understanding of the genre, but also his own sense of identity within the research community. Although he had felt uneasy taking on the gate-keeping role at the time, the role added to his "identity kit," giving him an opportunity to try on the roles of those he interacted with throughout the systems of research.

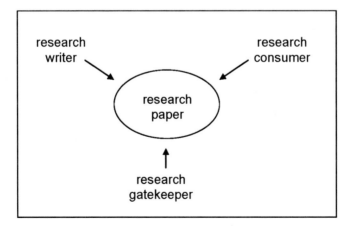

Figure 8.5. Roles and perspectives on the research paper.

****

In the last few months of my research, I began mapping Chatri's writing and seeing the increased overlap and entanglement of various genres. When I first shared these maps with him and explained my interpretation of his writing as becoming increasingly intertwined in multiple tasks, he exclaimed, "Yes!" He too was unable to pinpoint starting and ending points of the various tasks he was working on, and he clearly noted the numerous ways in which his interactions—in his research group, with his advisor and supervisor, at a conference, and with hundreds of texts—were accumulating and feeding into his understanding of disciplinary writing.

It seems to me that Chatri's story provides insight into two important concepts in genre knowledge building: identity and task. As case studies by Casanave (2002) and Ivanič (1998) have compellingly illustrated, identity transformation is central to understanding writers' relationships to the genres that they encounter and, therefore, their developing knowledge of those genres. Chatri's story echoes this point, illuminating how the interaction and tensions between individual and community identities can give rise to textual choices of stance and engagement. But it also illustrates how identity interacts with task. With task repetition, writers may gradually build new identities as they take on new roles and become more comfortable in old ones. With task accumulation, writers gain experiences, content knowledge, and identities to draw upon in subsequent tasks. I explore the relationships among these elements in the next and final chapter.

9 Building Genre Knowledge

Since the late 1980s, genre studies has been a vibrant interdisciplinary and international field of inquiry. Scholars focusing on the complexities of genre learning have drawn on overlapping theoretical orientations, including situated learning, sociocultural theory, activity theory, sociocognitive theory, structuration theory, and theories of discourse and rhetoric. While all of these orientations provide insight into the learning process, a comprehensive theory of how learners build genre knowledge—that is, a theory that takes into account diverse learners in diverse learning contexts—has not been developed. Indeed, an all-encompassing theory of this sort may be unrealistic and even undesirable. I tend to agree with Swales (2004) that it may be more useful to focus on the development of multiple theories that can help explain local situations rather than trying to develop a single theory that can do all things for all learners, teachers, and theorists. Cheng (2006b), for example, has called for a theory of genre learning for ESP learners, while scholars like Bawarshi (2003) have focused on developing theories of genre learning applicable primarily to L1 undergraduate writers.

Theory can of course be an intimidating term, and is admittedly one that I personally approach with some pause. Yet, theories help us to make sense of the world—they allow us to create order out what are unquestionably messy human behaviors. It is in this spirit that I outline in this final chapter a working theory of how writers build genre knowledge, particularly knowledge of very specialized genres used by disciplinary and professional groups. While I intend this model to be inclusive of both multilingual and monolingual writers, I think of it not as an overarching or all-encompassing theory. I am fully aware that the framework I outline reflects my own world of experience—as an ESP and EAP teacher of primarily adult learners, as a researcher attempting to integrate the disciplines of applied linguistics and rhetoric and composition, as a teacher of academic writing, and as an L1 writer of English living and working in the United States. So, what I lay out in the remainder of this chapter is intended to offer, in Atkinson's words, "*small* tools that *may* help people build their *own* understandings of social situations and power structures which will be relevant and useful in their own situations, including how to change them" (Atkinson, in press).

Drawing extensively on the model of genre knowledge described in chapter 1, this final chapter attempts to tease out the process of knowledge building by addressing three primary questions: How do writers move toward expert genre knowledge? What impacts the shape of genre learning? And, finally, can genres be taught? In addressing the first question, I return to consider the nature of genre knowledge, described in chapter 1 and explored throughout the book. I address specifically the strategies and resources that writers frequently draw upon as they learn genres, and I examine the ways in which this process may be influenced by different classroom and non-classroom contexts. Next, I turn to the parameters of individual, community, and task as a way to understand the variation in genre learning across writers and contexts. These parameters, I argue, can contribute to a theoretical understanding of genre learning that is sensitive to multilingual and monolingual writers, and to classroom and non-classroom contexts. Finally, I lay out three pedagogical principles that can support the development of genre knowledge in the writing classroom.

Moving Toward Expert Genre Knowledge

The framework I outline here grows primarily out of my understanding of the discipline-specific genres used in academic and professional contexts, though it has been informed by work in K-12 and U.S. first-year composition contexts. As described in chapter 1, knowledge of discipline-specific genres can be described as encompassing multiple, overlapping domains, each developed separately *and* simultaneously. Formal, rhetorical, process, and subject-matter knowledge work together to develop the expertise writers need to enact genres in effective ways. These four knowledge domains are best defined in expansive rather than restrictive ways, so that many different types of knowledge can fit within one or more of these larger domains.

Resources and Strategies of Genre Learning

As they carry out genre-related tasks, learners draw upon a range of resources and strategies that, over time, serve to build this multi-dimensional knowledge. The resources and strategies described below outline a general taxonomy of some of the common ways that learners build genre knowledge. The categories described here are based on my interpretations of empirical studies of genre learning (see Tardy, 2006), as well as my own research described in the previous chapters of this book. While the categories below are not exhaustive, they do suggest some of the more common resources and strategies that seem to aid writers in genre learning.

Prior Experience and Repeated Practice. As writers repeatedly encounter certain genres and discourses over time, they accumulate experiences and build repertoires that they can later draw upon when facing similar tasks. The writers in my study often compared new genres to those that they had encountered before, sometimes overgeneralizing and sometimes overlooking comparable genres. When writing cover letters, they noted similarities with the statements of purpose that they had written when applying to graduate school. When writing his master's thesis, Paul drew on his knowledge of research articles; when writing course project reports, Yoshi drew on his knowledge of project reports he had written in the workplace. While previous experiences that contradict current tasks may actually impede learning (Blakeslee, 1997), such tensions were not evident with these writers. As they re-encounter similar genres repeatedly, the relevant generic and discursive features become second nature, automatic, or tacit (Johnstone, Ashbaugh, & Warfield, 2002). As they become more comfortable with some features, such as form, writers begin to attend to other features, gradually forming more complex and contingent understandings of genre. Chatri's repeated experience with conference paper writing illustrates how this attention to new features over time re-informs prior knowledge.

Experience and practice are also closely linked to disciplinary participation, which plays an important role in developing disciplinary—and thus, rhetorical—genre knowledge (Haas, 1994), and may also lead to more routinized composing processes and greater efficiency in approaching writing tasks (Beaufort, 2004). Previous studies have shown that prior experience and repeated practice can have an impact on very young writers (Chapman, 1994; Kamberelis, 1999; Kamberelis & Bovino, 1999), undergraduate writers (Faigley & Hansen, 1985; Herrington, 1985; Ivanič, 1998; Spack, 1997), graduate student writers (Berkenkotter, Huckin, & Ackerman, 1988; Blakeslee, 1997), and workplace writers (Beaufort, 1999; Dias, Freedman, Medway, & Paré, 1999).

It is also important to note that while experience and practice may provide valuable resources, writers do not always benefit from them. For example, when writers are new to a particular community of practice, they may be unable to identify similarities between prior and present generic tasks. Similarly, many student writers lack repeated practice with genres simply due to limited assigned writing. When writers lack prior experience or repeated practice, they may turn to other resources, such as textual interactions, oral interactions, or mentoring.

Textual Interactions. As they interact with texts, writers gain exposure to different generic patterns and conventions, providing them with many potential resources for building their repertoire of expressions and discourse structures. Writers may use strategies of textual or discursive borrowing, they may take advantage of written feedback, or they may draw upon meta-genres or explicit guidelines for writing genres.

Textual borrowing (the incorporation of exact fragments of texts into one's own writing) is a strategy used by diverse learners in diverse contexts, including first and second language writers as well as academic and workplace writers (e.g., Gentil, 2005; Ivanič, 1998; Leki, 1995; McCarthy, 1987; Paré, 2000); findings of some studies do suggest, though, that the strategy may be more common for second language writers (Keck, 2006; Shi, 2004). For multilingual graduate students, textual borrowing seems to be particularly common when approaching new genres, with some writers keeping lists of useful formulaic expressions found in published writing (Angelova & Riazantseva, 1999; Gosden, 1996; Shaw, 1991). Yoshi, Chatri, and Paul borrowed from other texts when they were faced with unfamiliar genres for which they lacked a stockpile of conventional phrases or even the knowledge of what was conventional, as exemplified in the cover letter task described in chapter 3. Textual borrowing often provides writers with tried-and-true ways to introduce rhetorical moves (e.g., "The contribution of our work is . . ." or "I am attracted to your company because . . ."), developing their rhetorical knowledge as well as formal knowledge.

The writers in this book, like many multilingual writers in other studies (e.g., Li, 2006), described their borrowing as a learning strategy. Multilingual writers may borrow because of a lack of confidence in their writing skills or a lack of familiarity with a particular genre. Yoshi seemed to think of his extensive borrowing as a kind of crutch; John, on the other hand, was fairly confident in his writing abilities and only rarely borrowed exact textual fragments. While it is not appropriate from this research to generalize the influence of language proficiency on textual borrowing, it is certainly an area worthy of further study.

In addition to borrowing exact expressions from other texts, the writers here often borrowed discursive patterns, both explicitly and implicitly. Explicit analysis of texts' discourse patterns is common when writers approach unfamiliar genres for which they have no structural schemata or sense of appropriate arrangement. For example, when Paul faced the daunting task of organizing his master's thesis (chapter 7), he looked to models for help; Chatri did the same when writing up his research for an international conference (chapter 8). Models and samples may help writers attend to the content or structural patterns that are typical of the genre (Charney & Carlson, 1995) and can offer support in the absence of assistance from more expert writers such as instructors or advisors.

Writers may also engage in implicit discursive borrowing when they utilize knowledge gained through accumulated exposure to genres. Through repeated encounters (often as readers), they develop a tacit knowledge of those texts. The presentation slides described in chapter 5 present one example of this kind of implicit borrowing, as the writers organized their slides through a typical IMRD structure without even realizing that they had done so. In fact, the IMRD structure had become so automatic to them, that they did not even consider alternatives. Such borrowing (developed through exposure) seems to be characteristic of writers at a range of ages and levels. For example, in their studies of young L1 learners, Kamberelis (1999) and Kamberelis and Bovino (1999) found that children hold more implicit knowledge of story genres than of science report genres because they have so much more exposure to stories. For adult L2 learners, who tend to have more meta-awareness of their own learning, discursive borrowing may be incidental rather than implicit. That is, writers often appear to be quite conscious of the discursive structures that they encounter and use, particularly those structures with which they are less familiar. Over time, these structures take on an implicit nature in the sense that they become automatic. In other words, repeated generic encounters result in increased automaticity of response.

A third resource for building genre knowledge through interaction with texts is written feedback. Written feedback is not always available to writers, but when it is, it can play a key role in their development of genre knowledge. Writers may use written feedback from teachers, mentors, peers, or gatekeepers to build general or genre-specific writing knowledge (Connor & Mayberry, 1996; Li, 2006; Riazi, 1997) or to revise their strategy use or task approach (Angelova & Riazantseva, 1999; Leki, 1995). Paul and John both described written feedback as important in developing their writing skills. John, for example, felt that such feedback made him aware of certain features of his writing, even prompting him to reconsider issues like level of formality, form of figure captions, or issues of content and organization (chapter 6). Paul's written feedback from Dr. Xu prompted him to reflect on the rhetorical structure as well as language style. Aside from these instances, however, written feedback was rare—a situation that is likely typical for many writers in academic contexts. Despite the potential value of written feedback, then, its availability may be limited. Yoshi, for example, never received written feedback on his writing during my study, and Chatri's feedback came in the form of oral encounters and collaborative revision. This scarcity of written feedback, and the perceived value and desire for written feedback from disciplinary instructors, was also found in Leki's (2006b) study of 21 international graduate students.

Finally, writers draw on what Giltrow (2002) refers to as meta-genres, or genres that provide explicit guidance for writing within specific genres and communities. Meta-genres may include reference books, assignment guidelines and tips, Internet sites devoted to writing advice, or even templates or submission guidelines. The use of meta-genres has been identified as a strategy in other case studies of multilingual graduate writers (Angelova & Riazantseva, 1999; Dong, 1996; Riazi, 1997) and was used fairly extensively by two of the writers that I observed. When writing for WCGS, for example, Yoshi scoured the

Internet for samples of and guidelines for cover letters, résumés, and grant proposals. His printouts of these guidelines were highlighted, and he often took careful notes that were later turned into outlines and other organizing schemes to help him start writing. Yoshi also made extensive use of several English academic and scientific writing textbooks (written in Japanese), much like the junior Japanese scholars in Gosden's (1996) study. John too frequently turned to the Internet as a source of information about certain genres. He found sample statements of purpose and advice about writing these essays for graduate school. He also read numerous articles about cover letters, PowerPoint slides, and many of the sociopolitical influences on academic writing and academic life more generally. When John spoke with me, he frequently made reference to ideas that he had "read somewhere on the Internet." Although Chatri and Paul may also have turned to these instructional resources, they never referred to doing so.

Interactions with multiple texts, then, can provide writers with rich resources and strategies for building their understanding of particular genres. While textual interactions often contribute to writers' formal genre knowledge, they may also raise writers' awareness of particular rhetorical strategies used in certain genres and/or communities. Meta-genres can also build students' process knowledge of genres, and these networked genres often serve as a primary source for subject-mater knowledge building.

Oral Interactions. In addition to textual interactions, oral interactions (Ivanič, 1998) are important sources of genre knowledge development for many writers. Oral interactions can help familiarize learners with the thinking processes of a particular community by implicitly modeling those processes in interactions with experts—often instructors (Doheny-Farina, 1989; Freedman & Adam, 1996). Oral interactions can also help learners get "plugged in" to the network of tasks and activities within a given community (Winsor, 2001); increased access to the community in turn provides learners with more opportunities for learning about the community's genres (Flowerdew, 2000; Riazi, 1997; Shaw, 1991). Unfortunately, several studies of multilingual graduate students suggest that these students are often relatively isolated from important social networks, putting them at a disadvantage in comparison with their native-speaker counterparts (Dong, 1996, 1998; Shaw, 1991). What is crucial to note here is that not all learners have equal access to the social/oral interactions that can be so influential in genre learning. In other words, social interactions and social networking cannot be an assumed practice or resource. Any theory of genre learning therefore needs to take into account this variability.

In school settings, writers may seek out oral interactions with professors or peers to clarify tasks and increase their chances of success (Leki, 1995; McCarthy, 1987; Riazi, 1997). In my own study, John frequently used this strategy, asking Michele, a departmental secretary, his peers, and me questions like "How should I ask a professor for a letter of recommendation?" or "What should I say in an email to a professor that I want to work with?" He relied heavily on people as sources of information, often not trusting just one source, but instead canvassing many. Yoshi too made use of people, though in a more limited sense. He often asked me questions during our interviews, confirming his understanding of a particular genre's form, or asking about disciplinary practices in my field (a common occurrence among all four writers). For his course project in the fall of 2003, Yoshi and his partner went to their professor's office hours several times to share their ideas and ask for feedback. Yoshi felt these interactions confirmed that he and his partner were on the right track and increased his confidence in their work.

In many cases, the oral interactions that influence writers are not sought out but are incidental, as in Parks's (2000a) study of novice nurses or Spack's (1997) three-year study of an international student. These learners pick up what they can in the oral encounters that occur regularly in their day, rather than making specific attempts to engage in interactions to seek out information. Such incidental interactions can provide writers with valuable information. In casual conversations with their peers, for example, Chatri learned about the review process for conference papers and Paul learned about the average length of a master's thesis. Although much of the information they gleaned in this way was anecdotal, the writers understood it as such. Over time, this incidental information fed into their larger knowledge base, gradually adding little pieces to a complex puzzle.

Discussions that take place in disciplinary or writing classrooms or workgroups provide another resource for building genre knowledge. Through such discussions, writers are exposed to diverse reader reactions to texts and varying expectations for textual practices. Workgroup discussions can also be important in building writers' subject-matter knowledge, as it is here that they can share and test new ideas, respond to questions, and begin to think about their work in new ways. Changes in Chatri's approach to telling the "story" of his research (chapter 8), for example, were a result of questions posed to him by his advisor and others in his regular research group seminars. Discussions in writing classrooms often allow writers to compare perspectives from multiple disciplines and add more opportunities for influential oral interactions.

Mentoring and Disciplinary Participation. Many oral interactions also fall under the category of mentoring and disciplinary participation. Through mentoring and participation in disciplinary practice, writers can learn ways of thinking and working within their disciplinary communities. They gain invaluable rhetorical knowledge, as well as knowledge of genre procedures, form, and subject-matter content. At advanced professional stages, support from mentors can guide writers through increased practice, textual interactions, oral interactions, and collaboration, as shown in chapters 7 and 8 as well as many previous case studies (e.g., Beaufort, 1999; Haas, 1994; Parks, 2000a).

For Chatri and Paul, mentoring involved advising, modeling, and co-participation in disciplinary activities. Chatri often received explicit advice from both his advisor and post-doctoral supervisor through incidental discussions at work and more formal advice that his advisor posted on-line for all of his PhD students. Chatri remembered these suggestions and referred to them frequently. Both Paul and Chatri also developed discursive knowledge as their mentors implicitly modeled processes like writing, submitting, and reviewing articles. By watching others in their research groups carry out tasks such as submitting research papers, they learned about the processes and politics involved in such activities. Over time, the writers participated more actively in the work of their research groups, leading to increased textual and oral interactions. This increasing depth of participation—an example of LPP—was most clearly seen with Chatri, as he advanced from PhD student to candidate. Collaborative writing with his supervisor extended his knowledge of rhetorical appeals and generic procedures, and it helped him clarify his understanding of his subject matter. Other research of advanced academic writers (e.g., Blakeslee, 1997; Cho, 2004; Prior, 1998) similarly highlights the value of co-authorship in developing knowledge in these areas.

Mentoring is, of course, not a guaranteed path to success. The nature of mentoring relationships varies widely, influenced by numerous factors that may support or constrain learning—for example, the style of individual mentors (Belcher, 1994), the distribution of power and authority (Blakeslee, 1997; Gosden, 1996; Prior, 1991), previous cultural and educational experiences (Connor & Mayberry, 1996), goals and expectations (Fishman & McCarthy, 2001), and geographic and linguistic distance (Flowerdew, 2000). A survey study by Dong (1998) found L2 graduate students to voice a greater need for mentoring from their advisors than did their L1 peers, but those same L2 writers often had expectations of mentoring that diverged from their advisors.' Nevertheless, concerns about mentoring relationships are not experienced exclusively by L2 writers, nor do all L2 writers experience difficulties in this area.

However, it should not be assumed that all writers have access to mentoring or to increased disciplinary participation. Many graduate students working at the master's level lack these resources, as is also likely to be the case with many undergraduate writers and some workplace writers. As illustrated in a comparison of chapters 6, 7, and 8, there was a marked difference between those students who were actively mentored (Chatri and Paul) and those who were not (John and Yoshi), with the two groups encountering different genres and taking on different roles in genre activities. Yoshi and John were both master's degree students who were not working as RAs within research groups. As such, their disciplinary interactions were tied to the classroom, their instructors, their peers, and (in the case of John) their teaching. They did not conduct independent research outside of classroom requirements, and they did not engage in disciplinary genres outside of the classroom.

A lack of formal mentoring does not preclude the opportunities for being mentored into a discipline, but it is likely to limit or constrain a writer's opportunities for actively engaging in non-classroom disciplinary practice. Writing solely within a classroom context means that a writer's work is guided by constraints such as task guidelines, the presence of only a single reader, and evaluation in the form of a letter grade.

Shifting Roles Within a Genre Network. As writers increase participation in disciplinary or professional communities, they gain exposure to the multiple, interlinked genres that coordinate the community's activities. Such exposure builds learners' understanding of the repertoire of genres that a community uses and the ways in which these genres respond to one another to carry out particular goals. Exposure to these networks can be particularly valuable in building writers' process and rhetorical knowledge. But as writers begin to participate more centrally within a community, they will find themselves shifting roles and experiencing the genre networks from multiple positions of agency. For example, graduate students or junior scholars may be asked to review conference proposals, manuscripts, or textbooks, thereby experiencing the conference submission activity from a reader/evaluator position rather than a writer's position. Through participation in genre networks from these multiple vantage points, writers learn to contend with multiple purposes, exigencies, and positions of agency. In this way, shifting roles can increase insider knowledge, building a deeper and broader picture of the writing activities within the organization (Beaufort, 2000).

One powerful example of this important resource is found in Chatri's experience reviewing a manuscript for a journal edited by his advisor, as described in chapter 8. In completing this task, Chatri's role was to focus not on the research results of the paper, but instead on the author's process of obtaining these results and on the validity of the knowledge claims. Chatri admitted that the experience had changed much about his reading and writing. After this task, he began to read articles quite differently, focusing more on the work's contribution and trying to identify the evidence for any conclusions or knowledge claims. To his own writing Chatri subsequently brought a more sophisticated understanding of research genres, holding a very real sense of the referee's role and potential strategies for persuading the referee of the value of his work. Through exposure to the multiple research genres in his lab and to discussions of those genres, Chatri also gained a greater awareness of the many constraints on writing—e.g., time pressures or failed experiments—and an understanding that researchers write for a wide range of purposes, from sharing work with their disciplinary community to gaining tenure.

Adopting a network-based perspective of genre, as I've attempted to do throughout the chapters of this book, helps to illuminate the increased integration of the multiple textual and sociorhetorical influences on a writer's knowledge development, considering not only the genres that a writer encounters but the multiple perspectives that he or she gains through those encounters.

Resource Availability. As I followed the writers in this book through their experiences in multiple domains of writing, it became clear that they did not always use the same resources and strategies for knowledge building. Instead, resource and strategy use was largely contingent on the given situational context. When the students wrote cover letters for WCGS, for instance, Michele provided them with many sample letters; these textual resources were thus readily available so that explicit textual and discursive borrowing were efficient strategies to use in that context. When writing his lab reports for biomedical engineering, on the other hand, John did not have access to sample lab reports; in the absence of sample texts, he drew upon his own prior experiences as well as his instructor's written feedback as resources as he carried out the task repeatedly during the semester. When writers lack oral interactions or mentoring, textual interactions may take on increased use and value.

Acknowledgement that resource availability may determine, or at least influence, the resources and strategies that individual writers use is crucial for a theory of genre knowledge development. Much research of L1 writers, for example, has examined how writers learn genres in social organizations (e.g., Dias et al., 1999; Freedman & Adam, 1996; Smart, 2000; Winsor, 1996); in these organizations, co-participation and LPP tend to be powerful influences on such development. However, writers do not always have access to these resources in other settings, and such resources are socially constrained by class, race, gender, symbolic and material capital, and so on. It is therefore crucial to understand what writers do, or *can* do, with the resources that are available to them in a given task within a particular context.

Learning Genres Within and Across Multiple Domains

A benefit to studying writers who are participating simultaneously in classroom and non-classroom settings is that we can observe the varying availability of resources in these diverse contexts. As the snapshots in this book have shown, not all settings offer writers the same learning opportunities—and not all writers have the opportunities to participate in all settings. Although studies have tended to focus on only one of these domains, theoretical views of genre learning have, for the most part, failed to take learning domain into consideration. In practice, genre knowledge is developed in multiple domains, so it is useful to understand how these contexts overlap and intermingle for learners and also how they may be distinct.

Writing Classrooms. Writing classrooms vary widely in their shape and context. They include, for example, elementary language arts classes, foreign language classrooms, undergraduate composition courses, undergraduate writing across the curriculum and writing in the disciplines courses, graduate writing and EAP courses, and workplace training. What these contexts share is a central concern with developing students' written communication skills. In most writing classrooms, there is at least some attempt to build learners' meta-awareness of writing and to practice writing through activities and assignments.

A traditional writing classroom is likely to engage students in a range of textual interactions, such as sample texts, peer texts, assignment guidelines, and other meta-genres. Many classrooms—like the WCGS course described here—also create opportunities for meaningful oral interactions through discussions, conferences, or peer groups, all of which can support students' learning. Students are likely in writing classrooms to draw upon their own prior writing experiences, both in terms of their writing process strategies and also in terms of their understanding of genre conventions and expectations. Writing classrooms may also offer varying degrees of practice, through drafts or regular assignments in specific genres (such as response papers, summaries, or "the research paper").

In general, studies of genre learning situated within writing classrooms have focused less on students' active uses of strategies and resources and more on effects of various instructional approaches. However, genre-based pedagogies often aim to give students practice in a range of strategies. Through activities analyzing genre texts, students can practice explicit discursive borrowing; as they discuss disciplinary distinctions among genres used in different communities, they engage in oral and textual interactions that may benefit their learning. For John, Yoshi, Paul, and Chatri, such activities tended to be especially useful for genres with which they were unfamiliar.

Although the potential was not fully realized in the WCGS course I observed, writing classrooms also offer space for building students'

social resources and a meta-awareness of writing. Classrooms that incorporate ethnography of genres and communities, as suggested by
Johns (1997) and Reiff (in Devitt, Bawarshi, & Reiff, 2003a), take
students out of the classroom and engage them in non-classroom oral
interactions, potentially fostering mentoring or disciplinary participation to some degree. Classrooms in which students compile literacy or
genre portfolios (Devitt, 2004; Hirvela, 1997) raise writers' awareness
of the networked nature of genres and can turn their eyes toward the
various roles that writers play within genre systems. Classroom writing
also tends to build on students' prior knowledge and experiences, giving them opportunities to draw upon the genre knowledge they have
built over time as they expand their genre repertoires.

Much of the knowledge that students build in writing classes may
in fact be knowledge of form—not only is this often the focus of writing assignments, written feedback, and class discussion, but it is also
the aspect of writing that students often expect to improve through
classroom instruction. This may be especially true for second language
writers, who are often aware that their writing is frequently evaluated
in terms of form. At the same time, classroom learning is not limited to formal knowledge. As shown in chapter 3, however, writers
can build rhetorical and even process knowledge of genres within
classroom contexts. Though such knowledge is decontextualized and
partial, it nonetheless contributes to writers' gradually evolving genre
knowledge.

Disciplinary Classrooms. So-called disciplinary classrooms—classrooms
in which the major aim is to teach disciplinary content—afford learners somewhat different learning opportunities than writing classrooms.
In these environments, students often build knowledge through prior
experience and repeated practice (e.g., writing lab reports repeatedly
throughout a course or even throughout a multi-year curriculum), by
looking to meta-genres (such as assignment guidelines and discussions
of instructor's expectations) and through oral interactions that take
place with instructors and peers. Such resources and strategies are particularly valuable in building knowledge of content, process, and rhetorical strategies. Through disciplinary classrooms, instructors model
and students participate in the ways of thinking and doing that are
valued within the discipline and/or the local institution. Students may
learn through interactions with disciplinary texts, though such learn-

ing is likely to be less explicit and conscious than it may be in a writing classroom. In many cases, disciplinary classroom writing might be considered occluded (Swales, 1996), as students are often unfamiliar with the genre or expectations, and sample texts may not be readily available. Additionally, the quantity and quality of feedback provided in disciplinary classes is likely to vary more than in writing classrooms. In this study, for example, Yoshi received no substantive feedback on his writing during the entire two years of his master's program. When feedback is provided, on the other hand, it can be extremely valuable in giving student writers insights into the expectations of various genres.

Examining the differences in resources and strategy use between writing classrooms and disciplinary classrooms highlights a strong argument for writing across the curriculum (WAC) and writing in the disciplines (WID). WAC/WID approaches have the potential to blend the benefits of these different classroom spaces, giving students access to more resources and opportunities to engage in a wider range of writing strategies. In examining undergraduate writers with different access to writing-intensive disciplinary courses, Johnstone et al's (2002) study provides support for the value of WAC and WID particularly related to repeated practice in particular genre tasks over time.

Disciplinary Practice. Many studies of genre learning have taken place in non-classroom settings, especially workplace environments and academic research. Through this kind of disciplinary practice, learners have access to the resources that may be essential for genre learning: mentoring and oral interactions, repeated practice, scaffolded participation in disciplinary activity, and often intensive textual interaction. With increased disciplinary practice, learners often begin to take on various roles within the disciplinary community, experiencing the genre networks from multiple perspectives and gaining new insights into the values that influence rhetorical conventions and procedural practices. Social interactions provide a major resource for knowledge building, through collaboration, feedback, and mentoring. Theories such as distributed cognition and LPP provide useful short-hand for understanding the ways in which knowledge building occurs through these social interactions.

As shown in chapters 7 and 8, disciplinary practice helps writers gain essential content, process, rhetorical, and formal knowledge. Unlike the more controlled environments of classrooms, disciplinary participation is messy. Here, writers must contend with contested viewpoints and agendas, existing at a wide range of institutional and geographic levels. The stakes of writing in disciplinary practice are often high, with success or failure having material and social implications.

THE SHAPE OF GENRE LEARNING

When one "mucks around" long enough in the details of genre learning, it becomes clear that the process is not as predictable as writing instructors and researchers might hope. Individual learners prefer certain strategies over others; individual environments make available some learning resources but not others. Furthermore, different genres require unique knowledge. A monomodal genre intended for a wide audience, such as David Russell's (1997) example of a grocery list, may be learned fairly quickly and easily. A multimodal genre for a very specialized audience, like the presentation slides described in chapter 5, may be learned and re-learned over years, requiring sophisticated content knowledge, visual literacy, discipline-specific process knowledge, and a knowledge of the technology used to compose the genre (among many other things). A working theory of disciplinary genre learning should capture this variation in learning, across writers, genres, and contexts. Such a model might be built around the key parameters that shape the learning process in significant ways. I propose here the parameters of individual, community, and task to provide a framework for understanding the variability in genre learning. These parameters move beyond a simple cognitive model of knowledge building, emphasizing the social, cultural, and political nature of learning.

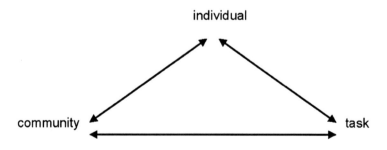

Figure 9. Parameters that shape genre knowledge development.

Individual

In this book, I have focused on the genre learning of multilingual writers because, as described in chapter 1, multilingual writers are, in many contexts, the "typical writer"—this is certainly the case in a global context but is also increasingly true in the context of U.S. higher education. By broadening the research and theoretical lens to be inclusive of a diverse range of writers, it becomes apparent that it is not enough to assume that learners who find themselves in a mentoring environment conducive to "picking up" a genre will do so. Rather, writers' learning processes are shaped by many individual factors. Writers have unique cultural profiles and perspectives, linguistic backgrounds, educational experiences, geopolitical contexts, and so on, all relevant to genre learning. As recent work has shown, individual identities also play a critical role in understanding a learner's development (Belcher, 1994; Casanave, 2002; Hirvela & Belcher, 2001; Ivanič, 1998; Norton, 2000; Prior, 1998). The stories shared in this book illustrate how identities can influence writers' composing processes—contrast, for example, John's one-draft composing process to Yoshi's painstaking planning—as well as their willingness to adopt or adapt certain disciplinary norms or conventions. John, for example, held a strong sense of personal writing style, which he exerted in his presentation slides, statements of purpose, and lab reports. He frequently made reference to his stylistic preferences and the ways in which he made his own writing unique. Like Paul (chapter 7), John felt that much of his style was formed early on:

> I thought that my English teachers probably influenced me the most in writing itself, but for formal writing, I think my dad influenced me the most, because he's an engineer, and he has this scientific form of writing. So he would help me out when I was like in elementary school. So he would say, like—even for simple experiments then—he would say, "You have to think of a hypothesis." And I would be like, "What's a hypothesis?" And that *really* influenced my style. (May 3, 2003)

Yet, as Bowden (1999) points out, an individual's style or voice as constructed through written words may belie his or her more personal sense of self, since writers create particular discursive identities (Ivanič, 1998) for given writing tasks. All of the writers in this book faced tension between self-identity and discursive identity at one time or another. Chatri, for example, struggled with his own identity as a graduate student and the discursive identity of an expert that he believed was necessary to adopt in disciplinary writing. Paul identified himself as both a novice and a non-researcher. He saw his strengths to lie firmly in practical application rather than academic research, and this sense of identity seemed to play a role in his consistent deferral to his advisor's feedback.

Yoshi's discomfort with typical U.S.-style discourse strategies for achieving self-promotional aims in cover letters was also notable. He explained that the frequent use of "I" and the over-confident manner would seem arrogant in Japanese, and he described feeling quite awkward in adopting this language. Nevertheless, Yoshi attempted to sound "American" in his cover letter, borrowing exact fragments of quite assertive sample letters. When faced with the contradiction between what he felt comfortable with and what he believed to be expected in a U.S. context, he chose to align himself with his target audience. These tensions that writers experience between their discursive identities and more personal self-identities—and the ways in which they choose to resolve these tensions—are central to understanding individual writing development. As Chatri's experiences show, awareness of genre expectations is not enough; writers may resist displaying a discursive self that conflicts with their personal sense of self, even when they are aware that doing so may have negative consequences.

A writer's individual history and current practice also play a crucial role in shaping his or her learning. Whenever a writer encounters a genre, he or she brings a repertoire of previous encounters as well as current goals. In some cases, a writer may have very similar prior experiences to draw upon; he or she may respond to the new situation in a similar way and be either successful (thereby confirming this understanding of the genre) or unsuccessful (prompting a change in a subsequent encounter). But writers' actions are always influenced by a delicate mix of their previous encounters and the many unique qualities of the present task and rhetorical context.

Community

Individuals use genres within social groupings; community is therefore also a central parameter within a theory of genre knowledge development. Such a model must consider an individual's participation within and relationship to the different social groupings involved. Is the writer a complete novice? Does the writer have access to peers or mentors? Does the writer collaborate with others? Does he or she feel like an active or "legitimate" member of the community, or like an outsider or imposter? How do other members of the community view the writer?

Writers of course participate in multiple social groupings. In my study, for instance, the writers were members of classroom communities (both disciplinary classrooms and WCGS), workplace communities, research groups, peer groups, and collaborative teams. They reacted differently in each of these groupings as both their roles and their goals shifted. For writers attempting to learn the valued genres of academic research, involvement in research and professional communities is critical—but even involvement in classroom communities can provide support along the way. Through participation in social groups, writers build subject-matter knowledge, they encounter multiple (often interlinked) genres, they navigate genre networks, and they learn how others in the group navigate those networks.

Theories of communities and culture therefore can offer valuable heuristics in understanding the complexity of this parameter. Curry and Lillis (2004) note that target communities are heterogeneously constructed along lines such as linguistic medium, geopolitical location, and disciplinary and ideological focus. Atkinson's (2004) theoretical mapping of the construct of *culture* further complicates the notion of community. Atkinson focuses on, among other elements, the notion of culture as product and process, compelling us to consider how the individuals and social structures "work *in relation to each other*" (p. 283, emphasis in the original). He argues that "culture exists co-constitutively in the world and in the head, and that heads and worlds may therefore not really be such separate and isolated locations after all" (p. 284). Perhaps most useful from Atkinson's exploration of culture—for the purposes of understanding genre learning—is his conceptualization of "big" and "small" cultures as multi-layered and overlapping. For instance, any individual may feel connected to a national culture (or cultures), academic or professional culture, class-room culture, and so on.

Though the mapping of various big and small cultures to some extent relies on the contested notion of received culture, at the same time it offers a useful framework for understanding the multiplicity of social settings that individuals participate in at any one time. When this map of overlapping cultures is overlain with the multiple identities that writers juggle, we gain some insight into the wide range of dynamics that individuals face when learning in different social settings. Devitt (2004) too sees culture, or "contexts of culture," as a valuable addition to genre theory in that it highlights the co-constitutive role of ideological and material contexts in genre.

Social groups are also steeped in power, and learning to contend with power relationships is another important part of genre learning. Within local contexts and communities, writers' interactions are shaped by power structures that in turn influence their identities and their learning. Leki (2006a) illustrates the importance that such interactions may have in academic contexts, while Katz (1998) has traced power, and its relationship with expertise, in a workplace environment. Communities are also unique in the ways that they share responsibilities, accept and mentor newcomers, and distribute power. Learners in the sciences, social sciences, humanities, corporate workplaces, and not-for-profit organizations will therefore find varying possibilities and paths to success. It becomes clear, then, that the interplay of local politics, symbolic and material capital, and community culture will result in unique learning experiences for writers across communities.

Task

In recent years, sociocultural theory has provided a rich vocabulary for understanding the importance of social interaction in human learning. Within genre theory, the term *activity* has become especially useful as a way of understanding repeated generic practice. Prior (1998) describes the relationship between writing and activity in this way:

> Actual writing happens in moments that are richly equipped with tools (materials and semiotic) and populated with others (past, present, and future). When seen as situated activity, writing does not stand alone as the discrete act of a writer, but emerges as a

confluence of many *streams of activity: reading, talk-ing, observing, acting, making, thinking, and feeling as well as transcribing words on paper.* (Prior, 1998, p. xi, emphasis added)

While activity is central in understanding the environments in which writers participate, task (defined here as a goal-oriented, rhetori-cal literacy event) may be a more useful construct for understanding the influences on genre learning. Tasks are critical to building genre knowledge because they present individuals with goals, constraints, exigencies, and social circumstances. It is within tasks that individuals juggle their personal sense of identity with their social identities, mak-ing decisions about alignments and possibilities for resistance. While some tasks will reward resistance, others most definitely value confor-mity. The nature of a given task and its rhetorical situation also affects resource potential for learners—that is, tasks make available or even encourage use of some resources and strategies and not others. Writers may have access to previous experience, textual samples, written feed-back, mentoring, collaboration, instruction, and so on. Shi (2004), for example, notes that the strategy of textual borrowing by L2 writ-ers is likely to be influenced by task type. Such resource availability will impact the ways in which writers develop knowledge, or perhaps even the type of knowledge that a writer *can* develop, through the task. The rhetorical goals of a task, the relationship between the writer and the audience, and any procedural constraints influence a writer's knowledge development. Further, there is an important distinction between those tasks in which writers engage in knowledge-telling ver-sus knowledge-transforming, and while both are likely necessary in long-term genre knowledge development, it is through the latter that writers' develop genre expertise (Geisler, 1994). In this vein, writing classroom tasks often engage students in tasks that are much less intel-lectually rigorous or challenging (Leki, 2006a; Leki & Carson, 1994) than those in their disciplinary classroom texts; this difference most certainly has an impact on the ways in which learners develop knowl-edge in the different contexts.

In her pioneering theoretical work in 1984, Carolyn Miller de-scribed genres as typified responses to recurring rhetorical situations, and she placed the idea of exigence (defined as social motive) at the core of situation. As I followed Yoshi, Paul, Chatri, and John through their various discursive tasks, I was struck with the critical importance of exigence on genre knowledge development. Following Miller's rhetorical definition of exigence as social motive *along with* the more literal definition of exigence as an urgent need or a situation that requires a response, task exigencies influenced the writers' attitudes, composing processes, use of resources, and, in the end, the extent to which they further developed genre knowledge. Exigencies are socially constructed by the writer's purpose(s), the audience, and the desired outcome, including the perceived "stakes" at hand.

Following writers through multiple domains, it became clear that high-stakes tasks were more likely to be pivotal in learning than low-stakes tasks. Paul's master's thesis (chapter 7) and Chatri's slide presentation to his research sponsors (chapter 8) are examples of high-stakes tasks with an important outcome riding on them, while the WCGS presentation slides (chapter 5) represent the other end of the continuum. When comparing WCGS writing to his disciplinary writing, Chatri differentiated the task exigencies succinctly, saying, "maybe we can call it double-standard. *This* standard for this kind of writing, *this* standard for this kind of writing" (January 23, 2004). When the stakes are high, writers may invest more time in composing, marshal more resources for knowledge-building, and, in the end, make very visible leaps in their genre knowledge. This differentiated investment in writing tasks—and the importance of high investment—has been found in with undergraduates, vocational students, and graduate students (Leki, 1995; Parks, 2000b; Prior, 1998).

Teaching Genre

As a writing teacher, the question of whether genres can be taught has been of central concern to me. Yet my research has now led me to wonder whether this question is somewhat misplaced. Written communication is, generally, generic—that is, writers must learn to manipulate many written genres in order to carry out social actions. Ideally, writers will also learn to flout, break, and change these genres as they gain access to and power within various social groups. If genres are so central to writing, the question of whether genres can be taught in the writing classroom becomes somewhat irrelevant. Genres must play a role in the writing classroom, whether that role be one of explicit teaching, awareness-raising, or even more implicit discussion or practice of written text. So, the relevant question for teachers might more aptly be re-framed: *how can writing classrooms contribute to genre learning?*

With the obvious exception of classroom genres, it is highly unlikely that writers can develop genre expertise solely within a classroom. Sophisticated genre knowledge requires interaction within the genre's sociorhetorical setting—genres are, after all, socially embedded textual instantiations. But this truism does not preclude a role for writing classrooms, which can strive to create contexts that facilitate genre learning. As argued in the previous sections of this chapter, most learners develop genre knowledge through their experiences in multiple, overlapping contexts, of which the writing classroom is often one. For teachers, the challenge becomes how to create a classroom environment that can aid writers in learning genres.

One powerful benefit of the writing classroom is that it provides learners with so many textual interactions. As students read source texts, samples, models, and peer writing, and as they compose drafts of their own writing, these texts become part of their experience and knowledge base. They broaden learners' exposure to and engagement in genres—both important resources for genre learning. Classrooms also offer students experience and practice, so that they gain opportunities to apply the same genre for new audiences and tasks. For many learners, writing classrooms provide the only opportunities for engaging in repeated practice, responding to feedback, and carrying out meta-discursive discussions and analysis of writing. As Devitt (2004) argues, the genres students experience in a classroom become a part of their genre repertoires and then "become available to them as antecedents for learning new genres, and inculcate in them particular perceptions of situations" (p. 203).

Another advantage of the classroom is found in its inherent limitation: classroom writing is simplified. The genre networks of classroom writing tend to be more contained than those found in workplace or research contexts (as illustrated in chapter 3, for example), the audience is often limited to a single individual, and the purpose of assigned tasks are often relatively straightforward—though certainly also fraught with power imbalances and hidden agendas, among other complexities. Writing classrooms allow writers to avoid worrying about concerns such as procedural conventions, medium or mode, or, for the most part, content expertise. While these concerns certainly do exist within the writing classroom, they tend to operate differently here as compared with non-classroom writing. Students can benefit from the opportunity to focus their attention primarily on rhetorical forms, especially when they are writing in unfamiliar genres, in unfamiliar communities and contexts, and/or in a second language. My argument here is somewhat paradoxical: the decontextualized and simplified nature of classroom writing tasks may give learners valuable opportunities to develop a kind of automatic facility with particular forms, allowing them to concentrate on the more complex rhetorical and situated application of those forms when they re-encounter the same genre in non-classroom contexts. Genre knowledge is not static, but instead seems to be constantly re-structured as writers face new demands, constraints, and possibilities.

At the same time, writing classrooms are obviously limited in their opportunities for developing knowledge of certain genres—particularly process knowledge, subject-matter knowledge, and rhetorical knowledge. The most fundamental difference within the classroom is the distinct exigencies that prompt and guide classroom tasks versus non-classroom tasks. With different audiences, goals, and outcomes, writing classrooms tend not to offer the kind of high-stakes tasks that fully invest writers and lead to new insights and pivotal points of genre learning. Rather, students' task engagement is often at the level of what Prior (1998) refers to as "passing."

The biggest challenge that remains for me as a writing instructor has been to balance the need to help my students write in ways that are deemed appropriate and successful within various social groups with the need to help my students manipulate, break, and change genres and the power relationships embedded in them. Work by scholars like Canagarajah (2002) and Benesch (2001) bluntly places the challenge in front of teachers. Canagarajah argues that classrooms can help students appropriate normative discourse patterns for their own goals and agendas, and he provides numerous examples for doing so. Though taking a less overtly "critical" approach, Devitt (2004) and Bawarshi (2003) similarly highlight possibilities for student agency in genre discovery and change.

Volumes like Freedman and Medway (1994a), Herrington and Moran (2005), and Johns (2002b), and monographs by Hyland (2004), Paltridge (2001), and Swales (Swales, 1990; 2004) clearly show that teachers have both an interest and investment in genre. At the same time, contemporary pedagogical scholarship expresses a unified view against teaching genre as static form. So, how can teachers facilitate an environment that fosters genre learning without trapping students into learning de-contextualized, template-like forms?

Current approaches to genre-based pedagogy share an emphasis on awareness-raising and an explicit connection between text form and dynamic, sociorhetorical contexts. In U.S. first-year composition classrooms, the goal of such a pedagogy may be not only to help students develop more sophisticated, even destabilized, genre theories (Johns, 2002a) but also to enrich the undergraduate curriculum and place writing instruction in a central role in doing so (Vandenberg, 2005). In professional/technical writing and ESP classrooms, the goal of genre-based pedagogy may be to build writers' genre repertoires and equip them with strategies for tackling the new genres that they encounter in their local contexts, in all their messiness. In both contexts, teachers may hope to foster writers' sense of agency and their ability to manipulate, even change, genres to serve their own purposes. Even with their differing goals, current pedagogies largely draw upon shared principles of genre theory (genre as dynamic, structured, social action) and learning (awareness-raising as a transferable meta-cognitive skill). In addition, I describe below three pedagogical principles teachers may find useful in promoting genre learning within the context of the writing classroom. While these principles come out of my understanding of multilingual writing development, they are intended to outline inclusive pedagogical practices—that is, practices that support *both* multilingual and monolingual writers.

1. *Build a genre-rich environment in which students have access to a range of strategies and resources.* One of the greatest benefits of writing classrooms are that they give learners time and space to interact with texts and to engage in discussions of those texts. Although students will not master genres within the short and limited duration of a single writing course, classrooms can give them valuable exposure and practice that can later be built upon. As a teacher, it is rarely possible to predict which genres each student will encounter in other environments; exposing students to a broad range of genres, then, can help to build their genre repertoire. Exposure to a range of genres also helps learners to see that arbitrary "rules" about writing rarely, if ever, apply across writing tasks and goals, to understand how writing is carried out through genres, which are simply, in Ken Hyland's words, "so-

cially recognized ways of using language" (Johns et al., 2006, p. 237). As students re-encounter genres in new environments, they can draw upon their classroom experiences while integrating new knowledge gleaned from unique contexts, thereby restructuring and complicating their genre knowledge.

Creating a genre-rich environment also means exposing learners to a range of instances of any given genre. Learners can benefit greatly from seeing how a single genre may be approached by different writers in unique rhetorical contexts. They may consider the ways in which writers individualize genres, blending disciplinary identities with unique expressions and voices. They may compare reactions to genre instances that intentionally break or flout conventions, or they may discuss how timing, geopolitical context, medium, or distribution practices may affect the reception of a genre. Sample texts can be found not just through published and public sources but also through the students' own prior writing, including writing completed in the classroom. Students can compile genre portfolios, in which they themselves gather multiple instances of a genre and perhaps responses and reactions to those genres. They may target occluded genres like lab reports, student papers, or emails to professors, locating samples through teachers and peers. Written reflection or analysis can push students to locate connections, patterns, and differences that are meaningful to them.

Exposure to many genres provides a valuable resource for writers, but teachers can facilitate genre learning even more by helping students develop strategies for learning from these texts. Within the classroom, students can practice effective textual borrowing, learning not only to identify conventional expressions but to manipulate these expressions in rhetorically effective ways. They can also learn to identify discourse patterns and their variations, and to modify existing patterns for unique rhetorical purposes. Parody is a particularly effective pedagogic tool for exploring the borrowing and rhetorical manipulation of generic forms (see, for example, Devitt, 2004; Swales, 2004). For example, in preparing parodies of social networking websites like MySpace, my undergraduate students were able to identify common lexico-grammatical features, content, images, and even audio, and to then employ these features in excess to poke fun of the genre. They considered issues of audience and identity, and explored the notion of rhetoric by identifying the boundary between imitation and exaggeration. Students can stretch, re-design, or re-purpose texts, practicing the strategies of textual and discursive borrowing in acutely rhetorical ways.

2. *Help students develop complex and dynamic views of texts—but also recognize that they may at certain points need to simplify texts for ease of learning.* One reason that genre has become such an intriguing concept for writing instructors is that it encompasses both the complexity of writing in unique rhetorical situations and the similarities among texts that are used to carry out comparable social actions. Several genre scholars have advocated for the role of ethnography in the writing classroom (Devitt, Bawarshi, & Reiff, 2003a; Johns, 1997; Johns et al., 2006) as a way for students to explore the relationship between text and context. As writers investigate social communities and their uses of writing, they learn how effective writing demands much more than grammatical correctness. Ethnographic investigations help them develop dynamic views of writing (Johns, 1997, 2002a), while also giving them access to the social groups that shape genres, as both Paltridge and Reiff describe in Johns et al. (2006). Ethnography is, then, a way to take students out of the contrived environment of the writing classroom to see the ways in which writing is socially situated. Perhaps one of the greatest benefits to ethnography as a pedagogical tool is its potential for critiquing genres and the power relations that they reinforce.

While ethnographic analysis of genres is ideal for developing students' multidimensional genre knowledge and helping them to see genres as socially situated responses, this approach may not always be appropriate. An ethnographic analysis, such as that outlined by Devitt, Reiff, and Bawarshi (2003b) and used in the WCGS classroom I observed, requires students to consider rhetorical, formal, process, and subject-matter dimensions of genres. While this complicated picture of writing is certainly characteristic of expert genre users, this complex knowledge is built up gradually through time, experience, and practice. It may be somewhat overwhelming for novices or for students facing new cultural and/or linguistic contexts to dive head-on into an investigation of generic complexity. As illustrated in chapter 4, some writers may benefit from a focus on only a limited range of generic features when they first encounter new genres. As they become comfortable with some features, they may expand their investigations to others, all the while developing richer understandings of the genre and its various layers of complexity. Such an approach requires that instructors develop an understanding of students' "genre readiness"—a concept that Swales (2001) has also found to be a useful one.

3. *Adopt a network-based view of genre.* While genre theory has increasingly recognized the extent to which genres exist within intertextual systems or networks, less interest has been given to the role of intertextuality in genre learning. As described earlier in this chapter and illustrated throughout the book, adopting a network-based view of genre learning can highlight crucial resources in the learning process. On one level, genre networks provide a framework for understanding the rhetorical processes through which genres are created, distributed, and responded to. Novices, for example, must learn the general paths and repertoires of communication that compose a social group's genre network. On another level, participation in genre networks means involvement in community practices and social worlds. As they travel through the various paths and nodes of genre systems, novices take on different perspectives, roles, and positions of agency; they act as writers, readers, and gatekeepers; they enact and change discourses.

Writing classrooms can adopt a network-based perspective into written discourse by highlighting intertextual links. Panel discussions or guest writers may describe their writing processes with an emphasis on the various genres and social interactions involved. By compiling genre portfolios, students can explore uptake among genres or the intertextual nature of an entire domain of discourse. Teachers can also take an intertextual orientation to course design and assignment sequencing— for instance, writing a conference proposal, a conference paper, a presentation, and a handout. Such activities and strategies can help make available to learners the intertextual and multimodal resources that can develop more dynamic knowledge of genres. These resources may be particularly valuable for multilingual students who feel socially, linguistically, or culturally isolated, or "off-networked" from the valuable streams of mentoring and disciplinary participation.

POSTSCRIPT

For the writers in this book—Chatri, Paul, Yoshi, and John—the actual word *genre* had very little meaning during the time I followed their writing; yet, numerous classroom and research genres became sites of struggle and success in reaching their professional and academic goals. Five years after having completed my research with these writers, I am heartened to see that they have continued down their pathways and forged new ones, learning and appropriating genres along the way. They have surely continued to contend with tensions related to individual and social identity, language, exigence, and task, as they work to take ownership over socially situated texts—it is these points of tension that are at the center of what has made genre a contested construct for practitioners. Despite its problematic normalizing effects, however, writing and writers are tied to genre, even as they purposefully break generic convention. As new technologies are developed, as historical moments cause new exigencies, and as writers forge new pathways, they encounter new genres, and, often, they build more sophisticated genre knowledge. The dynamic, contextualized, and sociorhetorical nature of genre is what makes it so problematic to address in the confines of a classroom, but at the same time makes it a concept that writing instruction cannot ignore.

Appendix A

The written texts that I collected varied somewhat by writer (see Appendix B), but in all cases, every assignment completed for their writing course was collected, often including multiple drafts. In addition, the writers shared with me with many texts they had completed prior to and during the study. These texts and my analyses of them should be considered as responses to unique rhetorical situations. They do not so much represent the writers' generic competence at a given point as they do competence within the specific constraints of any given task—constraints of time, subject-matter knowledge, co-authorship, or general attitude or priority assigned to the task. The writers opted not to share certain texts with me either because they were not happy with the quality, because they contained confidential research, or because they felt the texts were too intermingled with the ideas of others.

I analyzed the writers' texts in several different ways, including rhetorical analysis of the texts' goals, audience, and content; genre-networks analysis of the discursive practices surrounding the text; and text-based genre analysis of rhetorical and lexico-grammatical features such as rhetorical moves, first person pronoun usage, use of formal language, or use of visuals. Through intertextual tracing (Prior, 2004) the writers' texts were also compared to other textual and oral interactions that they had engaged in, following links and noting conflicts.

Oral interviews with each writer were held nearly once a month throughout the study (Appendix C). We most often met in a small conference room in the building that housed the English department. The first five interviews followed very similar structures with each of the four writers; however, interviews did vary slightly with each writer in terms of emphasis given to different topics, and, in some cases, touching on different topics entirely. Later interviews were much more individualized, as each writer was engaged in quite distinct writing activities after their writing course had been completed. The interviews often focused on texts that the writers had recently composed; they were asked to describe, for example, their process in producing and revising the texts, any feedback they received, or relationships among types of writing they were doing or had done. The interviews cannot be interpreted as exact representations of writers' knowledge at given points, but instead as displays of the writers' articulations of this knowledge within specifically co-constructed rhetorical spaces (Block, 2000; Chin, 1994). Additional interviews were held with the ESL writing course instructor at several points during the semester that I observed her class.

In all cases, I have increasingly noted the limitations of interviewing as I have continued to work to make sense of the data. Reviewing interview transcripts months and even years later, I see holes, misinterpretations, and missed opportunities for follow-up. I wonder how those interviewed might have responded differently on a different day, in a different setting, or if talking to a different person. I wish I could go back to re-do earlier interviews with some of the insights that I developed later in the study, such as the importance of genre networks in developing writers' knowledge. These gaps and deficiencies, again, are inherent to situated qualitative work.

In addition to the interviews and texts, the four writers and their writing instructor agreed to audio-record their teacher-student conferences (Appendix D). These conferences played an important role in WCGS and were held with each student at six points during the semester. Because most students did not know what to expect in the conferences, I did not audio-record the first two of these conferences. The teacher-student conferences proved to be a particularly important source of data as it was in this setting that the writers received feedback on their writing. In many cases, there were extensive discussions of various genres that the writers were learning, and at times the writers used these conferences to ask many questions and thereby develop their knowledge of particular genres or writing practices.

All of the oral interviews and conferences were subsequently transcribed, then coded and analyzed using ATLAS.ti qualitative coding software. Despite its somewhat misleading scientific and objective appearance, the use of a computerized coding program had tremendous heuristic value for me. It allowed for ease in code retrieval and the ability to create and revise coding networks, thereby facilitating the recognition of relationships among codes. I used two primary coding schemes—one to identify the writers' various dimensions of genre knowledge pertaining to specific genres, and the other to identify the sources of knowledge—for example, classroom discourse, teacher feedback, mentoring advise, or sample texts. Coding categories within these two schemes were largely derived from readings and re-readings of the data; however, additional codes were added based on available literature pertaining to genre knowledge (e.g., Beaufort, 1999; Berkenkotter & Huckin, 1995; Bhatia, 1999, 2004; Johns, 1997; Kress, 2003). These codes derived from outside of the data capture genre knowledge and sources of that knowledge *not* identifiable in the data, thereby offering potential insights into underdeveloped knowledge or underused resources for knowledge development.

In relation to the interview transcripts, I preserved the writers' exact language when transcribing all audiotapes. When quoting from the transcriptions throughout this book, any modifications to the original language is signaled by the use of brackets. The bracketed language is used for sake of clarity, when the original statements may be ambiguous to readers. In adding these modifications, I have drawn on the larger context of the interviews and my familiarity with the writers' linguistic expression developed during my time with them. However, I do recognize the potential for appropriating the writers' intended meaning and encourage readers to be mindful of the bracketed modifications.

In addition to the interviews and collected texts, I attended and audio-recorded every session of the 15-week WCGS course, taking extensive field notes regarding the discussion, student questions, and specific feedback from Michele. The course sessions allowed me to see another venue through which writers developed and also demonstrated knowledge of genres and writing practices within their disciplines. These course observations also became an important source for tracing the relationships between the various activities that the writers participated in and their actual writing.

My research was entirely dependent on the participation and consent of the WCGS course instructor and the four writers of focus. Benefits of participation for them have therefore been important concerns for me. Because I could not pay the four student writers for their involvement, I instead offered them English speaking practice through the interviews or through additional tutorials. None of the writers accepted my offer for additional speaking practice, but both Paul and Yoshi commented multiple times about the usefulness of the interviews in giving them practice speaking in English.

Because the writers were not paid, I often found it difficult to place too many demands on their time. Therefore, some data sources that may have been extremely insightful (such as more frequent interviews, or visits to their research groups or courses) were not pursued. In general, my approach was to explain to the writers what I was interested in; when I felt that they were hesitant to give me access to particular documents or writing settings, I did not press for access. In reflecting on my research practices now, I wish I had pressed more at times, but I also recognize that not doing so may have helped me to develop and retain the writers' trust and active participation in the research.

I became equally concerned about benefits of participation for Michele, the writing course instructor. While students were able to gain the benefit of having free access to additional English practice and, at times, an "informant" on U.S. educational culture, I was more uncertain about the benefits that the instructor would gain through participation. It is my hope that her involvement in the study raised her own awareness of her classroom practices and that her three interviews with me offered her useful reflection on her teaching. I further hope that the results of this research may benefit Michele, as she has had the opportunity to see in detail the writing practices of four of her students over time.

But one of the most difficult tensions that I face with my role as a researcher is the inescapable dilemma of my own representations of the writers and activities. What I can share here are merely my own versions of their stories, read through my eyes and various filters. Sharing my versions of their stories with the actual writers and the writing teacher was an important way for me to gain some outside perspective, but I nevertheless must acknowledge the extent to which the stories in the chapters of this book would surely be told in different ways had they come from someone else.

Appendix B

WRITERS' TEXTS COLLECTED

Writer	Texts written prior to WCGS	Texts written for WCGS	Texts written outside of WCGS during the study
John	-mock NIH proposal	-writer's autobiography, drafts 1–2 -CV, drafts 1–2 -cover letter, drafts 1–2 -presentation slides -statement of purpose, drafts 1–4	-class mock proposal project -class final projects (2) -informal lab report -formal lab reports (2) -letter to professor
Paul		-writer's autobiography, drafts 1–3 -résumé, drafts 1–2 -cover letter -presentation slides	-résumé (3) -cover letter (3) -article reviews (12) -class final projects (2) -homework (13) -thesis, drafts 1–4 -presentation slides (2)
Chatri	-conference paper -journal article (in Thai) -journal article -power point slides -conference abstract -EE final projects (2) -CV	-writer's autobiography, notes and final draft -CV, drafts 1–3 -cover letter, drafts 1–2 -presentation slides -conference abstract, drafts 1–2	-presentation slides (4) -outline for potential paper -manuscript review draft -research paper -conference paper, drafts 1–3 -journal manuscript -conference paper, drafts 1–2

Writer	Texts written prior to WCGS	Texts written for WCGS	Texts written outside of WCGS during the study
Yoshi		-writer's autobiography, final -résumé, drafts 1–3 -cover letter, drafts 1–2 -presentation slides -grant proposal, notes -grant proposal, drafts 1–2	-class final project, notes -class final project, drafts 1–3 -class article review -presentation for ESL class -class project report, drafts 1–4 -class presentation slides (3) -class homework problems (9) -class lab reports (11)

Appendix C

Writer	Interviews	
John	Interview #1: Sept. 4, 2002	Interview #6: Jan. 30, 2003
	Interview #2: Sept. 20, 200	Interview #7: Feb. 27, 2003
	Interview #3: Oct. 10, 2002	Interview #8: April 3, 2003
	Interview #4: Nov. 8, 2002	Interview #9: May 3, 2003
	Interview #5: Dec. 10, 2002	
Paul	Interview #1: Sept. 3, 2002	Interview #7: Feb. 26, 2003
	Interview #2: Sept. 19, 2002	Interview #8: April 2, 2003
	Interview #3: Oct.15, 2002	Interview #9: May 13, 2003
	Interview #4: Nov.22, 2002	Interview #10: June 26, 2003
	Interview #5: Dec. 12, 2002	Interview #11: Aug. 4, 2003
	Interview #6: Jan. 23, 2003	
Chatri	Interview #1: Sept. 13, 2002	Interview #11: Sept. 12, 2003
	Interview #2: Oct. 2, 2002	Interview #12: Nov. 7, 2003
	Interview #3: Oct. 16, 2002	Interview #13: Dec. 16, 2003
	Interview #4: Nov. 8, 2002	Interview #14: Jan. 23, 2004
	Interview #5: Dec. 2, 2002	Interview #15: Feb. 27, 2004
	Interview #6: Jan. 31, 2003	Interview #16: April 16, 2004
	Interview #7: Feb. 25, 2003	Interview #17: May 14, 2004
	Interview #8: April 4, 2003	Interview #18: June 11, 2004
	Interview #9: May 9, 2003	Interview #19: June 25, 2004
	Interview #10: Aug. 29, 2003	Interview #20: July 15, 2004
Yoshi	Interview #1: Sept. 11, 2002	Interview #10: Sept. 3, 2003
	Interview #2: Sept. 23, 2002	Interview #11: Oct.1, 2003
	Interview #3: Oct.16, 2002	Interview #12: Nov.5, 2003
	Interview #4: Nov.8, 2002	Interview #13: Dec. 15, 2003
	Interview #5: Dec. 4, 2002	Interview #14: Jan. 22, 2004
	Interview #6: Feb. 12, 2003	Interview #15: Feb. 26, 2004
	Interview #7: March 28, 2003	Interview #16: April 1, 2004
	Interview #8: May 9, 2003	Interview #17: May 10, 2004
	Interview #9: May 15, 2003	
Michele	Interview #1: Aug. 28, 2002	
	Interview #2: Sept. 20, 2002	
	Interview #3: Dece. 18, 2002	
	Email correspondence: Sept. 11, 2003	
	Email correspondence: Sept. 12, 2003	

Appendix D

Participant	Conference Dates
John	Conference #3: Oct. 2, 2002
	Conference #4: Oct. 16, 2002
	Conference #5: Nov. 8, 2002
	Conference #6: Nov. 20, 2002
Paul	Conference #3: Oct. 2, 2002
	Conference #4: Oct. 18, 2002
	Conference #6: Nov. 22, 2002
Chatri	Conference #3: Oct. 2, 2002
	Conference #4: Oct. 16, 2002
	Conference #5: Nov. 8, 2002
	Conference #6: Nov. 25, 2002
Yoshi	Conference #3: Oct. 2, 2002
	Conference #4: Oct. 18, 2002
	Conference #5: Nov. 9, 2002
	Conference #6: Nov. 25, 2002

Appendix E

This appendix includes the full cover letters composed by Paul in WCGS and later when applying for jobs. Underlines indicate fragments that appear in all three letters. Italics indicate fragments that appear in the two letters written for actual job applications.

Paul's WCGS Cover Letter, October 2002

Dear Mr./Mrs. Someone:

I am a MS. degree candidate in Computer Sciences (degree anticipated June 2003). I am writing in response to the Chief Software Engineer position posted on your company's web site. I understand that you seek a candidate who has experience in leading a large team to develop professional software. I hope you will agree that my qualifications and experience meet your needs.

Since the early 1990's, I have begun to develop software for companies as my part time job. Some of the products were recognized among the best of other similar products. When I was an undergraduate student, I also worked as the team leader to participate in a software contest and won 3rd prize. After I became the Senior Engineer in SinoTech Inc., I was leading over 80 software developers and art designers on 6 projects, which were completed before the deadlines successfully. The evaluation my company gave me is the employee with qualified skill and outstanding leadership.

I continue to work on using software engineering theories in real development processes, and I have obtained significant experiences through these practices. While I have continued to pursue more advanced theories, I have learned Extreme Programming for the first time in the Software Engineering course I took in Midwest University. I feel it was completely different from what I learned before and would like to follow its concept in practice.

I am attracted to your company because of the great chance for me to implement an innovative project, and lead hundreds of well-trained developers to team work together. I am looking forward to your reply to arrange an interview.

Paul's Job Application Letter for a Gaming Position, April 2003

Dear Sir/Madam,

I am a MS. degree candidate in Computer Sciences (degree antici-pated Aug. 2003). I am writing in response to the position posted on Monster's web site. I understand that you seek a candidate who has strong computer science background and lot of experiences in devel-oping professional software, games and most important, has deep love for game development. I hope you will agree that my qualifications and experience meet your needs.

I first became a computer/game lover since I was 12. I have game ex-periences on PC, Nintendo and PS. My favorite sports games almost all come from EA sports. Game is the most important reason I study computer science. After 5 years of college study in computer sciences, I have obtained not only considerable knowledge, but also plenty of experiences. Since the early 1990's, I have begun to develop software for companies as my part time job. Some of the products, e.g. on-line stock-quoting system(GUI figures are available on my homepage), were recognized among the best of other similar products. When I was an undergraduate student, I also worked as the team leader to participate in a software contest and won 3rd prize. After I became the Senior Engineer in SinoTech Inc. (www.SinoTech.com), I have been leading over 50 software developers and art designers on 6 projects. In addition to working as a team leader, my work also included *design-ing, coding and testing* through the whole development process. My projects include online games, online chat room, into which I put all my heart, and all of my projects were completed before the deadlines with very high quality. After one year, SinoTech has *become one of the top 10 portals in China* and my work was considered one of the key contributions.

Actually I have made several little games using DirectX when I was a undergraduate student. One of them called "torus" is available on my homepage. Although most of my games are 2D, the reason I can not go into 3D is only because I can not draw 3D objects as good as what I want.

<u>I am attracted to your company</u> not only <u>because of the great chance for me to</u> *work with leading edge technologies, and enhance my technical skills,* but also the chance to be really involved in developing a award-winning sports game. <u>I am looking forward to your reply to arrange an interview.</u>

Paul's Job Application Letter for a Handheld Devices Position, April 2003

Dear Sir/Madam,

<u>I am a MS. degree candidate in Computer Sciences (degree antici-pated Aug. 2003), Midwest University. I understand that you seek a candidate who has strong computer science background and lot of ex-periences in developing professional software, especially on embedded systems. I hope you will agree that my qualifications and experience meet your needs.</u>

I have been developing software products since 1997 when I was an undergraduate student. The products I developed include an online stock-quoting system, a database system, and games (Please see my homepage at http://www.cs.Midwest.edu/homes/xxx). I have worked one year in a starting up company, SinoTech Inc., and helped it *become one of the top ten portals in China* after one year. In that period, I was in charge of several projects in which *designing ,coding and testing* are all required. After I came to Midwest University, my research work is related to wireless networked handheld devices. My Master thesis is about analyzing energy consumption of IPSec on handheld devices, which in my experiment are Compaq iPAQs with StrongArm processor running Linux. I have done two and am currently doing one internship that also related to applications on handheld devices and cell phones running windows CE. The software product, WinMove, has been announced for its beta test (Please try it at http://www.winmove.com). In the development of WinMove, I was in charge of overall design, client module and part of server module.

I am attracted to your company because of the great chance for me to *work with leading edge technologies,* learn from other outstanding colleagues *and enhance my technical skills* and leadership skills. I am looking forward to your reply to arrange an interview.

Best Regards,

Notes

[1] Freedman (1993a) defines explicit teaching as "explicit discussions, specifying the (formal) features of the genres and/or articulating underlying rules" (p. 224).

[2] Freedman (1993a) has applied Stephen Krashen's (1985) distinction between "learning" and "acquisition" to genre development, arguing that genres are best acquired rather than learned. I have chosen to avoid this distinction by using the more general term "development" where possible. In cases where I do use "learning" or "acquisition," however, I do so with no intention of distinguishing between the conscious learning of rules and a more tacit process of language development.

[3] I base this claim primarily on the textbook market for first-year composition courses in the United States, which is presumably at least somewhat representative of classroom practice.

[4] The disciplinary "screen" between these two approaches is unfortunate and reflects a more general resistance of L1 composition studies to integrate and draw upon the work of second language studies. Matsuda (1999), Silva, Leki, and Carson (1997), and Silva and Leki (2004) provide more thorough discussions of such disciplinary divisions as they relate to L2 and L1 writing studies.

[5] Chatri's research in this area was a part of a larger research project on ASL, directed by a linguist. Without the disciplinary knowledge in ASL research, he had relatively little sense of how the research may be situated, in terms of its contribution, within that field.

[6] At this point in the semester, the group included only one native English speaker; a second was added later in the course.

[7] Dr. Xu is a pseudonym for Paul's advisor.

References

Allen, J., & Simmons, G. (2002). The digital design revolution. In N. Allen (Ed.), *Working with words and images: New steps in an old dance* (pp. 219–230). Westport, CT: Ablex Publishing Company.

Angelova, M., & Riazantseva, A. (1999). "If you don't tell me, how can I know?" A case study of four international students learning to write the U.S. way. *Written Communication, 16,* 491–525.

Atkinson, D. (2004). Contrasting rhetorics/contrasting cultures: Why contrastive rhetoric needs a better conceptualization of culture. *Journal of English for Academic Purposes, 3,* 277–289.

Atkinson, D. (2005). Situated qualitative research and second language writing. In P. K. Matsuda & T. Silva (Eds.), *Second language writing research: Perspectives on the process of knowledge construction* (pp. 49–64). Mahwah, NJ: Lawrence Erlbaum Associates.

Atkinson, D. (in press). Between theory with a big "t" and practice with a small "p": Why theory matters. In T. Silva & P. K. Matsuda (Eds.), *Practicing theory in second language writing.* West Lafayette, IN: Parlor Press.

Bakhtin, M. M. (1986). *Speech genres and other late essays* (V. W. McGee, Trans.). Austin, TX: University of Texas Press.

Bawarshi, A. (2003). *Genre and the invention of the writer: Reconsidering the place of invention in composition.* Logan, UT: Utah State University Press.

Bazerman, C. (1988). *Shaping written knowledge: The genre and activity of the experimental article in science.* Madison, WI: University of Wisconsin Press.

Bazerman, C. (1994). Systems of genres and the enactment of social intentions. In A. Freedman & P. Medway (Eds.), *Genre and the new rhetoric* (pp. 79–101). Bristol, PA: Taylor & Francis.

Bazerman, C. (2002). Genre and identity: Citizenship in the age of the internet and the age of global capitalism. In R. Coe, L. Lingard & T. Teslenko (Eds.), *The rhetoric and ideology of genre* (pp. 13–37). Creskill, NJ: Hampton Press.

Beaufort, A. (1999). *Writing in the real world: Making the transition from school to work.* New York: Teachers College Press.

Beaufort, A. (2000). Operationalizing the concept of discourse community: A case study of one institutional site of composing. *Research in the Teaching of English, 31,* 486–529.

Beaufort, A. (2004). Developmental gains of a history major: A case for building a theory of disciplinary writing expertise. *Research in the Teaching of English, 30,* 136–185.

Belcher, D. (1994). The apprenticeship model to advanced academic literacy: Graduate students and their mentors. *English for Specific Purposes, 23,* 23–34.

Benesch, S. (1995). Genres and processes in a sociocultural context. *Journal of Second Language Writing, 4,* 191–195.

Benesch, S. (2001). *Critical English for academic purposes: Theory, politics, and practice.* Mahwah, NJ: Lawrence Erlbaum Associates.

Bereiter, C., & Scardamalia, M. (1987). *The psychology of written composition.* Hillsdale, NJ: Lawrence Erlbaum Associates.

Bereiter, C., & Scardamalia, M. (1993). *Surpassing ourselves: An inquiry into the nature and implications of expertise.* Chicago: Open Court.

Berkenkotter, C. (2001). Genre systems at work: DSM-IV and rhetorical re-contextualization in psychotherapy paperwork. *Written Communication, 18,* 326–347.

Berkenkotter, C., & Huckin, T. (1995). *Genre knowledge in disciplinary communication.* Hillsdale, NJ: Lawrence Erlbaum Associates.

Berkenkotter, C., Huckin, T. N., & Ackerman, J. (1988). Conventions, conversations, and certainty: Case study of a student in a rhetoric PhD program. *Research in the Teaching of English, 22,* 9–44.

Bertin, J. (1973). *Semiologie graphique.* Paris: Gauthier-Villars.

Bhatia, V. K. (1993). *Analysing genre: Language use in professional settings.* New York: Longman.

Bhatia, V. K. (1996). Nativization of job applications in South Asia. In R. J. Baumgardner (Ed.), *South Asian English: Structure, use, and users* (pp. 158–173). Urbana, IL: University of Illinois Press.

Bhatia, V. K. (1999). Integrating products, processes, purposes and participants in professional writing. In C. N. Candlin & K. Hyland (Eds.), *Writing: Texts, processes and practices* (pp. 21–39). London: Longman.

Bhatia, V. K. (2004). *Worlds of written discourse: A genre-based view.* London: Continuum.

Biber, D. (1988). *Variation across speech and writing.* Cambridge, UK: Cambridge University Press.

Blakeslee, A. (1997). Activity, context, interaction, and authority: Learning to write scientific papers in situ. *Journal of Business and Technical Communication, 11,* 125–169.

Block, D. (2000). Problematizing interview data: Voices in the mind's machine? *TESOL Quarterly, 34,* 757–763.

Bowden, D. (1999). *The mythology of voice.* Portsmouth, NH: Boynton/Cook Heinemann.

Bracewell, R. J., & Witte, S. P. (2003). Tasks, ensembles, and activity: Linkages between text production and situation of use in the workplace. *Written Communication, 20,* 511–559.

Canagarajah, A. S. (1996). "Nondiscursive" requirements in academic publishing, material resources of periphery scholars, and the politics of knowledge production. *Written Communication, 13,* 435–472.

Canagarajah, A. S. (2002). *Critical academic writing and multilingual students.* Ann Arbor, MI: University of Michigan Press.

Canagarajah, A. S. (2003). *A geopolitics of academic writing.* Pittsburgh, PA: University of Pittsburgh Press.

Carter, M. (1990). The idea of expertise: An exploration of cognitive and social dimensions of writing. *College Composition and Communication, 41,* 265–286.

Carter, M., Ferzli, M., & Wiebe, E. (2004). Teaching genre to English first-language adults: A study of the laboratory report. *Research in the Teaching of English, 38,* 395–419.

Casanave, C. P. (2002). *Writing games: Multicultural case studies of academic literacy practices in higher education.* Mahwah, NJ: Lawrence Erlbaum Associates.

Casanave, C. P. (2003). *Controversies in second language writing: Dilemmas and decisions in research and instruction.* Ann Arbor, MI: University of Michigan Press.

Casanave, C. P. (2005). Uses of narrative in L2 writing research. In P. K. Matsuda & T. Silva (Eds.), *Second language writing research: Perspectives on the process of knowledge construction* (pp. 17–32). Mahwah, NJ: Lawrence Erlbaum Associates.

Chapman, M. L. (1994). The emergence of genres: Some findings from an examination of first-grade writing. *Written Communication, 11,* 348–380.

Charney, D. H., & Carlson, R. A. (1995). Learning to write in a genre: What student writers take from model texts. *Research in the Teaching of English, 29,* 88–125.

Cheng, A. (2006a). Analyzing and enacting academic criticism: The case of an L2 graduate learner of academic writing. *Journal of Second Language Writing, 15,* 279–306.

Cheng, A. (2006b). Understanding learners and learning in ESP genre-based writing instruction. *English for Specific Purposes, 25,* 76–89.

Chin, E. (1994). Ethnographic interviews and writing research: A critical examination of the methodology. In P. Smagorinsky (Ed.), *Speaking about writing: Reflections on research methodology* (pp. 247–272). Thousand Oaks, NJ: Sage Publications.

Cho, S. (2004). Challenges of entering discourse communities through publishing in English: Perspectives of nonnative-speaking doctoral students in the United States of America. *Journal of Language, Identity, and Education, 3,* 47–72.

Connor, U., & Mayberry, S. (1996). Learning discipline-specific academic writing: A case study of a Finnish graduate student in the United States. In E. Ventola & A. Mauranen (Eds.), *Academic writing: Intercultural and textual issues* (pp. 231–253). Philadelphia: John Benjamins Publishing Company.

Conrad, S. (2001). Variation among disciplinary texts: A comparison of textbooks and journal articles in biology and history. In S. Conrad & D. Biber (Eds.), *Variation in English: Multi-dimensional studies* (pp. 94–107). Harlow, UK: Longman.

Cope, B., & Kalantzis, M. (Eds.). (1993). *The powers of literacy: A genre approach to teaching writing.* Pittsburgh, PA: University of Pittsburgh Press.

Cumming, A. (1989). Writing expertise and second-language proficiency. *Language Learning, 39,* 81–141.

Currie, P. (1998). Staying out of trouble: Apparent plagiarism and academic survival. *Journal of Second Language Writing, 7,* 1–18.

Curry, M. J., & Lillis, T. (2004). Multilingual scholars and the imperative to publish in English: Negotiating interests, demands, and rewards. *TESOL Quarterly, 38,* 663–688.

Devitt, A. J. (1991). Intertextuality in accounting. In C. Bazerman & J. Paradis (Eds.), *Textual dynamics of the professions* (pp. 336–357). Madison, WI: University of Wisconsin Press.

Devitt, A. J. (2004). *Writing genres.* Carbondale, IL: Southern Illinois University Press.

Devitt, A. J., Bawarshi, A., & Reiff, M. J. (2003a). Materiality and genre in the study of discourse communities. *College English, 65,* 541–558.

Devitt, A. J., Reiff, M. J., & Bawarshi, A. (2003b). *Scenes of writing: Strategies for composing with genres.* New York: Pearson Education.

Dias, P., Freedman, A., Medway, P., & Paré, A. (1999). *Worlds apart: Acting and writing in academic and workplace contexts.* Mahwah, NJ: Lawrence Erlbaum Associates.

Doheny-Farina, S. (1989). A case study of one adult writing in academic and non-academic discourse. In C. B. Matalene (Ed.), *Worlds of writing: Teaching and learning in discourse communities of work* (pp. 17–42). New York: Random House.

Dong, Y. R. (1996). Learning how to use citations for knowledge transformation: Non-native doctoral students' dissertation writing in science. *Research in the Teaching of English, 30,* 428–457.

Dong, Y. R. (1998). Non-native graduate students' thesis/dissertation writing in science: Self-reports by students and their advisors from two U.S. institutions. *English for Specific Purposes, 17,* 369–390.

Dreyfus, H. L., & Dreyfus, S. E. (1986). *Mind over machine: The power of human intuition and expertise in the era of the computer.* New York: Free Press.

Faigley, L., & Hansen, K. (1985). Learning to write in the social sciences. *College Composition and Communication, 18,* 140–149.

Fishman, S. M., & McCarthy, L. P. (2001). An ESL writer and her discipline-based professor. *Written Communication, 18,* 180–228.

Flowerdew, J. (1993). An educational, or process, approach to the teaching of professional genres. *ELT Journal, 47,* 305–316.

Flowerdew, J. (2000). Discourse community, legitimate peripheral participation, and the nonnative-English-speaking scholar. *TESOL Quarterly, 34,* 127–150.

Freadman, A. (1994). Anyone for tennis? In A. Freedman & P. Medway (Eds.), *Genre and the new rhetoric* (pp. 43–66). Bristol, PA: Taylor & Francis.

Freedman, A. (1993a). Show and tell? The role of explicit teaching in the learning of new genres. *Research in the Teaching of English, 27,* 222–251.

Freedman, A. (1993b). Situating genre: A rejoinder. *Research in the Teaching of English, 27,* 272–281.

Freedman, A. (1999). Beyond the text: Towards understanding the teaching and learning of genres. *TESOL Quarterly, 33,* 764–767.

Freedman, A., & Adam, C. (1996). Learning to write professionally: "Situated learning" and the transition from university to professional discourse. *Journal of Business and Technical Communication, 10,* 395–427.

Freedman, A., Adam, C., & Smart, G. (1994). Wearing suits to class: Simulating genres and simulations as genre. *Written Communication, 11,* 193–226.

Freedman, A., & Medway, P. (1994a). *Learning and teaching genre.* Portsmouth, NJ: Boynton/Cook Publishers.

Freedman, A., & Medway, P. (1994b). Locating genre studies: Antecedents and prospects. In A. Freedman & P. Medway (Eds.), *Genre and the new rhetoric* (pp. 1–20). Bristol, PA: Taylor & Francis.

Fulkerson, R. (2005). Composition at the turn of the twenty-first century. *College Composition and Communication, 56,* 654–687.

Gee, J. P. (1999). *An introduction to discourse analysis: Theory and method.* New York: Routledge.

Gee, J. P. (2005). *An introduction to discourse analysis: Theory and method* (2nd ed.). New York: Routledge.

Geisler, C. (1994). *Academic literacy and the nature of expertise: Reading, writing, and knowing in academic philosophy.* Hillsdale, NJ: Lawrence Erlbaum Associates.

Gentil, G. (2005). Commitments to academic biliteracy: Case studies of francophone university writers. *Written Communication, 22,* 421–471.

Giltrow, J. (2002). Meta-genre. In R. Coe, L. Lingard & T. Teslenko (Eds.), *The rhetoric and ideology of genre* (pp. 187–205). Creskill, NJ: Hampton Press.

Giltrow, J., & Valiquette, M. (1994). Genres and knowledge: Students writing in the disciplines. In A. Freedman & P. Medway (Eds.), *Learning and teaching genres* (pp. 47–62). Portsmouth, NH: Boynton/Cook Publishers.

Gold, R. (2002). Reading PowerPoint. In N. Allen (Ed.), *Working with words and images: New steps in an old dance* (pp. 256–270). Westport, CT: Ablex Publishing Company.

Gosden, H. (1996). Verbal reports of Japanese novices' research writing practices in English. *Journal of Second Language Writing, 5,* 109–128.

Gosden, H. (1998). An aspect of holistic modeling in academic writing: Propositional clusters as a heuristic for thematic control. *Journal of Second Language Writing, 7,* 19–41.

Grabe, W. (2000). Notes toward a theory of second language writing. In T. Silva & P. K. Matsuda (Eds.), *On second language writing* (pp. 39–57). Mahwah, NJ: Lawrence Erlbaum Associates.

Graddol, D. (1997). *The future of English?* London: The British Council.

Haas, C. (1994). Learning to read biology: One student's rhetorical development in college. *Written Communication, 11,* 43–84.

Halliday, M. A. K. (1994). *An introduction to functional grammar* (2nd ed.). London: Arnold.

Hammond, J., & Macken-Horarik, M. (1999). Critical literacy: Challenges and questions for ESL classrooms. *TESOL Quarterly, 33,* 528–544.

Hansen, J. (2000). Interactional conflicts among audience, purpose, and content knowledge in the acquisition of academic literacy in an EAP course. *Written Communication, 17,* 27–52.

Hardt, D. (2005). *Identity 2.0.* Retrieved December 10, 2006, from http://www.identity20.com/media/OSCON2005/

Harklau, L., & Williams, G. (in press). Practicing theory in qualitative research on second language writing. In T. Silva & P. K. Matsuda (Eds.), *Practicing theory in second language writing.* West Lafayette, IN: Parlor Press.

Henry, A., & Roseberry, R. L. (1998). An evaluation of a genre-based approach to the teaching of EAP/ESP writing. *TESOL Quarterly, 32,* 147–156.

Henry, A., & Roseberry, R. L. (2001). A narrow-angled corpus analysis of moves and strategies of the genre: 'Letter of application.' *English for Specific Purposes, 20*, 153–167.

Herrington, A. (1985). Writing in academic settings: A study of the contexts for writing in two college chemical engineering courses. *Research in the Teaching of English, 19*, 331–361.

Herrington, A., & Moran, C. (2005). *Genre across the curriculum.* Logan, UT: Utah State University Press.

Hirvela, A. (1997). "Disciplinary portfolios" and EAP writing instruction. *English for Specific Purposes, 16*, 83–100.

Hirvela, A., & Belcher, D. (2001). Coming back to voice: The multiple voices and identities of mature multilingual writers. *Journal of Second Language Writing, 10*, 83–106.

Howard, R. M. (1995). Plagiarisms, authorships, and the academic death penalty. *College English, 57*, 788–806.

Howard, R. M. (1999). The new abolitionism comes to plagiarism. In L. Bauranen & A. M. Roy (Eds.), *Perspectives on plagiarism and intellectual property in a postmodern world* (pp. 87–95). Albany, NY: State University of New York Press.

Hyland, K. (1995). The author in the text: Hedging scientific writing. *Hong Kong Papers in Linguistics and Language Teaching, 18*, 33–42.

Hyland, K. (2000). *Disciplinary discourses: Social interactions in academic writing.* Harlow: Longman.

Hyland, K. (2003). Genre-based pedagogies: A social response to process. *Journal of Second Language Writing, 12*, 17–29.

Hyland, K. (2004). *Genre and second language writing.* Ann Arbor, MI: University of Michigan Press.

Hyon, S. (1996). Genre in three traditions: Implications for ESL. *TESOL Quarterly, 30*, 693–722.

Hyon, S. (2001). Long-term effects of genre-based instruction: A follow-up study of an EAP reading course. *English for Specific Purposes, 20*, 417–438.

Hyon, S. (2002). Genre and reading: A classroom study. In A. M. Johns (Ed.), *Genre in the classroom: Multiple perspectives* (pp. 121–139). Mahwah, NJ: Lawrence Erlbaum Associates.

Hyon, S., & Chen, R. (2004). Beyond the research article: University faculty genres and EAP graduate preparation. *English for Specific Purposes, 23*, 233–263.

Institute of International Education. (2008). *Open doors 2007: Report on international educational exchange.* Retrieved May 15, 2008, from http://opendoors.iicnetwork.org/page/113118/

Ivanič, R. (1998). *Writing and identity: The discoursal construction of identity in academic writing.* Philadelphia: John Benjamins Publishing Company.

James, M. (2008). The influence of perceptions of task similarity/difference on learning transfer in second language writing. *Written Communication, 25,* 76–103.

Johns, A. M. (1997). *Text, role, and context: Developing academic literacies.* Cambridge, UK: Cambridge University Press.

Johns, A. M. (1998). The visual and the verbal: A case study in macroeconomics. *English for Specific Purposes, 17,* 183–197.

Johns, A. M. (2002a). Destabilizing and enriching novice students' genre theories. In A. M. Johns (Ed.), *Genre in the classroom: Multiple perspectives* (pp. 237–246). Mahwah, NJ: Lawrence Erlbaum Associates.

Johns, A. M. (Ed.). (2002b). *Genre in the classroom: Multiple perspectives.* Mahwah, NJ: Lawrence Erlbaum Associates.

Johns, A. M., Bawarshi, A., Coe, R. M., Hyland, K., Paltridge, B., Reiff, M. J., & Tardy, C. M. (2006). Crossing the boundaries of genre studies: Commentaries by experts. *Journal of Second Language Writing, 15,* 234–249.

Johnstone, K. M., Ashbaugh, H., & Warfield, T. D. (2002). Effects of repeated practice and contextual-writing experiences on college students' writing skills. *Journal of Educational Psychology, 94,* 305–315.

Jolliffe, D. A. (1999). *Inquiry and genre: Writing to learn in college.* Boston: Allyn and Bacon.

Jolliffe, D. A., & Brier, E. M. (1988). Studying writers' knowledge in academic disciplines. In D. A. Jolliffe (Ed.), *Advances in writing research, volume two: Writing in academic disciplines* (pp. 35–77). Norwood, NJ: Ablex Publishing Company.

Kamberelis, G. (1995). Genre as institutionally informed social practice. *Journal of Contemporary Legal Issues, 6,* 115–171.

Kamberelis, G. (1999). Genre development and learning: Children writing stories, science reports, and poems. *Research in the Teaching of English, 33,* 403–460.

Kamberelis, G., & Bovino, T. D. (1999). Cultural artifacts as scaffolds for genre development. *Reading Research Quarterly, 34,* 138–170.

Katz, S. M. (1998). A newcomer gains power: An analysis of the role of rhetorical expertise. *Journal of Business Communication, 35,* 419–442.

Kaufer, D., & Geisler, C. (1989). Novelty in academic writing. *Written Communication, 6,* 286–311.

Kay, H., & Dudley-Evans, T. (1998). Genre: What teachers think. *ELT Journal, 52,* 308–313.

Keck, C. (2006). The use of paraphrase in summary writing: A comparison of L1 and L2 writers. *Journal of Second Language Writing, 15,* 261–278.

Koutsantoni, D. (2006). Rhetorical strategies in engineering research articles and research theses: Advanced academic literacy and relations of power. *Journal of English for Academic Purposes, 5,* 19–36.

Krase, E. (2007). "Maybe the communication between us was not enough": Inside a dysfunctional advisor/L2 advisee relationship. *Journal of English for Academic Purposes, 6,* 55–70.

Krashen, S. D. (1985). *The input hypothesis: Issues and implications.* New York: Longman.

Kress, G. (2000). Multimodality: Challenges to thinking about language. *TESOL Quarterly, 34,* 337–340.

Kress, G. (2003). *Literacy in the new media age.* London: Routledge.

Kress, G., & van Leeuwen, T. N. (1996). *Reading images.* London: Routledge.

Leki, I. (1995). Coping strategies for ESL students in writing tasks across the curriculum. *TESOL Quarterly, 29,* 235–260.

Leki, I. (2006a). Negotiating socioacademic relations: English learners' reception by and reaction to college faculty. *Journal of English for Academic Purposes, 5,* 136–152.

Leki, I. (2006b). "You cannot ignore": L2 graduate students' response to discipline-based written feedback. In K. Hyland & F. Hyland (Eds.), *Feedback in second language writing: Contexts and issues.* Cambridge, UK: Cambridge University Press.

Leki, I., & Carson, J. (1994). Students' perceptions of EAP writing instruction and writing needs across the disciplines. *TESOL Quarterly, 28,* 81–101.

Lemke, J. L. (1998). Multiplying meaning: Visual and verbal semiotics in scientific text. In J. R. Martin & R. Veel (Eds.), *Reading science: Critical and functional perspectives on discourses of science* (pp. 87–113). London: Routledge.

Lemke, J. L. (2002). Travels in hypermodality. *Visual Communication, 1,* 299–325.

Lerner, N. (2007). Laboratory lessons for writing and science. *Written Communication, 24,* 191–222.

Lessig, L. (2002). *Free culture.* Retrieved December 10, 2006, from http://www.lessig.org/freeculture/free.html

Li, Y. (2006). Negotiating knowledge contribution to multiple discourse communities: A doctoral student of computer science writing for publication. *Journal of Second Language Writing, 15,* 159–178.

Luke, A. (1996). Genres of power? Literacy education and the production of capital. In R. Hasan & G. Williams (Eds.), *Literacy in society* (pp. 308–338). New York: Longman.

Martin, J. R. (1993a). A contextual theory of language. In B. Cope & M. Kalantzis (Eds.), *The powers of literacy: A genre approach to teaching writing* (pp. 116–136). Pittsburgh, PA: University of Pittsburgh Press.

Martin, J. R. (1993b). Genre and literacy—Modeling context in educational linguistics. *Annual Review of Applied Linguistics, 13,* 141–172.

Martin, J. R., & Rothery, J. (1993). Grammar: Making meaning in writing. In B. Cope & M. Kalantzis (Eds.), *The powers of literacy: A genre approach to teaching writing* (pp. 137–153). Pittsburgh, PA: University of Pittsburgh Press.

Matsuda, P. K. (1999). Composition studies and ESL writing: A disciplinary division of labor. *College Composition and Communication, 50,* 699–721.

McCarthy, L. P. (1987). A stranger in strange lands: A college student writing across the curriculum. *Research in the Teaching of English, 21,* 233–265.

McLaughlin, B. (1990). Restructuring. *Applied Linguistics, 11,* 113–128.

McNabb, R. (2001). Making the gesture: Graduate student submissions and the expectations of journal referees. *Composition Studies, 29,* 9–26.

Merino, B. J., & Hammond, J. (2002). Writing to learn: Science in the upper-elementary bilingual classroom. In M. J. Schleppegrell & C. S. Colombi (Eds.), *Developing advanced literacy in first and foreign languages* (pp. 227–243). Mahwah, NJ: Lawrence Erlbaum Associates.

Miller, C. R. (1984). Genre as social action. *Quarterly Journal of Speech, 70,* 151–167.

Miller, C. R. (1994). Rhetorical community: The cultural basis of genre. In A. Freedman & P. Medway (Eds.), *Genre and the new rhetoric* (pp. 67–78). Bristol, PA: Taylor & Francis.

Miller, T. (1998). Visual persuasion: A comparison of visuals in academic texts and the popular press. *English for Specific Purposes, 17,* 29–46.

Norris, C., & Tardy, C. M. (2006). Institutional politics in the teaching of advanced academic writing: A teacher-researcher dialogue. In P. K. Matsuda, C. Ortmeier-Hooper & X. You (Eds.), *The politics of second language writing: In search of the promised land* (pp. 262–279). West Lafayette, IN: Parlor Press.

Norton, B. (2000). *Identity in second language learning.* London: Longman.

Paltridge, B. (1997). *Genre, frames and writing in research settings.* Philadelphia, PA: John Benjamins Publishing Company.

Paltridge, B. (2001). *Genre and the language learning classroom.* Ann Arbor, MI: University of Michigan Press.

Paltridge, B. (2002). Thesis and dissertation writing: An examination of published advice and actual practice. *English for Specific Purposes, 21,* 125–143.

Paré, A. (2000). Writing as a way into social work: Genre sets, genre systems, and distributed cognition. In P. Dias & A. Paré (Eds.), *Transitions: Writing in academic and workplace settings* (pp. 145–166). Creskill, NJ: Hampton Press.

Parks, S. (2000a). Professional writing and the role of incidental collaboration: Evidence from a medical setting. *Journal of Second Language Writing, 9,* 101–122.

Parks, S. (2000b). Same task, different activities: Issues of investment, identity, and use of strategy. *TESL Canada Journal, 17*(2), 64–88.

Parks, S. (2001). Moving from school to the workplace: Disciplinary innovation, border crossings, and the reshaping of a written genre. *Applied Linguistics, 22,* 405–438.

Pecorari, D. (2003). Good and original: Plagiarism and patchwriting in academic second-language writing. *Journal of Second Language Writing, 12,* 317–345.

Pennycook, A. (1997). Vulgar pragmatism, critical pragmatism, and EAP. *English for Specific Purposes, 16,* 253–269.

Prior, P. A. (1991). Contextualizing writing and response in a graduate seminar. *Written Communication, 8,* 483–533.

Prior, P. A. (1998). *Writing/Disciplinarity: A sociohistoric account of literate activity in the academy.* Mahwah, NJ: Lawrence Erlbaum Associates.

Prior, P. A. (2004). Tracing process: How texts come into being. In C. Bazerman & P. A. Prior (Eds.), *What writing does and how it does it: An introduction to analyzing texts and textual practices* (pp. 167–200). Mahwah, NJ: Lawrence Erlbaum Associates.

Räisänen, C. (1999). *The Conference Forum as a System of Genres : A Sociocultural Study of Academic Conference Practices in Automotive Crash-Safety Engineering.* Göteborg, Germany: Acta Universitatis Gothoburgensis.

Reppen, R. (1994). A genre-based approach to content writing instruction. *TESL Journal, 4*(2), 32–35.

Riazi, A. (1997). Acquiring disciplinary literacy: A social-cognitive analysis of text production and learning among Iranian graduate students of education. *Journal of Second Language Writing, 6,* 105–137.

Rowley-Jolivet, E. (2000). Image as text: Aspects of the shared visual language of international conference participants. *ASp, 27–30,* 133–154.

Rowley-Jolivet, E. (2001). "Here you can see . . .," the role of photographs in the economy of scientific conference presentations. In M. Memer & M. Petit (Eds.), *L'anglais de specialité en France: Mélanges en l'honneur de Michel Perrin* (pp. 113–124). Bordeaux, France: GERAS Editeur.

Rowley-Jolivet, E. (2002). Visual discourse in scientific conference papers: A genre-based study. *English for Specific Purposes, 21,* 19–40.

Rowley-Jolivet, E. (2004). Different visions, different visuals: A social semiotic analysis of field-specific visual composition in scientific conference presentations. *Visual Communication, 3,* 145–175.

Russell, D. H. (1997). Rethinking genre in school and society: An activity theory analysis. *Written Communication, 14,* 504–554.

Said, E. W. (1982). Opponents, audiences, constituencies, and communities. *Critical Inquiry, 9,* 1–26.

Samraj, B. (2005). An exploration of a genre set: Research article abstracts and introductions in two disciplines. *English for Specific Purposes, 24,* 141–156.

Samraj, B. (2006). *Argumentation and evaluation in master's theses in two disciplines.* Paper presented at the American Association of Applied Linguistics, Montreal, Canada.

Segalowitz, N. (2003). Automaticity. In C. J. Doughty & M. H. Long (Eds.), *The handbook of second language acquisition* (pp. 382–408). Oxford: Blackwell.

Sengupta, S. (1999). Rhetorical consciousness raising in the L2 reading classroom. *Journal of Second Language Writing, 8,* 291–319.

Shaw, P. (1991). Science research students' composing processes. *English for Specific Purposes, 10,* 189–206.

Shi, L. (2004). Textual borrowing in second-language writing. *Written Communication, 21,* 171–200.

Silva, T. (2005). On the philosophical bases of inquiry in second language writing: Metaphysics, inquiry paradigms, and the intellectual zeitgeist. In P. K. Matsuda & T. Silva (Eds.), *Second language writing research: Perspectives on the process of knowledge construction* (pp. 3–15). Mahwah, NJ: Lawrence Erlbaum Associates.

Silva, T., & Leki, I. (2004). Family matters: The influence of applied linguistics and composition studies on second language writing studies—past, present, and future. *The Modern Language Journal, 88,* 1–13.

Silva, T., Leki, I., & Carson, J. (1997). Broadening the perspective of mainstream composition studies. *Written Communication, 14,* 398–428.

Smart, G. (2000). Reinventing expertise: Experienced writers in the workplace encounter a new genre. In P. Dias & A. Paré (Eds.), *Transitions: Writing in academic and workplace settings* (pp. 223–252). Creskill, NJ: Hampton Press.

Spack, R. (1988). Initiating ESL students into the academic discourse community: How far should we go? *TESOL Quarterly, 22,* 29–51.

Spack, R. (1997). The acquisition of academic literacy in a second language: A longitudinal case study. *Written Communication, 14,* 3–62.

Smith, S. N. (2002, March). *Teaching students to analyze using semiotics.* Paper presented at Conference on College Composition and Communication, Chicago, IL.

Swales, J. M. (1990). *Genre analysis: English in academic and research settings.* Cambridge, UK: Cambridge University Press.

Swales, J. M. (1996). Occluded genres in the academy: The case of the submission letter. In E. Ventola & A. Mauranen (Eds.), *Academic writing: Intercultural and textual issues* (pp. 45–58). Philadelphia: John Benjamins Publishing Company.

Swales, J. M. (2000, September). *Further reflections on genre and ESL academic writing.* Paper presented at the Symposium of Second Language Writing, West Lafayette, IN.

Swales, J. M. (2001). Issues of genre: Purposes, parodies, and pedagogies. In A. Moreno & V. Caldwell (Eds.) *Recent perspectives on discourse* (pp.11–26). AESLA: The University of Leon Press.

Swales, J. M. (2004). *Research genres: Explorations and applications.* Cambridge, UK: Cambridge University Press.

Swales, J. M., & Feak, C. B. (1994a). *Academic writing for graduate students: A course for non-native speakers.* Ann Arbor, MI: University of Michigan Press.

Swales, J. M., & Feak, C. B. (1994b). *Academic writing for graduate students: Commentary.* Ann Arbor, MI: University of Michigan Press.

Swales, J. M., & Feak, C. B. (2000). *English in today's research world: A writing guide.* Ann Arbor, MI: University of Michigan Press.

Swales, J. M., & Lindemann, S. (2002). Teaching the literature review to international graduate students. In A. M. Johns (Ed.), *Genre in the classroom: Multiple perspectives* (pp. 105–119). Mahwah, NJ: Lawrence Erlbaum Associates.

Tardy, C. M. (2003). A genre system view of the funding of academic research. *Written Communication, 20,* 7–36.

Tardy, C. M. (2006). Researching first and second language genre learning: A comparative review and a look ahead. *Journal of Second Language Writing, 15,* 79–101.

Tufte, E. R. (2003). *The cognitive style of PowerPoint.* Cheshire, CT: Graphics Press LLC.

UK Council for International Student Affairs. (2008). *Higher education statistics.* Retrieved on May 15, 2008, from http://www.ukcisa.org.uk

van Leeuwen, T. N., Moed, H. F., Tijssen, R. J. W., Visser, M. S., & van Raan, A. F. J. (2001). Language biases in the coverage of the Science Citation Index and its consequences for international comparisons of national research performance. *Scientometrics, 51,* 335–346.

Vandenberg, P. (2005). Animated categories: Genre, action, and composition. *College English, 67,* 532–545.

Wenger, E. (1998). *Communities of practice: Learning, meaning, and identity.* Cambridge, UK: Cambridge University Press.

Winsor, D. (2001). Learning to do knowledge work in systems of distributed cognition. *Journal of Business and Technical Communication, 15,* 5–28.

Winsor, D. A. (1996). *Writing like an engineer: A rhetorical education.* Mahwah, NJ: Lawrence Erlbaum Associate.

Yates, J., & Orlikowski, W. (2002). Genre systems: Chronos and kairos in communicative interaction. In R. Coe, L. Lingard & T. Teslenko (Eds.), *The rhetoric and ideology of genre* (pp. 103–121). Creskill, NJ: Hampton Press.

Index

About the Author

Christine M. Tardy is an Assistant Professor of Writing, Rhetoric, and Discourse at DePaul University in Chicago, where she serves as Graduate Director and teaches courses in writing, teacher education, and applied linguistics. She has taught English as a second or foreign language in the U.S., Czech Republic, Japan, and Turkey. She has published extensively in the areas of genre and discourse studies, second language writing, and academic writing instruction.

CPSIA information can be obtained at www.ICGtesting.com
Printed in the USA
BVOW04s2205310714

361003BV00003B/426/P